JOURNAL FOR THE STUDY OF THE OLD TESTAMENT SUPPLEMENT SERIES
299

Sheffield Academic Press

Rethinking Contexts, Rereading Texts

Contributions from the Social Sciences to Biblical Interpretation

edited by
M. Daniel Carroll R.

Journal for the Study of the Old Testament
Supplement Series 299

Published by Sheffield Academic Press Ltd
Mansion House
19 Kingfield Road
Sheffield S11 9AS
England

Typeset by Sheffield Academic Press
and
Printed on acid-free paper in Great Britain
by Bookcraft Ltd
Midsomer Norton, Bath

British Library Cataloguing in Publication Data

A catalogue record for this book is available
from the British Library

ISBN 1-84127-058-X

CONTENTS

PREFACE

The idea for this collection of essays was born in a conversation one afternoon in Sheffield, England, during the spring of 1995. Gerald West, Mark Brett and I were participating in a consultation on the use of the Bible in ethics at the University.[1] The three of us were reminiscing about our time together as doctoral research students in the Biblical Studies Department there in the late 1980s under the tutelage of Professor John Rogerson. We all agreed that for each one of us he had been the ideal supervisor and *Doktorvater*: a constant encourager, a stimulator of creativity and a promoter of our work. What a privilege it would be to be able to do something together with him, as both appreciative former students and, now, professional colleagues.

During our time in Sheffield one of the foundational contributions of Professor Rogerson to each one of us had been to cultivate an interest in interdisciplinary approaches in order to better understand the Bible and to make it relevant to the modern world. Throughout his career, the Professor himself has modeled an extensive interaction with the social sciences. He has published methodological surveys of the history of the use of anthropology in Old Testament studies, presented biographies of key individuals of the last century who pioneered the application of the social sciences to biblical research, and employed a number of social science perspectives in his own work on issues of Old Testament exegesis, ethics and theology.

It was agreed that any collaborative venture, therefore, should reflect that interest in interfacing biblical studies and the social sciences. When Professor Rogerson agreed to take part in this project, he suggested the addition of two other former students, Stanley Porter and Jonathan Dyck. The essays in this volume reflect the diverse backgrounds of the contributors and the variety of avenues of research each one has taken

1.   The papers of that consultation were published in J. Rogerson, M. Davies and M.D. Carroll R. (eds.), *The Bible and Ethics: The Second Sheffield Colloquium* (JSOTSup, 207; Sheffield: Sheffield Academic Press, 1995).

since that initial contact with the University. It is our sincere hope that the work offered here will stimulate others to explore new vistas in biblical studies with the aid of the multiple insights which the social sciences can provide.

Philip R. Davies, also a member of the Biblical Studies Department and one of the editors at the Press, was quick to accept the idea of this project and always was helpful in responding to any queries. It was he who suggested that the book appear in the JSOT Supplement series in order to guarantee a wider audience. I would also like to thank Fraser Hess of the Information Systems Department at Denver Seminary for his technical assistance. Most of all, I owe a deep debt of gratitude to my wife Joan and my two sons, Matthew and Adam. Throughout many late nights and long weekends over the last several months they have been so very patient with me as I have worked on this project. Without their support, it could never have become a reality.

M. Daniel Carroll R.
Denver, Colorado
May 1999

ABBREVIATIONS

AB	Anchor Bible
AnnRevAnth	*Annual Review of Anthropology*
ASSR	*Archives des sciences sociales des religions*
BASOR	*Bulletin of the American Schools of Oriental Research*
BETL	Bibliotheca ephemeridum theologicarum lovaniensium
Bib	*Biblica*
BibInt	*Biblical Interpretation: A Journal of Contemporary Approaches*
BIS	Biblical Interpretation Series
BSO(A)S	*Bulletin of the School of Oriental (and African) Studies*
BZAW	Beihefte zur *ZAW*
CBQ	*Catholic Biblical Quarterly*
ConBOT	Coniectanea biblica, Old Testament
CR:BS	*Currents in Research: Biblical Studies*
CrSoc	*Cristianismo y Sociedad*
CritAnth	*Critique of Anthropology*
CritInq	*Critical Inquiry*
CTL	Cambridge Textbooks on Linguistics
CurrAnth	*Current Anthropology*
DDD	K. van der Toorn, B. Becking and P.W. van der Horst (eds.), *Dictionary of Deities and Demons in the Bible*
FN	*Filología neotestamentaria*
HAT	Handbuch zum Alten Testament
HeyJ	*Heythrop Journal*
HSAT	A. Bertholet (ed.), *Die Heilige Schrift des Alten Testaments* (2 vols., Tübingen, 1922–23)
HSM	Harvard Semitic Monographs
HSS	
HTR	*Harvard Theological Review*
HTS	Harvard Theological Studies
HUCA	*Hebrew Union College Annual*
ICC	International Critical Commentary
Int	*Interpretation*
JAAR	*Journal of the American Academy of Religion*
JAOS	*Journal of the American Oriental Society*
JBL	*Journal of Biblical Literature*
JJS	*Journal of Jewish Studies*

Rethinking Contexts, Rereading Texts

JLT	*Journal of Literature and Theology*
JNSL	*Journal of Northwest Semitic Languages*
JSNT	*Journal for the Study of the New Testament*
JSNTSup	*Journal for the Study of the New Testament*, Supplement Series
JSOT	*Journal for the Study of the Old Testament*
JSOTSup	*Journal for the Study of the Old Testament*, Supplement Series
JTS	*Journal of Theological Studies*
JTSA	*Journal of Theology for Southern Africa*
NCB	New Century Bible
Neot	*Neotestamentica*
NICNT	New International Commentary on the New Testament
NTTS	New Testament Tools and Studies
OBT	Overtures to Biblical Theology
Or	*Orientalia*
OTG	Old Testament Guides
OTL	Old Testament Library
OTS	*Oudtestamentische Studien*
OTWSA	*Die Outestamentiese Wekgemeenskap in Suid-Africa*
PEQ	Palestine Exploration Quarterly
PMLA	*Proceedings of the Modern Language Association*
RB	*Revue biblique*
RIBLA	*Revista de Interpretación Bíblica Latinoamericana*
RILP	Roehampton Institute London Papers
SBG	Studies in Biblical Greek
SBLDS	SBL Dissertation Series
SBLMS	SBL Monograph Series
SBLSS	SBL Semeia Studies
SBT	Studies in Biblical Theology
SBTS	Sources for Biblical and Theological Study
SJOT	*Scandinavian Journal of the Old Testament*
SJT	*Scottish Journal of Theology*
SNTSMS	Society for New Testament Studies Monograph Series
SocComp	*Social Compass*
ST	*Studia theologica*
SUNT	Studien zur Umwelt des Neuen Testaments
TAPA	*Transactions of the American Philological Association*
TRE	*Theologische Realenzyklopädie*
TynBul	*Tyndale Bulletin*
UF	*Ugarit-Forschungen*
VT	*Vetus Testamentum*
VTSup	*Vetus Testamentum*, Supplements
WBC	Word Biblical Commentary
WUNT	Wissenschaftliche Untersuchungen zum Neuen Testament
ZAW	*Zeitschrift für die alttestamentliche Wissenschaft*
ZRGG	*Zeitschrift für Religions- und Geistesgeschichte*

LIST OF CONTRIBUTORS

Mark G. Brett
Professor of Old Testament, Whitley College, University of Melbourne, Australia

M. Daniel Carroll R.
Professor of Old Testament, Denver Seminary, USA; Adjunct Professor of Old Testament and Ethics, Seminario Teológico Centroamericano, Guatemala

Jonathan Dyck
Lecturer in Biblical Interpretation, Trinity College, University of Dublin, Republic of Ireland

Stanley E. Porter
Head of the Department of Theology and Religious Studies, Centre for Advanced Theological Research, Roehampton Institute London, UK

John W. Rogerson
Emeritus Professor, Department of Biblical Studies, University of Sheffield, UK

Gerald O. West
Professor in Biblical Studies, School of Theology, University of Natal; Director of the Institute for the Study of the Bible, Pietermaritzburg, Republic of South Africa

INTRODUCTION:
ISSUES OF 'CONTEXT' WITHIN SOCIAL SCIENCE APPROACHES TO BIBLICAL STUDIES

M. Daniel Carroll R.

1. *Engaging the Social Sciences in Biblical Studies*

In general terms, social-scientific criticism has as its twin goals to explicate the complex socio-cultural realities described or reflected in a number of ways in the biblical text and to explore the social dimensions of the interpretive process. Variety has been a hallmark, as a wide range of theories and models, primarily from the disciplines of sociology and anthropology, have been utilized with fruitful results in biblical research.[1]

Even though recent years have witnessed a veritable explosion in the number of publications which employ these methods, interest in the field can be traced back at least two hundred years. Within the province of Old Testament studies, Rogerson believes the first attempt to use a comparative method in order to understand the Bible to have been made by J.G. Michaelis in the mid-eighteenth century (1984: 3-5). Elliott points to pioneers in New Testament scholarship in the middle of the nineteenth century (1993: 3). Those initial endeavors, which would have lacked solid theoretical foundations and wide practical confirmation, mark the beginning of a long history of the development and application of an increasingly sophisticated set of analytical tools (cf. Hahn 1966: 44-82, 157-84; Rogerson 1978, 1995a; Wilson 1984: 10-29; Elliott 1993: 17-35). Some of these efforts, for example, can be grouped as falling within the broad categories of structural functionalism or conflict theory (see Mayes 1989; Malina 1993: 20-25); others appear more to appeal to social theory in a broader sense than to offer concrete

---

1. One could also mention other disciplines, such as psychology, but their impact and use has in no way been as prevalent.

models (e.g. Rogerson 1990, 1995b). Whatever the classification, however, the impression gained is one of great potential for an increasingly
more profound understanding of the biblical text and its impact on its
readers.

Today several introductions to social science approaches are available for both Old (e.g. Wilson 1984; Clements 1989; Mayes 1989;
Matthews and Benjamin 1993; Overholt 1996) and New Testament
studies (e.g. Malina 1986, 1993; Holmberg 1990; Elliott 1993; Esler
1994; Rohrbaugh 1996), several of which provide helpful surveys of the
history of research, detailed case studies, and full and up-to-date bibli-
ographies. Anthologies of classic works and more recent significant
contributions have also begun to appear (e.g. Lang 1985; Carter and
Meyers 1996; Horrell 1999). Perhaps the most conspicuous lacuna in
some of these works is the failure to acknowledge adequately (if at all)
the important implications of social theory for the production of the
biblical materials and its reception, interpretation and appropriation—
whether today or in the past. In other words, the possible contexts of the
biblical text are multiple, and we ignore any of them at our peril. My
discussion will highlight three. Before I begin my discussion two caveats are in order. First, for the sake of theoretical clarity I have distinguished three general categories of contexts, but in actual scholarly
practice different combinations of the three often can be employed
together in concert. Second, the following is in no way intended to be
comprehensive; rather, my aim is simply to point out some important
trends within contemporary scholarship; this, in turn, will help set the
backdrop for the essays in this volume.

2. *The Social Sciences and the Many Contexts of Biblical Texts:*
An Orientation

a. *The Text within its Context*
The greatest amount of social science research historically has been
done at the service of the investigation of biblical backgrounds. Any
number of the social sciences are drawn on to try to illuminate the
social, economic, political and cultural aspects of life in ancient Palestine. Though these theories and models are based on research into modern phenomena, some sort of continuity across the millennia must be
presupposed if they are to have any utility at all. At the same time, the
temporal, cultural and geographical distance between contemporary
societies and the ancient world require as well that the researcher recog-

nize that results are necessarily suggestive, not definitive. That is, the social sciences can provide heuristic frameworks for the interpretation of the biblical data, which must be constantly evaluated until more viable and comprehensive perspectives become available.

These studies are usually considered to be complementary (yet also at times corrective) of more traditional historical and grammatical analyses, which were not designed to explore some of those dimensions (cf. Elliott 1993: 107-109). Old Testament scholars have turned to the social sciences, for instance, for help in comprehending *cultural values and codes*, such as kinship and genealogies, social status, corporate personality, purity and uncleanness, and honor and shame; *social roles*, like those of the priests, prophets, judges and kings; and the *institutional organization and ethos* of the cult and the monarchy. In the last several years much attention has been given to *historical processes*, such as the rise of Israel as a cultural entity and nation state. Questions about *gender*—that is, the identity and place of women—have also generated a growing realm of research. Parallel topics within the time frame of the first century CE have also occupied New Testament studies. In addition, other particular features of social life of that era that also have been explored include the nature of peasant societies, millenarian and other sectarian movements, household and hospitality mores, and patronage and clientism.

While the enormous contributions of social science approaches to illuminating textual particulars are widely appreciated, at the same time not a few scholars have raised important questions of methodological concern. To begin with, some have underscored the fact that research is never neutral. Therefore, those appealing to social scientific methods should be aware of and open about their vantage point and the commitments that will affect their work. Modern presuppositions, whether philosophical or ideological, can affect the choice of social theory and the interpretation of the pertinent data. Research might be used as well to further a more transcendent political cause and/or theological agenda dear to the scholar (note e.g. Sasson 1981; Herion 1986; Pasto 1998; Provan 1995; cf. Carroll R. 1992: 34-36, 46-47). Others have argued that the paucity of available data from the ancient world demands the very circumspect use (if at all, according to some) of modern sociological theories. Researchers, in other words, should recognize the very real limitations of their efforts at investigating and explaining a world thousands of years removed from the possibility of direct corroboration or refutation (Rodd 1981; cf. Carroll R. 1992: 32-34).

Perhaps the most serious allegation is that biblical scholars often have demonstrated an inadequate grasp of the social sciences and thus can misunderstand or inappropriately apply them. This weakness has been evident from the very start of their utilization in biblical studies (see Rogerson 1978, 1985, 1986, 1989; cf. Lemche 1990; Carroll R. 1992: 36-44).[2] A striking example of a sustained critique of what he considers a misinformed endeavor to use the social sciences in the reconstruction of ancient Israelite society and religion is Lemche's detailed analysis of Gottwald's massive *The Tribes of Yahweh* (Gottwald 1979; Lemche 1985). This assessment is all the more sobering, as Gottwald is one of a handful of biblical scholars who have dedicated considerable time and effort to employ social scientific models in his research (note Gottwald 1979, 1985, 1993a). Ironically, one of Gottwald's principal aims in that work was to introduce this sort of approach into the study of early Israel with a seriousness not seen before in Old Testament studies and to point out how previous research either had been naive or had willfully ignored relevant issues, because of certain theological convictions and the compartmentalization of research due to overspecialization.

Each of these observations deserves attention. Nevertheless, it must be stressed that those who promote and employ social science criticism increasingly are cognizant of these very real dangers. Along with the encouragement to explore new areas, one now finds lists of safeguards and suggestions for greater theoretical perspicacity and methodological skill (see, e.g., Wilson 1984: 28-29; Rogerson 1985; Holmberg 1990: 1-17, 145-57; Elliott 1993: 87-106; Carter and Meyers 1996: 23-28). The conviction is that the achievements already attained and the possible insights to be gained in the future far outweigh any call to bridle too severely the social sciences' application to biblical studies.

---

2.   Interestingly, on the other side of the equation, so to speak, those from the social science disciplines who have ventured into biblical studies have been criticized for their lack of expertise in that field. On the one hand, the sociologist Max Weber has exercised a great influence on biblical scholarship. At the same time his shortcomings in biblical studies have also been duly noted. (Cf., e.g., Petersen 1979; Rodd 1979; Lang 1984; and Carroll R. 1992: 26-36). M. Douglas, an anthropologist whose work has influenced both Old and New Testament studies, begins a recent publication with the admission of her lack of training in biblical studies and an expression of gratitude for those biblical scholars who have been willing to help educate her, the 'ignorant enquirer' (1993: 16-17).

b. *Contexts for the Text*

A second key context, to which social sciences have contributed increased awareness and sensibility, is that of the reader and community of interpreters. This new appreciation is evident from several different perspectives.

First, the social sciences have been taken up by movements around the globe, which have tried to voice the protests and aspirations of the marginalized. Latin American liberation theology was a pioneer in calling for a hermeneutics of suspicion, a suspicion that challenged ecclesiastical hierarchical structures, pastoral practice, the reading of biblical texts and the formulation of theology. All of this was grounded in the demand for an epistemological break away from the dominant interpretive lenses to a conversion to 'doing theology from below' in commitment to and solidarity with the poor and oppressed (cf. Carroll R. forthcoming).

The need to better understand Latin American existence, the hope of a deeper level of *concientización* (i.e. conscious and critical awareness) of the harsh realities of the peripheral nations of the world, and the desire for concrete direction for social and political praxis led liberationists to the social sciences, in particular to various aspects and currents of Marxism. The use of Marxism by liberationists has been selective and critical, but some of those categories that have been appropriated are dependency theory, praxis, capital as fetish, the organic intellectual and the hope for a socialist state (cf. Gotay 1985; Girardi 1986; Dussel 1985, 1988, 1993; Kee 1990). A landmark piece in this new orientation for biblical studies was Juan Luis Segundo's articulation of the 'hermeneutical circle' (Segundo 1976: 7-38). The Bible thus was read anew for an agenda of liberation. The social science framework not only defined the social location and purpose of the interpreter, but also dramatically influenced the choice of texts, their interpretation and the choice of methodologies (cf., e.g., Rowland and Corner 1990; Carroll R. 1992: 291-306, 312-19). Latin American liberationist biblical scholars, such as Elsa Tamez, Jorge V. Pixley, and Severino Croatto, in time acquired a hearing in the more developed countries and have impacted the way biblical research will be done in the future. This story of the importance of the appeal to the social sciences in transforming the self-understanding of the interpreter could be repeated in African–American,

African (especially South African),[3] and Asian biblical studies. A more recent development is the emergence of biblical studies from indigenous points of view (note, e.g., Carroll R. 1995a; Richard 1996; Cook 1997).

A second orientation comes from the gender perspective, which would encompass the concerns of women in the West and other countries and of various ethnicities. These feminist and womanist biblical studies have utilized the social sciences in order to expose the patriarchal dimensions of human reality. Accordingly, there arises the demand to resist and contest conventional approaches, which are criticized for not grasping this essential component of social existence and of the academic guild itself. Reading consciously as women has led, among other things, to the observation of different kinds of textual details and themes, the rereading and re-evaluation of biblical narratives, and inquiries into the essence and function of religious language in the Bible and in ecclesiastical traditions (cf., e.g., Ruether 1983; Fiorenza 1984). One of the fruits of gender-sensitive biblical studies was the publication of *The Women's Bible Commentary* (Newsom and Ringe 1992).

The recognition of the value of being cognizant of the social impact of the reception of biblical texts also has moved into other areas of research. For example, scholars are now investigating the role of the Bible in the colonial and imperialist policies of various nations and social movements in the past (cf. Rivera 1992; Carroll R. 1995a: 195-200; Prior 1997). Coming from another tack, Smith-Christopher has championed attempts to show how certain modern cultures approximate the life experiences of the world of the biblical text and hence can help scholars arrive at a closer approximation of the original textual meaning (Smith-Christopher 1995). Lastly, issues of postmodernism, which eschews metanarratives in favor of multiplicity and contextuality, raise questions about the social location of interpreters in ways that some might consider inimical to the liberation enterprise: Is it possible now to claim that any specific interpretive stance is to be privileged? How does one call for responsible interpretation (and what would that mean?) in a hermeneutical environment pushing for absolute plurality (Segovia and Tolbert 1995b; Batstone *et al.* 1997)? Each of the trends mentioned in

---

3. One work that merits particular mention in this vein is West 1995a. The author describes and analyzes biblical studies in South Africa in dialogue with African–American and Latin American liberation studies and North American feminism.

this paragraph would make use of different social sciences in distinct ways to fulfill its aims. Once again, the necessity of social scientific criticism, in all of its diversity, is made manifest.

c. *The Context behind the Text*
A final context to be explored briefly is the context of the production of the biblical material. What is in view, in other words, are discussions of the ideology of the text that would be related to the sociology of literature in tandem with sociological reconstructions. In the past critical scholarship in its presentation of the redaction of texts always has alluded to the possible contexts of oral traditions, sources and literary forms, editors and the like. Social scientific criticism, however, has allowed for a more complex exploration and explanation of those contexts. This approach, though, also has led to different valuations of the biblical tradition. This phenomenon is connected in part in some cases to the previous category: textual ideologies are deemed undesirable and worthy of rejection, because of the moral commitments and values of scholars within the contexts of their chosen communities.

The effort to uncover these textual ideologies can have several facets. Some highlight socio-economic and political components. The ideology of the received text, for many of a liberationist persuasion is unacceptable. What is sought out then is an original core of material, or even an originating impulse within this material, that is ideologically commendable and relevant for today. This sort of thrust can be traced, for instance, in Gottwald (e.g. 1979: 703-709, 1993a: 291-383, 1995), Pixley (1987, 1992), and Mosala (Mosala 1989; cf. West 1995a: 70-74, 135-46), who believe that the foundational message of the Bible is one of liberation for the oppressed. This 'true' faith and the force of its social demands were either diminished or buried with the accretion of other material in an editorial process controlled by elites. The task of scholarship, therefore, is to find a way back to the earlier level of tradition. Others would not be so generous with the text and would claim that any attempt to reclaim the ideology of the text (whatever that might be) would be misdirected: 'the Bible never generated an ideology of freedom' (R.P. Carroll 1995: 37).

A similar pattern is evident in feminist and womanist approaches, whose primary attention is to gender issues. In this case, a spectrum of opinions surface regarding the worth of a text that these scholars see as inherently patriarchal and reflective of the worldview of its male authors (cf. Ringe 1992). While some hold that it is still possible to use the Bible in spite of these limitations (e.g. Cahill 1995; Ringe 1995; Bird 1997: 239-64), others would 'prefer doing away with the notions of canon and biblical authority altogether' (Exum 1995: 264) because the text is perceived to be hopelessly and irretrievably androcentric.

Recent research on ancient Israelite history and its representation in the Old Testament also is probing the ideology of the text. Davies, for instance, would claim that the entire Old Testament is a late creation of the Persian period, constructed by political and religious elites to provide for themselves a history and sacred legitimation. In his view, scholarship has too naively embraced the theological history of the Bible as fact. He attempts to articulate—admittedly sometimes in a speculative manner—the ideology of those elites (Davies 1992). Scholars involved in trying to understand the religion of ancient Israel are questioning, too, the religious ideology of the received text, which defends monotheism while decrying the veneration of other gods and certain kinds of cults. This picture, it is said, is neither reliable nor a fair representation of what religious life truly would have been like for the early periods of Israelite history.[4] Interestingly, Keel and Uehlinger link their efforts to uncover goddess worship and other religious trends of Israel's past to feminist interests and Third World religious practices and beliefs in the present (Keel and Uehlinger 1998: 409).

3. Conclusion

To enter the world of the social sciences and their use in biblical studies is to become acquainted with a veritable plethora of methods, models and concerns. I have tried to enumerate, howbeit in summary fashion, some of the contexts of the Bible to which social scientific criticism has contributed an understanding and sensitivity: the context described or assumed by the text, the context in which the text is read and applied, and the context lying behind its production. It is obvious that there are all sorts of avenues of future research to be explored and refined, as well as many disagreements among scholars regarding priorities, interpretations, and estimations of the value of the Bible for these kinds of studies.

4.   For a fuller discussion, see in this volume my essay 'Re-examining "Popular Religion": Issues of Definition and Sources. Insights from Interpretive Anthropology'.

What is also clear is that social science approaches necessarily will draw upon and impact other disciplines. For instance, it is impossible to speak of the contexts of the reception of the Bible and not interact with literary theory and philosophical hermeneutics. Making decisions about the contemporary viability of the text, whether positive or negative, moves very quickly into issues of theology and religious traditions. Said another way, interdisciplinarity breeds yet greater interdisciplinarity. This can be a salutary development as different fields interact with and enrich biblical studies.

The essays in this volume reflect some of the variety of approaches mentioned in this introduction, and all reveal an awareness of the several contexts pertinent to the social sciences. The authors appeal to theories from many different social sciences and offer new readings and interpretations that ideally can encourage further dialogue and research in both Old and New Testament studies. This volume is divided into two parts. The first set of essays includes aspects of the personal journeys of the authors into the realm of the social sciences. Each as well suggests fresh insights into how they might serve biblical research. The second set of essays contains three extensive case studies. These are applications of a social science model introduced in the preceding chapter.

Part I

THE POTENTIAL AND PITFALLS OF SOCIAL SCIENCE APPROACHES

THE POTENTIAL OF THE NEGATIVE:
APPROACHING THE OLD TESTAMENT THROUGH
THE WORK OF ADORNO

John W. Rogerson

1. *Introduction*

The use of social-scientific models in Old Testament interpretation is not an end in itself, neither is it adherence to a fashion. In my own case it began early in my teaching career when I felt the pressing need to gain a vantage point from which I could survey from outside, as it were, the academic discipline of biblical studies into which I had been inserted as a student and which had shaped the beginnings of my teaching. In the event, it was social anthropology that gave me the needed vantage point. I found in social anthropology a self-critical awareness that I missed in biblical studies; and as I began to compare what was being written about the interpretation of culture and societies in social anthropology with what was being produced in Old Testament studies, I became convinced that the latter discipline badly needed the former. The result was two books and several articles (Rogerson 1970a, 1970b, 1974, 1987).

More recently I have turned to sociology in the broad sense of social and political theory. This move has been partly personal in that the growing awareness within biblical studies of the past twenty years that it is not possible to separate academic study from political commitment has led me to question my political stances. This has led in turn to an attempt to understand the roots of modernity and of the functioning and values of modern Western society. However, what has been in part a personal quest for understanding has proved to be illuminating for interpreting the Old Testament. In particular I have tried to argue that the interpretation of modernity by Jürgen Habermas can be used profitably in Old Testament study (Rogerson 1990, 1995a). In the past twelve months, without in any way abandoning Habermas, I have concentrated on the man whose *Assistent* in Frankfurt Habermas once was, Theodor W. Adorno. To some, including possibly Habermas himself, this could be regarded as a retrograde step; a move from Habermas's theory of greater explanatory power to Adorno's seemingly limited and negative position (cf. *inter alia* Habermas 1987). Yet I have been impressed by Adorno's profound sincerity, and by his willingness to think the un-thinkable; and I have found his pessimism compelling as we leave one horrendous century and enter a new one with little hope that human inhumanity will be in any way mitigated by human action.

Twelve months of study of Adorno and some of the secondary liter-ature has left me with two convictions: that my grasp of Adorno is fragile and that compared with those who have had longer to engage with his thought my efforts are likely to seem superficial. However, this may be an advantage in that those unfamiliar with Adorno's work may find their way into it more easily via something that is elementary than something that is more profound. Yet I hope that what follows will be illuminating in itself and for Old Testament interpretation. The extent, and thus the limitation, of my engagement with Adorno and the sec-ondary literature will be indicated by the next footnote.[1]

---

1.   The Wissenschaftliche Buchgesellschaft in Darmstadt has recently issued (1998) a special inexpensive edition of the *Gesammelte Schriften* (hereafter *GS*) of Adorno in 20 volumes, to which must be added the further volumes of nach-gelassene Schriften published by the Adorno Archiv in Frankfurt. The main works, namely, *Dialectic of Enlightenment, Minima Moralia, Negative Dialectics* and *Aes-thetic Theory* have been translated into English, albeit not always entirely satisfac-torily. However, the bulk of Adorno's writings remains untranslated. Among treat-ments in English, the most recent is by S. Jarvis (1998). A general work by M. Jay (1973) places Adorno in the context of the Institute for Social Research. An inter-esting account of Adorno's American exile followed by an interpretation of his thought is provided by P.U. Hohendahl (1995). S. Benhabib (1986) contains much illuminating material on Adorno. The two most helpful German works that I have read are G. Schweppenhäuser (1996) and U. Kohlmann (1997). An interesting dis-covery has been the sharp criticisms of Habermas by scholars who consider that he is responsible for distorting the work of Adorno and of his fellow author (of *Dialec-tic of Enlightenment*) Max Horkheimer. The conference held in Frankfurt in 1983 in memory of Adorno on what would have been his eightieth birthday (L. von Friede-burg and J. Habermas [1983]) was countered by a symposium held in Hamburg the following year which was highly critical of the 1983 conference. See M. Löbig and G. Schweppenhäuser (1984). A further conference by what might be called the anti-Habermas camp was held in Berlin in 1989 and published as F. Hager and H. Pfütze (1990). Titles which barely conceal their antagonism to Habermas and support for

2. *The Life of Adorno in Context*

Adorno was born as Theodor Ludwig Wiesengrund in September 1903 in Frankfurt am Main. His mother, Maria, was a singer and his father, Oscar, a wine merchant. Born into a Jewish family, Oscar had been baptised as a Protestant. His son was later increasingly drawn back to his Jewish roots, especially following the German persecution of the Jews and the Holocaust. Two interests dominated Adorno's formative years: music (where his mother's influence can be seen) and philosophy. While still in his teens Adorno spent many Saturday afternoons reading Kant's *Critique of Pure Reason* with Siegfried Kracauer, to whom he had been introduced by a friend of his parents.[2] In 1919 he began to study musical composition at a conservatory in Frankfurt, and in 1921 entered the University of Frankfurt to study philosophy, psychology and sociology.

Only three years later he gained a doctorate for a thesis on Husserl's phenomenology and in the following year (1925) went to Vienna to study composition with Alban Berg. Here he met Arnold Schönberg and Georg Lukács, among others. Back in Frankfurt, from 1927 he edited a musical journal dedicated to avant-garde music and worked on his *Habilitationsschrift*, the postdoctoral thesis needed to gain an academic position in a German university. His supervisor was Paul Tillich, the subject was Kierkegaard's aesthetic theory, and the thesis was accepted in 1931.[3] Meanwhile Adorno had begun to work with the Institute of Social Research in Frankfurt, founded in 1923 and directed

Adorno and Horkheimer include G. Bolte (1989), C. Rademacher (1993), and P. Moritz (1992). A recent work on Adorno's social theory is D. Auer, T. Bonacker and S. Müler-Doohm (1998). Adorno's aesthetic theory is discussed in B. Scheer (1997: 169-87), while his negative dialectics is treated in J. Ritsert (1997: 147-82).

2.   See Adorno's account of how Rosie Stein introduced him to Kracauer in 'Der wunderliche Realist: Über Siegfried Kracauer' in *GS* 11: 388-408. Siegfried Kracauer (1889–1966) studied architecture and philosophy at Darmstadt and took a doctorate in engineering in Berlin in 1915. He then worked as an architect in Frankfurt among other places. From 1921 he edited the Feuilleton section of the *Frankfurter Zeitung*. With the advent of Nazism he moved to Paris, and emigrated to the United States in 1941, where he founded materialist film criticism and wrote on the history and theory of film. See *Neue Deutsche Biographie*, 12 (Berlin: Duncker & Humbolt, 1980), pp. 630-31.

3.   The thesis was published as *Kierkegaard: Konstruktion des Äthetischen* in 1933. The edition in *GS* 2 reprints the third, 1966, edition.

since July 1930 by Max Horkheimer, whom Adorno had first met in his student days in 1922 (Jay 1973: 25).

With the assumption of power by the National Socialists in 1933 Adorno's right to teach in a university was abrogated, and from 1934 to 1937 he commuted between Frankfurt and Oxford, where he was an advanced student at Merton College. In 1938 he was officially appointed to the staff of the Institute of Social Research and emigrated, together with other members, to the United States. He dropped the surname Wiesengrund and adopted his mother's surname Adorno. Adorno's American exile, spent from 1941 in Los Angeles, saw the publication of the joint work with Horkheimer, *Dialectic of Enlightenment*,[4] the writing of *Minima Moralia*[5] and the completion of the research embodied in *The Authoritarian Personality* (Adorno *et al.* 1950).

Adorno returned to Germany in 1949 to take up the post of *Ausserordentlicher Professor* (professor without an established chair) in Philosophy at Frankfurt, and from 1950 he and Horkheimer headed the refounded Institute of Social Research. Among the important publications of the following years the *Negative Dialektik* and the posthumous *Ästhetische Theorie* are particularly noteworthy.[6] As the student protest movement began to gather strength in the 1960s Adorno came to be regarded by the radicals as one of their guiding lights. However, his response to the student unrest in 1969, when he called in the police to protect the Institute against a student sit-in, disillusioned many. Adorno died unexpectedly of a heart attack while on holiday in Switzerland in August 1969.

4.   The *Dialektik der Aufklärung* appeared in a mimeographed edition in 1944 as a publication of the Institute of Social Research. In 1947 it appeared as a book published by Querido in Amsterdam. A revised edition was published by the Fischer Verlag in Frankfurt am Main in 1969. It also exists in the collected works of both Horkheimer (1987: 13-290) and Adorno (*GS* 3).

5.   Adorno (1951). Revised editions appeared in 1962 and 1964. The edition in *GS* 4 reprints the 1964 edition with an Appendix (*Anhang*) of material from the 1951 edition that Adorno removed from the later editions. The English translation by E.G.N. Jephcott (Jephcott 1974) does not include the *Anhang*.

6.   The *Negative Dialektik* was published in Frankfurt in 1966 by Suhrkamp with a second edition the following year. See *GS* 6, English translation by E.B. Ashton (Ashton 1973). *Ästhetische Theorie* appeared under Suhrkamp's imprint in 1970 (second edition 1972). See *GS* 7. English translation by C. Lenhardt (1984) Retranslation by R. Hullot-Kentor (1996).

3. *The Philosophy of Adorno and its Relevance for Old Testament Studies*

One of the aims of *Dialectic of Enlightenment* is to describe the anatomy of human reason. The Enlightenment is not presented as an intellectual movement in the Europe of the seventeenth to eighteenth centuries. The Enlightenment is rather a feature of human rationality that has been present since humans began the struggle against nature to survive, by seeking ways of overcoming it. However, any success in controlling part of nature has been paid for in two ways. First, there has been no human control of a part of nature without the domination of some humans by others. An obvious example from the Ancient Near East[7] is that the construction of irrigation systems in order to take full advantage of water resources in areas affected by drought entailed the organization of labour, which necessitated hierarchical domination. The struggle between humanity and nature is therefore reproduced in a struggle between humans and humans. The second price paid was that what is called in *Dialectic of Enlightenment* inner (i.e. human) nature has had to be controlled either by self-discipline or by coercion.

These positions are outlined in the opening section of *Dialectic of Enlightenment* and in the first of the two Excursuses, that concerning the *Odyssey* (Horkheimer 1987: 67-103; Adorno, *GS*: 61-99). This part of the *Dialectic* was written by Adorno early in 1943, and Horkheimer's contribution was to shorten it slightly. The publication in 1998 of Adorno's original longer version makes this text mandatory for any study of Adorno (Adorno 1998). Among other things, its footnotes are more considerable than in the jointly authored version, and this mitigates to some extent Jarvis's reasonable observation that the references in *Dialectic of Enlightenment* are thinly sown (Jarvis 1998: 20). The most striking part of the Excursus is the exposition of the incident in which Odysseus navigates his vessel past the sirens by filling his men's ears with wax so that they cannot hear the sirens, and by having himself tied to the mast so that he cannot respond to what he hears. The incident symbolizes the dialectic of human rational engagement with nature. The party in the ship survives because, through the exercise of hierarchical authority, the men are deprived of their hearing. Their leader is also deprived of his freedom to respond to the alluring sounds and reve-

---

7.   My own illustration, not one from *Dialectic of Enlightenment*.

lations of the sirens by ordering his men to tie him to the mast and to ignore any orders to set him free, while the danger lasts (Horkheimer 1987: 82-83; Adorno, *GS* 3: 77-78; R. Tiedemann 1998a: 59-60 with one additional phrase). Adorno describes this, and other strategies in the *Odyssey* to defeat the like of Polyphemus and Circe, as *List* (cunning). These characters in the story represent forces that humanity must overcome in order to survive.

However, what is found in the mythical world of Homer[8] is also a feature of modern life. It is one of the Enlightenment's myths that myth is a thing of the past. On the contrary, human engagement with nature requires that humans dominate and control other humans, and that they subordinate their inner (human) nature to this task. The failure of enlightenment rationality to realize these things indicates the extent to which it has itself fallen prey to myth, in the sense of lack of critical self-understanding. Ultimately, Adorno will argue that all forms of human domination, and especially that represented by capitalism, are manifestations of an inescapable characteristic of human rationality. It has been rightly said that what is contained in *Dialectic of Enlightenment* is not a history of domination but a primordial history, an *Urgeschichte*.[9]

The mention of *Urgeschichte* can be taken as an immediate clue to turn to the Old Testament; but before this is done it can be pointed out that Adorno could have illustrated his points from texts other than Homer's *Odyssey* among writings from the ancient world.[10] The dialectic between nature and culture is evident in *The Epic of Gilgamesh*, for example. By getting the wild man Enkidu tamed and 'cultured', so that he can assist Gilgamesh in his fights against Humbaba and the bull of heaven, Gilgamesh robs him of his freedom and makes him aware of the terrors of death (Pritchard 1969: 72-97). The dialectic between

8.   Adorno's use of the notion of myth is, perhaps deliberately, ambiguous. See R. Tiedemann 1998b.

9.   H. Schnädelbach, 'Die Aktualität der Dialektik der Aufklärung', in H. Kunnemann and H. der Vries (eds.), *Die Aktualität der Dialektik der Aufklärung* (Frankfurt am Main: Campus Verlag, 1989), pp. 20, 29, cited in Jarvis (1998: 41).

10.   That he chose Homer arose from an engagement with Nietzsche, Rudolf Borchardt, Gilbert Murray and others. This becomes clear from the extensive discussion at the beginning of the original version of Excursus I, material that was not included in the published version. See Adorno 1998: 38-45.

culture and nature is also central to C. Lévi-Strauss's (post-Adorno) *Mythologiques* (Lévi-Strauss 1964).

In Genesis 2–4 the dialectic is as follows. In ch. 2 the man and woman are in harmony with each other and with the world of nature. Their world is, however, a static world. The alternative, a world in which humans develop agriculture and animal husbandry, build cities and become skilled in metal-working and music (Gen. 4.1-2, 17, 21-22) is a world of conflict—conflict between humans (Gen. 3.8-23; 4.1-8, 23-24) and between humans and nature (3.15, 17-19). It is often said that the opening chapters of Genesis are never explicitly referred to elsewhere in the Old Testament and that they were therefore unimportant for its editors/compilers. However, the anatomy of what it means to be human in Genesis 1–11 is presupposed in many other parts of the collection, including the laws that enjoin compassion and fair treatment of fellow Israelites, foreigners and the natural order (e.g. Exod. 23.4-13). Whatever Gen. 1.26-27 may mean when it speaks of humankind being made in the image and likeness of God, the immediately following chapters present a sombre view of the anatomy of being human that is as realistic as that of Adorno.

Another matter addressed in the first Excursus is sacrifice (Horkheimer 1987: 73-83; Adorno *GS* 3: 66-76; Adorno 1998: 48-59 with additional material). This topic enables Adorno to connect a number of themes that are central to his concerns: *List* (cunning), exchange, the suppression of individuality by external factors and the need for self-renunciation (*Entsagung*), and the evils of German fascism. These connections are arguably most clearly seen in the original, longer version in the *Frankfurter Blätter*. In a remarkable passage that did not appear in the published version, Adorno drew an implicit comparison between Odysseus and Hitler, sharply criticizing the tactics used by the former to survive during his journeyings and blaming Odysseus's need to appear finally in his own palace as a beggar for his subsequent violent behaviour towards the suitors gathered there. Adorno continued:

> The period between that of the triumphing beggar Odysseus and the all-powerful ascetic Hitler was that of the middle way, the way of moderation, self-discipline, patience, the balancing of good fortune (*Glück*) and bad fortune (*Unglück*) over a long time period, as the philosophers urged so insistently during the whole bourgeois era. The result was that in popular consciousness the term 'philosopher' became identical with 'self-renouncer'. The middle way together with philosophy and humanity came to an end, however, when rulers used fascism to tear the prospect

of good fortune away from the self-renunciation of the oppressed and made once more into a fetish the fulfilment of sacrifice, the dangerous life in the service of privilege, as it had once been in antiquity.[11]

From this passage a number of connections can be identified. Adorno believed that one of his tasks was to revise philosophy so that it was no longer an ally of that middle way, which (in his view) led from the dialectic of rationality in antiquity to the horrors of modern fascism. How he proposed to do this will be discussed later. Secondly, he was able to attack the idea of renunciation (*Entsagung*), which for him was the way in which the dialectic of enlightenment forced people to subordinate their inner (human) nature and thus deny their individuality. Fascism merely took that process to a logical conclusion by demanding complete self-renunciation in the service of a higher cause—a cause that included eliminating supposed inferior races such as the Jews. A self-denying thus became the means of denying life to others.

But the self-renunciation, this completing of self-sacrifice, was also an instance of the false value of exchange that was fundamental to sacrifice in general, and which was given practical expression in modern capitalism by the undervaluing of the labour of working people. In the immediate context of fascism, individuals were persuaded or forced to exchange their individuality for the achievement of the ambitions of a dictator. In the Odysseus stories his men were forced to exchange their individuality for the successful voyage of Odysseus to his home island. However, this unequal exchange fundamental to self-sacrifice was also fundamental to sacrifice per se. When a sacrifice was offered to a deity, there was necessarily an unequal exchange. An animal or an offering of food or drink was not an exact equivalent for the offerer himself. Further, sacrifice involved a degree of *List* (cunning) on the part of the

11. Adorno (1998: 58-59), my translation. The German is: 'Das Zeitalter zwischen dem triumphierenden Bettler Odysseus und dem allvermögenden Asketen Hitler war das des mittleren Weges van Mäßigung, Selbstdisziplin, Geduld, der Aufrechnung von Glück und Unglück in die Totalität der Zeit, wie ihn während der gesamten bürgerlichen Ära die Philosophen so beharrlich empfohlen haben, daß der Begriff des Philosophen im populären Bewußtsein mit dem des Entsagenden übereinkam. Als aber die Herrschenden im Faschimus die Entsagung der Unterworfenen von der Aussicht auf Glück losrissen und den Vollzug des Opfers, das gefährliche Leben, im Dienst des Privilegs wiederum zu dem Fetisch machten, der es in der Vorzeit einmal gewesen war, hatte der mittlere Weg samt Philosophie und Humanität das Ende erreicht.'

offerer, since the sacrifice's purpose was to enable the offerer to make
the deity subject to the offerer's wishes (cf. Horkheimer 1987: 74;
Adorno *GS* 3:68; Adorno 1998: 50-51).[12] Adorno thus maintained that
the linked notions of sacrifice and exchange (exchange is described as
secularized sacrifice) pointed to a fundamental contradiction in human
rationality (Horkheimer 1987: 73, Adorno *GS* 3: 67; Adorno 1998: 49).
The two functions were essential to human survival in the struggle with
nature and its personified forces, and in the organization of social relationships, but they entailed cunning and unequal and distorted exchange.

There is much here for the interpreter of the Old Testament to pon-
der, bearing in mind that what we have here in Adorno is an *Urgeschichte* and not an historical or social account of sacrifice. It must also
be borne in mind that the Old Testament, in the wilderness wandering
narratives, has an account of a journey of people that can be compared
with the Odysseus story.

On the question of sacrifice, the prophetic denunciations of the cult
highlight precisely those factors that Adorno wishes to expose: deceit,
including self-deceit, and distorted and unequal exchange. In a famous
passsage in Mic. 6.1-8 the question is posed 'with what shall I come
before the LORD?' The answer is that the most exaggerated offerings
will be inappropriate, because nothing can be of equal value to the
practice by individuals of justice and mercy towards others, and faith-
fulness towards God. Adorno's point that the purpose of sacrifice is to
subordinate the deity to human aims is both affirmed and denied in the
Old Testament. It is affirmed in the prophetic denunciations of those
who believe that the mere performance of sacrifice will ensure God's
favour (e.g. Isa. 1.12-15, Amos 4.4-5). It is denied (a denial that proves
Adorno's point) in the articulations of God's transcendence, a transcendence that is above manipulation by human offerings and which makes
them not only redundant but offensive (e.g. Psalm 50).

It is striking, indeed, that texts such as Psalm 50 which condemn

12. 'Alle menschlichen Opferhandlungen, planmäßig betrieben, betrügen den
Gott, dem sie gelten: sie unterstellen ihn dem Primat der menschlichen Zwecke,
lösen seine Macht auf, und der Betrug an ihm geht bruchlos über in den, welchen
die ungläubigen Priester an der gläubigen Gemeinde vollführen' ('All human acts
of sacrifice, carried out systematically, deceive the deity for whom they are meant.
They subordinate the deity to the primacy of human aims, and destroy its power.
The act of deceiving the deity passes intact to the things that unbelieving priests
inflict upon the believing congregation.' [my translation])

sacrifice so strongly should lay such stress upon the need for human justice. The psalmist condemns those who promote theft and adultery, who indulge in evil gossip and slander, who introduce conflict into the family (Ps. 50.18-26). The opposing of sacrifice to social justice in the Old Testament has long been a discussion point in Old Testament studies. However, it takes on a new dimension in the light of Adorno's work. If Adorno's analysis of the dialectic of human rationality is correct, that dialectic had already implicitly been recognized in the Old Testament and its implications for justice in human relationships had been spelled out.

This conclusion leads to a perhaps awkward point for anyone approaching the Old Testament via social science methods. Since at least the time of William Robertson Smith, Old Testament scholars have enlisted the aid of social anthropology to enable them to make a positive evaluation of ancient Israelite sacrifice. Their motives have been mixed. Robertson Smith himself had a theological agenda in wanting to establish that the basic aim of Semitic sacrifice was to establish communion between the deity and worshippers and that the expiatory aspect of sacrifice was a later (and thus less authentic) development (Smith 1927: 213-440).[13] An approach via Adorno seems to put the matter back where it was in the late nineteenth century, when scholars such as George Adam Smith saw prophets such as Isaiah of Jerusalem as proto-Protestants, wanting to abolish the sacrificial cult and to stress social justice.

If Adorno is followed, however, this is not a reversion to nineteenth century veiled polemic against Catholic-type forms of Christianity. The ghastly twentieth century lies between that era and our own, with the Holocaust (an appropriate and terrifying word in this particular context) being the apogee of its barbarism. If there is a dialectical relationship between sacrifice and the exercise of power, that leads to such things as the Holocaust and the other barbarities of the twentieth century, this needs to be exposed; and if the Old Testament, even implicitly, makes the same connections, this enhances its value as a text that can address today's world. What becomes apparent from reading Adorno is that social scientific methods cannot be neutral when faced with social

13. Lectures VI–XI. As a member of the Free Church of Scotland Smith believed that personal religion was preferable to that mediated by a priestly cult, as he supposed it to be in Catholicism, for example.

reality; and that fact must also affect the uses of them made by Old Testament scholars.

The next task is to survey briefly the accounts of the wilderness wanderings in Exodus and Numbers, in comparison with the story of Odysseus. The first point to note is that Moses has nothing like the control over his (admittedly very large) group that Odysseus has over his men. Also, their aims are different, that of Odysseus being to get himself back to Ithaca, while Moses has the task of getting his people to the promised land. Odysseus has absolute power over his men, Moses faces frequent rebellions. If Odysseus loses men, as is necessary if he is to pass Scylla and Charibdis safely, it is to ensure this ultimate survival. Moses' task is to get his people safely to their destination, and if any of them are lost (as in the rebellon of Korah and his supporters in Numbers 16) it is not so that Moses can survive, but because groups have taken the law into their own hands. Odysseus achieves his goal of reaching Ithaca. Moses gets his people to within sight of the promised land but is not allowed to enter it himself.

No doubt this comparison between the two accounts of journeyings is superficial and proves nothing. Yet it is interesting that in the legal sections that are inserted into the wilderness wanderings attempts are made to emphasize and to protect the individuality of Israelites. In a society in which the inequality of the exchange of labour for its value resulted in slavery, strenuous efforts were made, in theory if not in practice, to mitigate these effects and to restore individual Israelites to their full dignity. Slavery was limited to a period of six years (Exod. 21.1-11; Deut. 15.12-18) and, in the most ambitious legislation of all, the Jubilee in Leviticus 25, all kinds of provisions are stipulated which are designed to counteract the economic distortions inherent in Israelite society which lead to the impoverishment and degradation of some Israelites.

I want to turn now to this matter of the individual and to pursue it further. In Adorno's writings the matter of individuality is bound up with his dissatisfaction with traditional philosophy and his revision of what he sees as its central task. Human thought has tried to understand the world by subsuming its manifold appearances under various categories. Binary oppositions such as light/dark, hard/soft have played their part in this. Adorno's objection to this is that by placing particulars into specific classes, the uniqueness and individuality of the particulars have been lost.[14] In the context of human society, individuals have lost their individuality through the need to perform in ways appropriate to class or profession. Thus Adorno's attack upon philosophy is not merely an intellectual matter. Rightly or wrongly he believes that there is a link between Western philosophy's classification of particulars in terms of generalizations and the inhumanity that fails to treat each human individual as a unique 'other'. Precisely what philosophy should do, according to Adorno, will be discussed later; but his aim is that, in philosophical thinking and social practice there should be what has been called 'the coercionless synthesis of the manifold' (Jarvis 1998: 32). This, whether practically attainable or not, would be a process in which people and objects would form a harmonious whole without losing their uniqueness. Elsewhere, as will be explained later, Adorno stresses the importance of non-identity.

A text in the Old Testament that comes to mind in this connection is the Song of Songs. While this text is probably made up of poems from various contexts, running through the collection as a whole is the theme of the constraints placed upon the man and the woman by the social conventions of their society. This constraint is most clearly expressed in 8.1-4:

> O that you were like a brother to me
> that nursed at my mother's breasts!
> If I met you outside, I would kiss you,
> and none would despise me.
> I would lead you and bring you into the house of my mother,
> and into the chamber of her that conceived me.
> I would give you spiced wine to drink,
> the fruit of my pomegranates.
> O that his left hand were under my head,
> and that his right hand embraced me!
> I adjure you, O daughters of Jerusalem,
> that you stir not up nor awaken love until it pleases.

The woman complains that, whereas social convention would allow her to express her affection for a full brother in public and that nobody would think it wrong if she were to take her brother into her domain, such actions would be impossible if the male were her lover. It could be argued, of course, that such social conventions existed in order to

---

14. See Adorno, 'Zu Subjekt und Objekt', in *GS* 10.2: 741-58; *GS* 6: 176-93, ET pp. 174-92; Adorno 1967; Schweppenhäuser 1996: 59-66.

protect her and to prevent her from being harmed by unscrupulous males; but it has to be acknowledged that such conventions are also part of the mechanisms by which men control women. A passage which follows several verses later indicates this clearly (vv. 8-10):

> We have a little sister,
> and she has no breasts.
> What shall we do for our sister,
> on the day she is spoken for?
> If she is a wall,
> we will build upon her a battlement of silver;
> but if she is a door,
> we will enclose her with boards of cedar.
> I was a wall,
> and my breasts were like towers;
> then I was in his eyes
> as one who brings peace.

Although there are many problems of interpretation (are the words 'we have a little sister' spoken by the woman's brothers, or is the woman mimicking their words in order to refute them in v. 10?), even the most generous reading cannot escape from the fact that brothers played a part in arranging the marriages of their sisters (cf. Gen. 24.50, 55).[15]

There is, in Song of Songs, a powerful tension between the desire of the man and woman to develop a relationship which is one of equality and mutual respect, and social conventions which prevent such activity. The man and the woman are not allowed to be themselves; their relationship must conform to what social convention, in the service of male control, permits. They must practise self-renunciation (*Entsagung*). This is perhaps why the woman adjures the 'daughters of Jerusalem' not to stir up or awaken love before it is time for it to be expressed as convention allows. Passions aroused prematurely can only be frustrating and destructive. The woman is left to fantasize: 'O that his left hand were under my head, and that his right hand embraced me!' (v. 3).

Read from the perspective of Adorno, the tension in Song of Songs

---

15. Some commentators take the verses to mean that the woman's brothers wish to get the best possible price for her when she is married. See, for example, the references in Murphy (1990: 198). This view seems to rest upon an inadequate understanding of the functions of bride-wealth, which can be reserved for the woman by her family in case she is wrongly divorced and which can protect against wrongful divorce. See further Royal Anthropological Institute (1951: 116-22).

between the desire of the man and women to enjoy a relationship of equality and mutual respect, a non-coercive synthesis of their unique-ness, and the hindrances set up by social conventions, is not a call for 'free love'; but a yearning for a different world. What sociologists call passionate and romantic love (cf. Giddens 1992: 37-47), and which has taken many forms in human history from ballads to magazine stories, is a deeply rooted expression of natural human desires—desires frustrated in many ways by factors beyond the control of human beings. They are fantasies that enable people to cope with the realities of their world; and it would be folly to deny that the origins, collection and modern appeal of the Song of Songs have nothing to do with human fantasizing about passionate love.[16] Such fantasizing is, however, a desire to escape from the world; to enjoy something that the world as it is denies to people. Applying Adorno's views to Song of Songs makes it possible to read its poems as a desire not for escape, but for transformation. This, in turn, requires a consideration of the way in which negative critical thinking is central to Adorno's view of the task of philosophy as well as to his notions of Utopia.

Earlier in this essay it was pointed out that Adorno was critical of the attempt of philosophy to understand reality by organizing into concepts and categories the manifold of particulars that are presented to indi-vidual human perception. This does not mean that Adorno believed that philosophy should no longer attempt this. Rather, he believed that phi-losophy had not gone far enough, that it needed both to analyse experi-ence into concepts and categories and to expose the inadequacies of these procedures and the part that they had played and continued to play in the domination by humans of nature and other humans. The only escape that Adorno could envisage from human entrapment in the dialectic of enlightenment and its practical implications was the exer-cise of a critical negativity which exposed the true nature of the dialec-tic of human rationality and sought to negate it by stressing non-identity (i.e. the impossibility of subsuming two particulars under one category without robbing both of part of their uniqueness), and the priority of

---

16. See Giddens (1992: 37), where passionate love is characterized as 'marked by an urgency which sets it apart from the routines of everyday life in which, indeed, it tends to come into conflict. The emotional involvement with the other is pervasive—so strong that it may lead the individual, or both individuals, to ignore their ordinary obligations. Passionate love has a quality of enchantment which can be religious in its fervour. Everything in the world seems suddenly fresh.'

objectivity over subjectivity. At the same time this was not a call for an isolated individualism. 'Dialectical thought opposes reification in the further sense that it refuses to affirm individual things in their isolation and separateness: it designates isolation as precisely a product of the universal'.[17] Returning briefly to Song of Songs, the import of this quotation is that, if what was envisaged was simply an escape from an unchanged world, this would amount to an affirmation of that unchanged world; the escape would be a product of the unchanged world. For the man and the woman to be able to express their devotion to each other in a way that affirmed, in harmony, the uniqueness of each, a world would be required in which all other relationships and institutions similarly harmonized without coercion all the unique features of humans and other species. What such a world would be like could be stated only in terms of negatives, in the negation of the world as we know it.

Early in *Minima Moralia* Adorno wrote:

> There is nothing innocent left. Small exclamations of pleasure, the observations about life that seem exempt from the responsibility of [rigorous] thought, contain not only a degree of perverse foolishness, an insensitive self-blindness, but directly serve the interests of their exact opposite. Even the tree that blossoms lies, when its blooms are seen but not the shadow of terror. Even the innocent 'how lovely' becomes an excuse for the scandal of an existence that is quite other than lovely. There is no beauty or comfort left except in looking at horror, withstanding it, and in the unmitigated consciousness of negativity holding fast to the possibility of what is better (my translation).[18]

---

17. Adorno, *GS* 4: 8. ET by Jephcott (1974: 71). 'Das dialektische Denken widersetzt sich der Verdinglichung auch in dem Sinn, daß es sich weigert, ein Einzelnes je in seiner Vereinzelung und Abgetrenntheit zu bestätigen: es bestimmt gerade die Vereinzelung als Produkt des Allgemeinen.'

18. *GS* 4: 26, ET, p. 25. 'Es gibt nichts Harmloses mehr. Die kleinen Freuden, die Äußerungen des Lebens, die von der Verantwortung des Gedankens ausgenommen scheinen, haben nicht nur ein Moment der trotzigen Albernheit, des hartherzigen sich blind Machens, sondern treten unmittelbar in den Dienst ihres äußersten Gegensatzes. Noch der Baum, der blüht, lügt in dem Augenblick, in welchem man sein Blühen ohne den Schatten des Entsetzens wahrnimmt; noch das unschuldige wie schön wird zur Ausrede für die Schmach des Daseins, das anders ist, und es ist keine Schönheit und kein Trost mehr außer in dem Blick, der aufs Grauen geht, ihm standhält und im ungemilderten Bewußtsein der Negativität die Möglichkeit des Besseren festhält.'

Returning again briefly to the Song of Songs, it would have to be read as follows if the above quotation were taken seriously: the sublime evocations of nature that the book contains must not be taken as descriptions of the world as we know it. To respond in this way would simply be to affirm the shadows which parts of the book undoubtedly cast, such as the actual or imagined beating and stripping of the woman by the watchmen when they find her searching for her lover (Song 5.7).

To deny those shadows and the tangible horrors that cast them, the evocations of nature must be seen as the result of a process of consciously negating the actual world so that a better world can be hoped for. It would then be possible to see Song of Songs as an *Urgeschichte* and to contrast it with Genesis 3 (cf. Trible 1978: 144-65).

The use of negativity to hope for a better world is a theme that must now be explored further from an Old Testament viewpoint. It is striking that in one of the most vivid descriptions contained in the Old Testament of a new heaven and a new earth, the hope is expressed largely in negatives:

> no more shall be heard in it [Jersualem] the sound of weeping and the
> cry of distress.
> No more shall there be in it an infant that lives but a few days,
> or an old man who does not fill out his days...
> They shall not build and another inhabit;
> they shall not plant and another eat;
> ... They shall not labour in vain,
> or bear children for calamity (Isa. 65.19b-20, 22a, 23a).

Furthermore, where the passage contains positive formulations, some of them deliberately describe a world that is not the world of human experience:

> The wolf and the lamb shall feed together,
> the lion shall eat straw like the ox;
> and dust shall be the serpent's food.
> They shall not hurt or destroy in all my holy mountain says the LORD
> (Isa. 65.25).

These expressions of hope, combining as they do the negation of the world as it is and invoking a world different from that of human experience, lead back to the opening chapters of Genesis, where it cannot be stressed too strongly that the world of Genesis 1 is not the world of our experience. The world of Genesis 1, a world in which humankind and all the animals are vegetarians (Gen. 1.29-30), is a world at peace with

itself. Again, the world of Genesis 2 is not one in which the man is in
conflict with the natural order and its animals. He is not the human as
described in *Dialectic of Enlightenment*, needing to overcome nature in
order to survive and thereby needing to dominate and control other
humans—although he becomes that from ch. 3 onwards. The opening
chapters of Genesis make more theological sense when read in the light
of Adorno's negativity than when they are used to support either a
'Christian doctrine of creation' or a 'creation spirituality'.

An approach along the lines of negativity can also be made to passages about the Day of the LORD. These are entirely cast in negative
terms, and refer to human wickedness and injustice (cf. Zeph. 2.17); but
they have a cosmic dimension and imply the destruction of the present
created order. Thus, Zephaniah begins

> 'I will utterly sweep away everything
> from the face of the earth' says the LORD.
> 'I will sweep away man and beast;
> I will sweep away the birds of the air
> and the fish of the sea.
> I will overthrow the wicked;
> I will cut off mankind
> from the face of the earth' says the LORD (Zeph. 1.2-3).

Similarly Isa. 2.12-14 states that

> the LORD of hosts has a day
> against all that is proud and lofty,
> against all that is lifted up and high;
> against all the cedars of Lebanon, lofty and lifted up;
> and against all the oaks of Bashan;
> against all the high mountains,
> and against all the lofty hills.

No doubt these implicit condemnations of aspects of the natural world
are not directed against them as such but against them as used by or to
symbolize human achievement. But what is envisaged is not a tamper-
ing with the world in order to improve it but the destruction of a world
that cannot be improved.

Where positive statements are made in visions of the last days or the
Day of the LORD, they are based upon the negative of the present order.
Thus the statement that nations will 'beat their swords into plough-
shares and their spears into pruning hooks' (Isa. 2.4) envisages a situation which is the negation of what is currently the case.

What is the value of reading these and similar passages in the light of Adorno's negative dialectics? I can only give a personal answer to this question, along the following lines. If the material is read without any religious belief or political conviction being brought to bear, one has to say something like: 'This is what the prophets/writers of the Old Testament believed. They despaired of their own world and believed that God would create a better one. They expressed this belief in terms of the images and thought-forms available to them. Their hopes were not fulfilled; the world continues as before.' If, say, a liberal Christian faith is brought into play, something such as the following can be said: 'the prophets/writers of the Old Testament were mistaken in thinking that the world would be transformed within the contingencies of time and space. However, if one thinks in terms of eternity, or the afterlife (possibilities that were not available to the Old Testament writers), the transformation can be understood as something that happens beyond rather than in the world of human experience.' This last position, however, gives no direction for political action in the here and now; and the same would be true of the conservative type of Christian belief that holds that there will be a divine transformation of this world at a future date.

An approach to this material via negative dialectics could lead to something like the following statement: the prophetic/Old Testament negation of the world of human experience is a counterpart to the exercise of negativity that must characterise contemporary political action. We must, as Adorno says, 'fashion perspectives that displace and estrange the world, reveal it to be, with its rifts and crevices, as indigent and distorted as it will appear in the Messianic light'.[19] This is a programme for ideological criticism with implications for political praxis. But it is not the kind of ideological criticism that adopts the holier-than-thou perspective of today's world in condemning such things as patriarchy or class divisions in ancient Israel. Such criticism is merely another form of domination and self-deception.[20] The kind of ideological criticism that stems from negative dialectics takes its as its starting-point the rifts and crevices, the distortions and indigence of our own

19. Adorno, *GS* 4: 283, ET p. 247. 'Perspektiven müßten hergestellt werden, in denen die Welt ähnlich sich versetzt, verfremdet, ihre Risse und Schründe offenbart, wie sie einmal als bedürftig und entstellt im Messianischen Licht daliegen wird.'

20. Adorno (1951, para. 152), 'Vor Mißbrauch wird gewarnt' (Warning: not to be misused), *GS* 4: 280-83, ET pp. 244-47.

world and of our part in it. It then becomes possible to engage in an ideological criticism that is in solidarity and sympathy with the negative dialectics of the Old Testament writers and with their attempts to create within the limitations of their situations, what I have called elsewhere 'structures of grace' (Rogerson 1995b). It becomes possible, in sympathy with parts of the Old Testament, 'to contemplate all things as they would present themselves from the standpoint of redemption'.[21]

The final text to be considered in the light of Adorno is Ecclesiastes, whose presumed author I shall call by his Hebrew name of Qoheleth. A recent detailed monograph on the book proposes that the work derives from a teacher of young adults, who were faced by the questions posed to Judaism by Hellenism from the late fourth century BCE onwards (Fischer 1997). Whether or not this is correct, some conclusions can be drawn from the text about the problems that disturbed Qoheleth.

He was troubled by the lack of justice in the world: a lack of justice that was beyond human control and a lack of justice that was caused by human action. Of the former he wrote:

> Again I saw under the sun that the race was not to the swift, nor the battle to the strong, nor bread to the wise, nor riches to the intelligent, nor favour to the men of skills; but time and chance happen to them all (Eccl. 9.11).

In other words, the universe is not a moral universe, if by that is understood a world in which reward is proportionate to virtue and effort. This 'natural' injustice is compounded by the human perversion of justice:

> I saw under the sun that in the place of justice, even there was wickedness, and in the place of righteousness, even there was wickedness (3.16).

And again:

> I saw all the oppressions that are practised under the sun. And behold, the tears of the oppressed, and they had no one to comfort them! On the side of the oppressors there was power, and there was no one to comfort them (4.1).

21. *Minima Moralia, GS* 4: 283, 'Philosophie, wie sie im Angesicht der Verzweiflung einzig noch zu verantworten ist, wäre der Versuch, alle Dinge so zu betrachten, wie sie vom Standpunkt der Erlösung aus sich darstellten' (ET, p. 247, 'The only philosophy which can be responsibly practised in face of despair is the attempt to contemplate all things as they would present themselves from the standpoint of redemption.')

What was the reason for this state of affairs? Time and again Qoheleth answers that there are no answers to these and other questions.

> However much man may toil in seeking, he will not find it out; even though a wise man claims to know, he cannot find it out (8.17).

What can be known for certain is that the human lot in the world is an unhappy business (1.13). Humans are not only the victims of capricious 'natural' injustice and human injustice; they are also imprisoned in patterns of life that leave them little room for freedom. The famous poem beginning:

> For everything there is a season, and a time for every matter under heaven:
> a time to be born, and a time to die...(3.1-2)

describes processes over many of which humans in ancient Israel had little control. It goes without saying that people do not control the time of their birth and death; but neither did they control the agricultural seasons for planting and reaping in the ancient world, nor the times of war (which had to be fought at the time of year when an invading army could live off the land; cf. 2 Sam. 11.1), nor when it became necessary to mourn the death of others. Although not all of the antitheses of Eccl. 3.1-8 can be read as clearly in this way, sufficient of them can be in order to yield a sombre picture of a humanity subject to an inexorable timetable laid down by 'nature' (birth, death), the need to use nature (planting, reaping, building) and the calls of inter-human relationships (mourning, loving, making war). As an addendum to this there comes the terrifying allegory of the infirmities and weaknesses of growing old and of dying (12.1-7).

Yet there are those who can escape from some, at least, of these grim realities, namely, those who lord it over others (8.9). Qoheleth himself claims to have been in this position (ch. 2). He was able to build houses, to plant vineyards and to lay down gardens and parks. In doing this he would have employed labourers; and he certainly claims to have had male and female slaves as well as singers and concubines (if this is what the Hebrew *shiddâ* means, and the text is not corrupt). These privileges brought no advantage, but only the realization that 'all is vanity and a striving after wind' (2.17).[22]

---

22. It is not necessary to suppose that these claims are literally true in the sense that Qoheleth actually possessed the wealth implied in ch. 2. The chapter could just

Looked at from an Adorno perspective, Qoheleth shares the pessimism of Adorno, a pessimism that is a realism that refuses to deceive
itself into supposing that the world is better than it is, or that its 'rifts
and crevices' can be satisfactorily explained. He evidently suffers in
spirit with those who are oppressed by the powerful, and despairs that
corruption and injustice occupy the seats of power. When he considers
the plight of humanity in general, he sees them controlled by an inexorable timetable of natural and human constraints which only death
ultimately brings to an end. Like Adorno in *Minima Moralia*, if he sees
a tree in bloom, he will not say 'how lovely'! Aware of the shadows
cast by many distressing aspects of life, he will say 'all is vanity'.

One of the puzzling aspects of the book of Ecclesiastes is the way in
which Qoheleth appears to contradict himself when speaking of God.
On the one hand, Qoheleth appears to say that the perilous state of
affairs which he describes is God's ordinance. An example is 1.12b, 'it
is an unhappy business that God has given to the sons of men to be
busy with'. On the other hand, there are statements that look to God for
a correction of the undesirable state of affairs. Thus, after the complaint
that justice is in the place of wickedness (3.16), Qoheleth continues 'I
said in my heart, God will judge the righteous and the wicked, for he
has appointed a time for every matter and every work' (3.17). Yet this
in turn has to be qualified by the observation in 8.10, 'then I saw the
wicked buried; they used to go in and out of the holy place, and were
praised in the city where they had done such things'.

Qoheleth was too much of a realist to believe that in practice, the
wicked were ultimately punished and the righteous rewarded. He did
not observe this in the present world, and the only world beyond this
one that was available to him was the shadowy afterworld of Sheol, in
which the wise and foolish and righteous and wicked shared the same
fate. Indeed, humans shared the same fate as animals (2.13, 3.19-20,
9.2)! Even the hint that the wicked are punished by living a shorter life
than they would have done had they not been wicked (8.13) is contra-
dicted by observations such as 7.15, 'there is a wicked man who pro-
longs his life in evil-doing', and 8.14, 'there are righteous men to whom
it happens according to the deeds of the wicked, and there are wicked
men to whom it happens according to the deeds of the righteous'.

Qoheleth's ambivalence towards God—his realistic despair that the

as well be an ironic comment on the ultimate worthlessness of material things.

righteous will ultimately gain any advantage in God's world contrasted with his hope that God will judge the righteous and the wicked (3.17), and coupled with his admonitions to trust in God (5.1-7)—has led to the view that the book as we have it has suffered from interpolations by a later editor or editors who added the positive statements about God to make the book more orthodox.[23] In what follows it is not my intention to engage with this particular matter.[24] From a dialectical point of view, however, the ambivalences of the final form of the text are interesting.

God, according to the book of Ecclesiastes, is on the one hand the creator of a world in whose recurrent cycles no purpose can be discerned, and is responsible for placing in this world a humanity whose lot is 'an unhappy business'—a lot exacerbated by the human corruption of justice, by the oppression of humans by others, and by the apparent failure of God or human systems to punish or curb the prowess of the wicked. It is a world in which a man's achievements can be reversed by his descendants, or in which great acts of wisdom can be quickly forgotten (9.13-15). On the other hand, God is the one who is looked to to judge the righteous and the wicked, from whose gift it comes that people should eat and drink and take pleasure in their toil (3.13), who has made everything beautiful in its time (3.11), whose works endure for ever (3.14), who is the giver of joy (5.19-20) and who will ensure that it will go well with those who fear God (8.12).

How can this paradox be explained? Qoheleth may be drawing upon Jewish 'wisdom' teaching in order to stress the positive side of God as the author of human good fortune.[25] But it is also possible to see his positive view of God as an exercise in negative dialectics. Having exhausted the possibilities of human resources for understanding the world of his experience (1.12–2.17) and having come to hate life, the only way of retaining hope in a world where so much counted against it, was by 'looking at horror, withstanding it, and in the unmitigated consciousness of negativity holding fast to the possibility of what is

23. A good example is Eissfeldt, who regards 3.17, 'I said in my heart, God will judge the righteous and the wicked', as one of a number of interpolations (1965: 499).

24. While I accept that verses at the end of the book such as 12.9-10 are later additions, I have no opinion on whether verses such as 3.17 were added later for theological reasons.

25. See the summary by L. Schwienhorst-Schönberger in E. Zenger *et al.* (1995: 268-69).

better'.[26] For Qoheleth, this possibility was articulated in terms of appropriate 'wisdom' categories.

It must be stressed that Adorno himself did not read Ecclesiastes in this way. In an explicit reference to Qoheleth (whom he called Solomon) Adorno wrote:

> The old suspicion that magic and superstition continued to flourish in religions has, as its reverse side, the suspicion that the heart of the positive religions, the hope for the life to come, was never as important as its concept demanded. Metaphysical speculation joins with that of the philosophy of history: it entrusts only to a future without life's miseries the possibility of a correct consciousness even of those Last Things. The curse of these miseries is that they do not force us beyond mere existence but rather adorn it, confirming it as a metaphysical authority. The statement 'all is vanity' in connection with which the great theologians since Solomon have pondered upon immanence, is too abstract to guide us beyond immanence (my translation).[27]

This difficult passage has to be read in the context of Adorno's atheism and his negative attitude to metaphysics as stated in the 'meditations' with which the *Negative Dialectics* concludes.[28] There also has to be considered Adorno's view that religion only serves to support and not to change the kind of world that led to Auschwitz.[29] These are salutory

26. See n. 19.

27. *Negativ Dialektik*, GS 6: 390, ET, pp. 397-98. 'Der alte Verdacht, in den Religionen wucherten Magie und Aberglauben fort, hat zur Kehrseite, daß den positiven Religionen der Kern, die Hoffnung aufs Jenseits, kaum je so wichtig war, wie ihr Begriff es forderte. Metaphysiche Spekulation vereint sich der geschichsphilosophischen: sie traut die Möglichkeit eines richtigen Bewusstseins auch von jenen letzten Dingen erst einer Zukunft ohne Lebensnot zu. Deren Fluch ist es, daß sie nicht sowohl über bloße Dasein hinaustreibt, als es verbrämt, selber als metaphysiche Instanz befestigt. Das Alles ist eitel, mit dem seit Salomo, die grossen Theologen die Immanenz bedachten, ist zu abstrakt, um über die Immanenz hinauszugeleiten'.

28. See the article by W. Müller-Lauter 'Atheismus II', *TRE* 4 , pp. 398-99.

29. The passage referred to in n. 28 continues later (*GS* 6: 390, ET, p. 398) with the words: 'Denn die Grundverfassung der Gesellschaft hat sich nicht geändert. Sie verdammt die aus Not auferstandene Theologie und Metaphysik, trotz mancher tapferen protestantischen Gegenwehr, zum Gesinnungspaß für Einverständnis'. The official translation is: 'For there has been no change in society's basic condition. The theology or metaphysics which necessity resurrected are condemned, despite some valiant Protestant resistance, to serve as ideological passports for conformism'.

thoughts not only for theologians but also for Old Testament scholars using social scientific methods. What profit is there in doing this, if in the end society remains basically unchanged and the work serves only as an ideological passport to confirm an unjust world? The importance of Adorno is that his writings never let you remain content with the world as you find it, or with your position within it. This is part of his abiding value for anyone studying the Old Testament seriously.

READING THE BIBLE IN THE CONTEXT
OF METHODOLOGICAL PLURALISM:
THE UNDERMINING OF ETHNIC EXCLUSIVISM IN GENESIS[*]

Mark G. Brett

1. *Introduction: Preliminary Considerations*

No one currently writing on the Bible can claim to have mastered all
the disciplines that are potentially relevant to reading the book of Genesis. Scholars are faced with a choice: they can locate themselves within
specific traditions of professional research, or they can attempt to foster
a dialogue between the disciplines. My approach in reading the book of
Genesis is perhaps an extreme example of the latter: this essay combines older styles of historical scholarship with a pastiche of narratology, reader-orientated criticism, anthropology, the so-called new historicism and postcolonial theory. The pluralism proposed here is not a
new method but rather a dialogical style of engagement with the text,
which begins by confessing the variety of readers' questions, contextual
concerns and interpretative frameworks and then enters into a reading
process, expecting to be enriched by the conversation, and perhaps even
'enraptured' by it (Rorty 1992: 106-107).

Being enraptured by a conversation need not, however, imply the
total eclipse of a reader's subjectivity. For this reason, I will not indulge
the formalist fantasy of interpretation, which constructs an ideal reader,
entirely fabricated by the dictates of a text. How a text engages us, and
perhaps even changes us, is shaped at least in part by our 'horizon of
expectation', which includes not just the focused questions of an explicit
interpretative tradition but also the customarily unacknowledged backgrounds of culture, gender, class and institutional matrixes that are

[*] This chapter is a revised version of part of M.G. Brett, *Genesis: Procreation
and the Politics of Identity* (London: Routledge, 2000).

inevitably part of a reader's subjectivity.[1] Thus, in recent years, there has been a shift in reader-orientated studies towards flesh-and-blood audiences, the analysis of scholarly discourses, and even towards so-called 'autobiographical criticism' (e.g. Veeser 1996; Kitzberger 1998).

While it would be impossible to articulate all the features of my 'horizon of expectation', it is worth registering at this point some of the interrelationships between my biography and the traditions of criticism which will be represented here. As is commonly the case in an age of globalization, my own subjectivity is constituted by an heterogeneous collocation of identity markers. To highlight Australian citizenship, for example, would be important but complex: although born in Australia, I was brought up in Papua New Guinea, and when, for a few years, I went to boarding school in Australia I perceived the country of my birth as not just foreign but as hostile. My undergraduate degree, in philosophy and history, was taken in an Australian university (Queensland), but subsequently I have absorbed a range of educational subcultures, studying the Hebrew Bible within an American seminary (Princeton), a German faculty of theology (Tübingen), and an English faculty of arts (Sheffield). Each of these institutional matrixes are remarkably different in their history and ethos, each with their own story of ideological contestation. Each institution has made its own mark, layering its influence on a biography which begins with expatriate identity and has taken shape within the postcolonial contestations of both Papua New Guinea and Australia. All of this forms a background to my political commitments—to civic republicanism in Australia, reconciliation with Aboriginal communities, and the affirmation of multiculturalism in public discourse. My biography does have some affinity with the tone of methodological pluralism, but I doubt whether the identity pastiche determines, in any strong sense, the details of an interpretation. Nor is it necessary that anyone with a similar biography would arrive at the same commitments.

I also belong to a nonconformist denomination of Protestantism, which has been constituted, in part at least, by an assertion of religious freedom over against the established church (Hill 1988), and one might suggest that this would help to explain the overall argument. Jewish scholars have certainly identified Protestant prejudices at work in some

---

1.   See Brett (1991a: 123-43) for a discussion of the notion of epistemological 'horizons' reflected variously in the work of Karl Popper, Hans-Georg Gadamer and Hans-Robert Jauss.

of the supposedly historical research on Genesis (Levenson 1993: 25-32, 56-61). It is worth noting, however, that very few of my scholarly mentors have been nonconformist Protestants. Among those who might agree to religious self-descriptions at all, they would call themselves Anglican, Roman Catholic or Jewish. Among the mentors who resist religious self-descriptions, it would be necessary to revert to professional role descriptions (like literary critic or anthropologist) or interdisciplinary schools of thought (like poststructuralist, feminist or postcolonialist theory).

Reading Genesis as a Protestant, it is ironic to find how resolutely the book resists the Reformation's presumption of textual perspicuity. The laconic style of Genesis, its opacities and ambiguities, suggest that we can only ever engage with it partially; we can never exhaust the full depths of its history and the peregrinations of its meaning. This precludes the pretensions of scholarly objectivity that have too often marred the historical biblical scholarship of the last two centuries, pretensions which are redolent with the confident epistemological tones of both Protestantism and the Enlightenment.

But the epistemological modesty that has slowly been gaining ground in recent years need not collapse into total skepticism or failures of rigour (cf. Miller 1987). Whatever one's religious or nonreligious commitments, a genuine conversation with the primary text requires neither full understanding nor full agreement. Disciplined understandings and agreements, however partial or unstable, are more valuable than either sweeping dismissals of canonical texts or pre-fabricated religious readings that are all-too-credulous. There is no reason why a reader cannot play the role of an anthropologist, feeling their way into the weave of a foreign culture, or the role of literary critic, illuminating the nuances of the language. Indeed, the recent contributions of anthropologists and narratologists have greatly enriched professional biblical scholarship. Neither the holiness of the text nor the religious convictions of the reader need determine interpretative outcomes in advance. Genuine conversations are more unpredictable than that.

2. *Situating Genesis*

This preliminary discussion of my horizon of expectation has highlighted the themes of heterogeneity and contestation. To focus now on the particular text at issue, my overarching argument will be that the book of Genesis is itself shaped by contestation—in the diversity of its cultural influences, in its representation of ethnic relations, and in its numerous narratives which explicitly and implicitly question the political authorities of the day. In his recent *History of Israelite Religion in the Old Testament Period*, Rainer Albertz argues that although the religion of Genesis is depicted in the Bible as historically prior to the distinctively Israelite religion of Yahwism, Genesis should be understood 'not as a preliminary stage but as a substratum of Yahweh religion' (1994: 29). This argument is, at least in part, explained by the fact that the final editing of the book took place only in the fifth century BCE, during the period of Persian imperial rule (1994: 24).[2] Instead of assuming that the sources of Genesis survive relatively intact and that biblical interpretation should focus on their reconstruction, my approach will be more synchronic: the hypothesis is that the received Hebrew version of Genesis can be quite directly related to the politics of the Persian period.

My thesis is that the final editor of Genesis has set out to undermine the theologically legitimated ethnocentrism found in the books of Ezra and Nehemiah, expressed in particular by the notion of the 'holy seed' (Ezra 9.1-2). It is not important to my case that the historical careers of these two Persian emissaries be reconstructed in detail; I will simply assume that the polemics against foreign marriages in the books of Ezra and Nehemiah are in some sense representative of a dominant ideology of the fifth century, emanating from the native administrators of Persian rule. The resistance of Genesis can, I will suggest, be read both in theological and in economic terms: theologically, the final editor is, through a retelling of Israelite origins, proposing a less ethnocentric understanding of Israelite identity. But this theological difference may well be related to economic issues insofar as the discourse of the 'holy seed' was part of a strategy to control land tenure within this administrative district of the Persian empire.

Some preliminary matters need to be clarified at this point, both

---

2.   Here Albertz cites the innovative work of Blum (1990), but for at least a century now it has been commonplace to suggest that the literary sources of Genesis were combined and edited only after the exile in Babylon (587–538 BCE). Even Israel Knohl, who dates the literary sources much earlier than most biblical scholars, is willing to concede that the final editing of the Pentateuch took place during the Persian period, when many of the Israelite 'exiles' returned from Babylon to Judah (1995: 100-103, 201).

methodological and historical. First, I need to note some historical studies which provide a framework of my reading of the text. The assumption here is not that history can be grasped in some naive objectivist
sense, but only that critical historical discourses can provide interpretative frameworks for articulating the social energies which are not
explicit in the biblical text (cf. Greenblatt and Gunn 1992). Secondly, I
need to clarify the kind of reading strategy—inspired especially by
postcolonial theory—which allows my interpretation to be a legitimate
one, even though there is no explicit polemic in Genesis against Ezra
and Nehemiah.

For my present purposes, a key work on the period is Kenneth Hoglund's *Achaemenid Imperial Administration in Syria-Palestine and the
Missions of Ezra and Nehemiah* (1992). Perhaps the most significant
aspect of Hogland's work is the argument that the fortification of Jerusalem under Nehemiah (see Neh. 2.8, 7.2) was part of a wider imperial
response to the Egyptian revolt against the Persian empire fomented in
the mid-fifth century by a certain Inaros and supported by a Greek
coalition, the Delian League. The rebuilding of the walls of Jerusalem
was comparatively unusual within the widest context of Persian policy,
since such walls could be turned to advantage in the case of indigenous
revolt. However, after reviewing the archaeological evidence, Hoglund
argues that the threat presented in this period by the Egyptians and the
Greeks apparently resulted in a proliferation of imperial fortresses
throughout the Levant, and Nehemiah's citadel can best be understood
as part of this defensive strategy (1992: 209-10).

Hoglund suggests that the prohibition against foreign marriages in
Ezra and Nehemiah served related interests of imperial social control.
The focus on genealogical purity is seen as a way of establishing the
legitimacy of land tenure, thereby asserting control of land and property. The biblical evidence for this comes particularly from Ezra 10.8
where the text suggests that anyone failing to attend the prescribed
convocation would face severe penalties: 'by the instruction of the
officials and the elders, all his property is forfeited, and he is excluded
from the assembly of the exiles'. Furthermore, the letter from Artaxerxes in Ezra 7 concludes by saying that anyone who does not obey
the law of Ezra's God would suffer severe consequences, including the
confiscation of property (7.26). Ezra's ethnic version of holiness was
contested by a number of theologies of the Second Temple period—
notably in the latter parts of Isaiah and in the book of Ruth—but

Hoglund's work has made clear the connections between the administrators' theology and the economics of the Judean restoration. Along with other scholars, he has shown that the rhetoric of the 'holy seed' may well have been a particular construal of Israelite tradition which served the imperial interests.

Hoglund's work converges, in some respects, with a view expressed recently by the anthropologist Mary Douglas (1993), although her argument focuses on biblical material which can be read as *resisting* the imperial governors. She argues that the ostensibly Priestly concern with ethnic purity that underpins the prohibition on foreign marriages in the Persian period, cannot be derived directly from the Pentateuch. In particular, the book of Numbers stands against the idea that the 'holy seed' might be a clearly defined group, established by legitimate birth. Drawing attention, for example, to Num. 15.22-31 and 19.10, she points out that the purity system is there specifically designed to include the non-native *gerim* ('aliens' or 'sojourners'), and unlike the tendency of Deut. 23.3, there are no blanket rulings against strangers simply by virtue of their ethnicity.[3] Douglas concludes that Numbers opposes the separatism of Ezra and Nehemiah: 'the concern of the priestly editor is to constrain a populist xenophobia' (1993: 39). Recent biblical scholarship is perhaps less willing to speak of Priestly theology as a unified system, but certainly by the time of the Persian period, many would agree that the so-called Priestly texts in Numbers and Leviticus have declared aliens to be on the same legal footing as native-born Israelites.[4]

Jan Joosten's recent study of the Holiness Code concludes that in view of the extensive marriage laws in Leviticus 17–26 it is significant that there is no prohibition against marrying non-Israelite women (1996: 85). Lev. 21.14 is the 'exception that proves the rule'; it is binding only on priests. Rolf Rendtorff has similarly raised the possibility that the Priestly laws concerning the *gerim* were shaped and edited in opposition to the marriage policies of Ezra (1996: 86-87). Thus, the work of Mary

---

3. 'The defilement system described in Leviticus and Numbers protects the sanctuary; it does not organize social categories. Admittedly, it separates priests from laity, but only in respect of access to the sanctuary' (Douglas 1993: 155).

4. Knohl draws a distinction between the earliest layer of the Priestly tradition, which he calls the Priestly Torah, and a later Holiness School to whom he ascribes the ethical concern with aliens (1995: 21, 53, 93). This diachronic distinction does not affect Douglas's thesis, since Knohl asserts that the Holiness School influenced Priestly tradition even before the exile in Babylon.

Douglas converges with a number of recent studies on the Pentateuch in a way which lends an initial plausibility to my account of Genesis as resistance literature.

In view of these recent studies, it seems that the older scholarly tendency to associate Ezra's idea of the 'holy seed' with Priestly tradition is misguided. Assuming for the moment that a Priestly tradition can be reconstructed from the text of Genesis—an assumption which is, in fact, not necessary to my reading of the book—it is worth drawing attention to one key text which has consistently been identified as part of this tradition. The promises to Abraham in Genesis 17 are associated with a body-marking that has often been thought to be a definitive indicator of identity: the practice of male circumcision. 'For the generations to come every male among you who is eight days old must be circumcised, including those born in your household or bought with money from a foreigner—he who is not of your seed' (17.12). The so-called Priestly text explicitly includes persons bought from foreigners—those who are 'not of your seed', and a reader from the Persian period might well have heard a resonance here which undermined the notion of the 'holy seed' in Ezra 9.1-2. The implications of this suggestion will be explored below, where I offer an interpretation of Genesis 17 without assuming that it comes from a coherent Priestly tradition.

If the final text of Genesis is to be read in a more focused way against the background of the Persian period, then the possibility arises that the editors of Genesis saw an analogy between two 'native' administrators of imperial rule, Ezra and Joseph. Indeed, the concluding chapters of Genesis make good sense if we read the character of Joseph negatively. The analogy suggests that the Persian audience of the Joseph story would have been suspicious of any representative of the Persian monarchy who made extravagant claims to divine wisdom (Gen. 41.39, cf. 41.8) and providence (50.20) while expropriating property (Gen. 47). Ezra 7.25-26 has Artaxerxes praising Ezra's divine wisdom, legitimating the imperial desire that those who disobey the law should be banished or have their goods confiscated. A covert polemic against Persia would be all the more subtle since it appropriates a story set in Egypt, that is the immediate enemy of the Persian administration. Any criticism of Egypt would ostensibly have served Persian interests, but the cunning of Genesis may be that Egypt in the Joseph story can be read as a cipher for Persia.

3. *A Methodological Orientation*

This summary of my argument brings together a number of different hypotheses about the interpretation of Genesis, and they are not all of the same kind. Each interpretative hypothesis requires further specification in terms of its goals, the limits of its claim and the framing of the relevant evidence. For example, my approach does not logically exclude the reconstruction of literary sources and editing; it is just that they are largely irrelevant to the purposes of this particular interpretation. Nor do we claim that the editors of Genesis invented all their narratives; it is more likely that their work is a subtle hybrid construction. My argument could even include the possibility that earlier layers of these traditions were in some sense xenophobic, but the final editors have organized their materials so as to exclude this possibility. Since, however, the editors were thereby calling into question the official ideology of the imperial governors, opposition had to be formulated with extreme subtlety. James Scott's *Domination and the Arts of Resistance: Hidden Transcripts* (1990) and Homi Bhabha's *The Location of Culture* (1994) would lead us to expect that resistance is often exercised behind the back of powerful ideologies. The work of Scott and Bhabha, an anthropologist and a literary critic, respectively, converge to provide a model of agency exercised at the margins, at times paradoxically absorbing much of the dominant discourse (cf. West 1995b; Brett 1996b). It is this form of resistance that I have in mind. In order to be clear about this kind of editorial agency, we will need to turn now to an account of what methods are appropriate in interpreting it. In effect, this account provides a limited defence of methodological pluralism, specifically with respect to goal of interpreting the final form of Genesis.

One contemporary mode of biblical interpretation, which I will argue is relevant to my project, but limited in its application, is best described by the term 'narrative poetics'. This mode is concerned primarily with the communicative devices which constitute the most explicit layers of the text; the focus is on the details of dialogue, the development of characters, the flow of the plot, the nuances of repetition, and on the variety of 'points of view' represented by each character and by the narrator. This mode of reading, pioneered in particular by the literary critics Robert Alter (1981) and Meir Sternberg (1985), was at first perceived to be thoroughly antagonistic towards the older styles of historical criticism that dissected the text of Genesis into successive layers of oral and literary composition. And, indeed, some practitioners of narrative poetics were scathing in their condemnation of historicist scholars whose only tool for dealing with literary complexity, it seemed, was a scalpel.

Alter and Sternberg have provoked much self-examination among biblical specialists, and the influence of historicism has waned significantly in the last decade. However, in their reaction against the atomistic reconstructions of historical critics, Alter and Sternberg promoted a style of formalism, which excluded not only questions about the history of a text's composition but also about the location of a text within sites of ideological contestation. Alter, in particular, has resisted interpretative practices which move beyond the aesthetic limits of a text to engage with ideological matrixes within which the Bible was produced and read (e.g. Alter 1990; cf. Alter and Kermode 1987). Sternberg (1992) has become embroiled in a similar kind of debate about the possibility of ideologically neutral poetics, defending his impartiality against the idea that readers' identities are an ineluctable part of all interpretation (Fewell and Gunn, 1991).

A pluralist approach to methodology would suggest that some of this conflict—but not all of it—is misplaced. If there are a variety of valid interpretative goals, then it follows that there will be a corresponding variety of methods which are proper to those goals. Our study of Genesis will illustrate that biblical critics now have a wide range of interpretative interests, from aesthetic to social-scientific, and many of these interests are compatible even where they have often been perceived to be in conflict. To be sure, there are cases where, for example, fresh observations at the level of narrative poetics have placed older hypotheses in doubt. In other words, I am not arguing for the kind of genial pluralism which overlooks any genuine cases of disagreement. However, we need to arbitrate between competing methods on a case-by-case basis, specifically with reference to the goals of a particular interpretation.

At this point it may be helpful to provide an example of what appears to be a genuine methodological disagreement and then show how it could represent simply a difference of focus, rather than irrevocable disagreement. In Gen. 27.46, Rebekah complains to her husband about the possibility that her son might marry a Hittite woman: 'If Jacob takes a wife from among the women of the land, from the Hittite women like these, what will life mean to me?' Historical critics have long been in the habit of dissecting the surrounding narrative into a 'doublet'—two literary sources which offer competing reasons for Jacob's trip to his uncle Laban (e.g. Gunkel 1910: 386; Emerton 1988: 398). In the first, Gen. 27.1-45, Jacob's life is threatened by his own deceit in stealing his brother's blessing, and he needs to find refuge from Esau's anger; Rebekah suggests that her brother Laban's house as a good place to hide (27.43). In the second text, Gen. 26.34-35 and 27.46–28.5, Jacob needs to contract an endogamous marriage, that is, a marriage within the kinship group. The second text has been consistently identified with the so-called 'Priestly' tradition which is usually dated late in Israel's history and associated by many scholars with a theologically legitimated ethnocentrism, such as can be found in Ezra 9.1-2. In summary, such an argument would suggest that Rebekah's (implied) plea for an endogamous marriage in Gen. 27.46 betrays the supposed ethnocentrism of the Priestly tradition.

There is, however, another way of construing this conflict of interpretations which makes the history of composition irrelevant. A narratological analysis might suggest that this conclusion has been reached too quickly and with far too many assumptions. Gen. 27.1-45 depicts Jacob's theft of the blessing that properly belongs (according to an implied principle of primogeniture) to his older brother Esau. Esau's rage is entirely justified, but so is a mother's concern for the wellbeing of her younger son; she counsels Jacob to run for his life. In a patriarchal society, however, it is natural that a father's permission should be sought. The narrator has chosen not to tell the reader of Isaac's reaction to Jacob's deceit, so the possibility is left open that he may have disagreed with Rebekah's reasoning in 27.42-46. The received text of Genesis moves naturally from Rebekah's manipulation of Isaac for Jacob's sake in 27.1-45 to her manipulation of Isaac in 27.46. Her expression of concern for endogamous marriage could simply be a ruse designed to obtain paternal permission for Jacob's flight, exploiting the tension with her Hittite daughters-in-law (rather than a general xenophobia) that was mentioned in 26.34-35.

We have here, then, what appears to be a genuine disagreement between the historicist perspective on the one hand (that fuses Rebekah's speech in 27.46 with Priestly ethnocentrism) and a narratological analysis on the other (that sees 27.46 as simply a ruse on a par with 27.5-13). In the first case, Rebekah's speech is taken to be a transparent window on Priestly ideology, and ethnocentrism is attributed both to her character as well as to a reconstructed Priestly writer. In the second case, Rebekah's character is marked by tricksterism, rather than by ethnocentrism; there is no necessary connection between Rebekah's speech and the narrator's ideology. The division of the story into two separate sources is not required.

My proposal to read Rebekah consistently as a trickster does not logically require the historical unity of these chapters (cf. Carr 1996: 321-22). On the contrary, it may well be that there is a history of composition behind the received text of Genesis; the heterogeneous elements of the text speak strongly for this view, even if there is no one reconstruction of that history that has secured a scholarly consensus. Practitioners of narrative poetics characteristically tend to read the text as if it were a unity, whether or not this was historically always the case. They have been charged with historical naiveté for doing so, but it is quite possible to understand their work as a contribution to the question of what the received or 'final' Hebrew text might mean—ironically a somewhat neglected topic in the last two centuries of professional biblical criticism. Sometimes this quest for the meaning of the received text has been expressly opposed by literary critics to the historical question of what the final editor might have 'intended', but I will argue below that authorial intention is a legitimate interpretative goal as long as we are clear what we mean by intention. The standard historicist hypothesis for understanding Rebekah's motivation in 27.46 does not actually deal with the question of what the final editor may have intended to communicate in preserving the whole of Genesis 26–28 in just this way. In short, the standard historicism has neglected at least one legitimate historical question—the purpose of the final editor— which might be answered by considering the contributions of narrative poetics. The standard assumption has been that the final editor merely collects up the traditions with no apparent purpose other than antiquarianism, but to say that this assumption unjustifiably reduces the interpretative options would be something of an understatement.

I have begun here to deconstruct the opposition between narratological analyses and the old historicism: on the one hand, narratology does not logically require unified texts, and on the other hand, the old source-critical dissections of the biblical text have habitually excluded a legitimate historical question—the communicative purpose of the final Hebrew text. Yet it is precisely the final text which has been the focus of narratologists. Is it plausible, then, to construe narrative poetics as a contribution to this particular historical question?

My study advocates a model of pluralism which suggests that narratology can make a potential contribution to this question, but there are a range of factors beyond the aesthetic limits of the text which would have to be considered also. The purposes of the final editor of Genesis can also be illuminated, for example, by comparative anthropological studies of kinship (which range far and wide beyond the limits of the biblical text), but before I consider these anthropological perspectives I need to look more philosophically at the concept of intention and at the relevance of 'historical context'.

If we are to be concerned with the communicative purpose of the final form of Genesis, we have to be clear about the nature of this interpretative goal. The concept of intention is highly complex, and a methodological pluralism which wants to defend intentionalist criticism will need to be aware of the conceptual problems involved; many of the attacks on authorial intention have exploited these conceptual ambiguities. Scholars have meant at least three, quite different things by authorial 'intention' or 'purpose':

(1)   an explicit communicative intention,
(2)   an implied or indirect communicative intention,
(3)   a motive.

Initially, we may take (1) and (2) together, and distinguish a communicative intention (what an author or editor is trying to say) from a motive (why it is being said). The motives behind a communicative act may be complex, contradictory and even unconscious, never coming to expression in language at all. This domain is the focus of psychoanalytical criticism. At the level of language, on the other hand, an author's intention may be relatively explicit in the text or it may only be implied—something which must be inferred from the often unstated circumstances of utterance. These unstated circumstances may include literary allusions and the like, but also non-linguistic features of the communicative context.

Thus, one can distinguish between explicit communicative intentions and indirect communicative intentions, although in practice the distinction may be more of a continuum (cf. Brett 1991b). Analyses of indirect communication have been provided especially in the linguistics literature on pragmatics (e.g. Levenson 1983; Leech 1983), but also in anthropological studies of communication (e.g. Gumperz 1977; Sperber and Wilson 1986). Situated on the border between anthropology and biblical studies, Mary Douglas's work on Numbers can be cited as an example of such an interest in indirect communication. The important point here is that an interpretation of communicative intention need not restrict itself to the explicit communicative features embedded in a text but may need to encompass the unspoken features of a reconstructed historical situation, or at least those features of the situation which may be relevant to an author's purpose. An interest in indirect communication inevitably leads into the domain of hypothesis; interpretation in this area will require finely balanced judgments of probability.

As already suggested, the three senses of 'intention' blend into each other to such an extent that it is sometimes practically impossible to distinguish between them. But a conceptual distinction is always possible, and the lack of conceptual awareness on this issue has led to a great deal of confusion, both in biblical studies and in literature studies generally. As Annabel Patterson (1990: 146) has rightly observed, much of the controversy about literary intention in the last four decades could have been avoided if the participants had been clearer in their uses of the term 'intention'. Further, if the various schools of interpretation that have conspired against authorial intention had been more modest in the formulation of their goals, some of the antagonism could have been ameliorated. The case for critical pluralism requires that we distinguish the immodest claims of these anti-intentionalist schools (e.g. new criticism, structuralism and poststructuralism) from claims which might be, at certain points, complementary.

My argument about intentionality is, for example, quite compatible with the theory of reading made famous by the literary critic Stanley Fish. While some critics have read Fish to be recommending only methods of interpretation which focus on readers rather than authors, this view of his work is quite misleading. Apart from one early essay, Fish's theoretical arguments have been focused on the epistemology of interpretation, not the goals of interpretation (see Brett 1993). He is concerned with general philosophical reflections on the nature of reading, no matter what school of criticism. The idea that interpretation takes places within communities is meant to encompass all forms of interpretation, not just the enlightened few who gather under the banner of 'the reader'. Concerning authorial intention, his point is simply that an author's mind cannot be known directly, as if it were a bit of evidence independent of the process of interpretation. If he makes the point that 'interpretation creates intention' (1980: 163), it is not that interpreters need to give up all quests for intention. Indeed, in *Doing What Comes Naturally*, Fish even suggests that we cannot do without some notion of intention: 'One cannot understand an utterance without at the same time hearing or reading it as the utterance of someone with more or less specific concerns ... someone with an intention' (1989: 15). This statement does not depart from his original position, since he clarifies the point by saying 'Intentions are not self-declaring, but must be constructed from evidence that is itself controversial' (1989: 98-100).

My case for pluralism necessarily rejects any naive intentionalist approach which would regard a reader's intuition about authorial psychology as a relevant source of evidence; the author's mind is clearly not accessible. It does not follow, however, that interpretation of a biblical text needs to be restricted to the evidence available in a single text. On the contrary, if we are interested in indirect communicative intention (examples of which would be irony, parody, allusion and other forms of covert communication), it is necessary to consider evidence from the situation of authorship, insofar as this can be reconstructed. To be sure, in the case of the Hebrew Bible the historical situation of the author or editor must always be reconstructed from evidence that is itself controversial. We can only ever have better and worse hypotheses, arguments which are more and less coherent, interpretations which are based on more and less evidence.

In addition to this epistemological self-consciousness, the case for critical pluralism would also need to refute any theories of interpretation which made immodest claims for the unique validity of particular interpretative interests. Thus, although my concern with Genesis reflects an interest in communicative intention, it does not subscribe to the kind of arguments advanced by E.D. Hirsch which suggest that quests for intention can claim some kind of moral high ground (e.g. 1976: 7; 1967: 24-25). I would argue that good ethical grounds can be adduced for a variety of interpretative interests (Brett 1995b), and therefore we should not pre-empt the ethical debate by endorsing a generalized claim that the author's intention is always to be respected.

Similarly, in order to be coherent, a critical pluralism needs to reject some of the more extreme claims of literary formalism. While accepting that there is a mode of poetics that focuses on the conventional communicative devices evident in the surface of the text, I would reject the new critical idea that the interpreter of a successful poem should not make reference to non-linguistic evidence; as already indicated above, there are other potentially appropriate sources of evidence beyond the sources imagined in Wimmsatt and Beardsley's classic statement of new criticism. They argued that scholars should restrict themselves to essentially linguistic resources—'grammars, dictionaries, and all the literature which is the source of dictionaries' (1972: 339)—but the unspoken features of a reconstructed historical situation may well turn out to be relevant to an author's purpose, as the discipline of pragmatics has revealed.

Even Sternberg's poetics can ironically be seen as a revised version of formalism, in the tradition of the so-called new criticism. While he has elegantly demolished some of the anti-historicism among his fellow literary critics, the contribution of historical research turns out to be largely irrelevant to the details of his exegesis. Although he has illuminated the dynamic tensions between what is said and what is not said in a narrative, the tension carried by the not-said is conceived entirely in literary terms as a 'gap' which will be filled out by the unfolding of the narrative. All the questions left over, not specifically answered by the text, are relegated to the nonliterary rank of 'blanks'. But it is precisely the domain of the blank, the 'never-said', which must be considered relevant to any examination of ideological contestation. The domain of the not-said is potentially rich with indirect communication. This point is crucially relevant to any thesis which might suggest that the ethnic politics of Persian period militated against explicit strategies of communication.

Having briefly located the quest for communicative intention against this background—bringing together considerations from poetics, pragmatics and reader theory—it now remains to deal with the challenges brought forward by structuralism and poststructuralism which threaten to undermine the very idea of authorial agency. These movements have been highly influential not just within literary criticism but within the human sciences generally. A critical pluralism that wants to preserve intentionalist criticism will need to defend this enterprise against any critical theory which seeks to dissolve individual agency into larger structures of culture or cultural hybridity. Once again, it will be possible only to sketch in the theoretical issues which bear most closely on the present discussion.

First, it is necessary to differentiate between Ferdinand de Saussure's pioneering work in linguistics, *Cours de linguistique générale* (1916), and the applications of his work in anthropology, notably by Claude Lévi-Strauss in influential works such as *Structural Anthropology* (1963). In this latter work, Lévi-Strauss was inspired by the advances made in linguistics, in particular in the science of phonology which had succeeded in reducing the sounds used in all known languages to a small number of binary phonetic contrasts. Lévi-Strauss argued, similarly, that it was possible to analyse social phenomena, like marriage and kinship, across various traditional societies and reduce them to a small number of structural principles (cf. Rogerson 1978: 102-14). In recent studies of Genesis, for example, there has been much discussion of an idea stemming from Lévi-Strauss that the ideal marriage from the point of view of the groom would be with a daughter of the mother's brother, that is, matrilineal cross-cousin marriage (see Donaldson 1981; Prewitt 1990; Oden 1987: 106-30). This is a possible reading of Genesis 27–28, discussed above, in which Jacob is advised to find a wife from among the daughters of his mother's brother.

Steinberg (1993: 8-14) has rightly questioned whether there is really sufficient evidence to sustain such an hypothesis in the case of Genesis. She suggests, on the contrary, that the final text of Genesis reveals the ideal to be a form of 'patrilineal endogamy' in which both the father and the mother descend from Abraham's father, Terah. The system is called patrilineal since the line of the father defines the bounds of the lineage, but it has a 'collateral' or sibling feature that includes women. Rebekah, like all the 'proper' wives, also stems from the patrilineage of Terah, since her father Bethuel is the son of Nahor. Thus, the collateral patrilineage of Terah looks like this:

	Terah		
Haran	Abram		Nahor
Lot			Bethuel
	Isaac	=	*Rebekah* and Laban
	Esau and Jacob	=	*Rachel and Leah*

I will examine the implications of this argument in due course, but the important question arising at this point is methodological: what kind of interpretative question is answered by Steinberg's thesis? And in precisely what sense does her thesis differ, as she claims, from the kind of structuralism descended from Lévi-Strauss?

Steinberg distances herself from Lévi-Strauss by distinguishing social 'structure' from 'social organization'. In aligning herself with studies of social organization, she means to place a greater emphasis on the 'individual decisions made in adapting to external circumstances' while, at the same time, abstracting a pattern that reflects reiterated individual choices (1993: 9-10). She implies that structuralist anthropology operates without enough attention to the complex realities of individual agency, and cites Raymond Firth in support of her perspective:

> A structural principle is one which provides a fixed line of social behaviour and represents the order which it manifests. The concept of social organization has complementary emphasis. It recognizes adaptation of behaviour in respect of given ends, control of means in varying circumstances, which are set by changes in the external environment or by the necessity to resolve conflict between structural principles. If structure implies order, organization implies working towards order (Firth 1964: 61).

This passage from Firth, and Steinberg's use of it, reflects the tension in recent social theory between social structures and individual agency. Firth is careful here to affirm the 'complementarity' between his position and any stronger emphases on structure which would make individual agencies redundant. Whether he succeeds in maintaining such an eirenic balance we may leave as an open question. It may be possible to sustain this idea of complementarity if structuralism is seen as having an extremely abstract depth of focus, on analogy with comparative grammar, rather than a detailed focus on the intricacies of individual agency and particular speech acts. At least in biblical studies, even where structuralist interpretations have begun from particular texts, it seems that their purpose has been to suggest a wider context of oppositions and schema within which an author is unwittingly implicated (e.g. Barthes 1977). But structuralism is not alone in this regard: other schools of social thought have also tended to relegate the discourse of actors to the margins of analysis, whether they have emphasized the systemic unity of societies, or whether they have viewed societies as the product of fundamental socio-economic conflicts (Mayes 1989).

There has, however, been a marked tendency in recent social theory to give more attention to individual agency, or at least to intentional action (Handel 1993). Mary Douglas's reading of Numbers, as well as James Scott's account of covert resistance, provide examples of anthropological work which promises to provide a *rapprochement* between the social sciences and the older humanism of biblical scholarship that focused on matters of language, text and authorial intention.

It is doubtful, however, whether Steinberg's work on Genesis can be read as part of this quest for a more balanced account of agency. In the end, she replaces one structure with another: matrilineal cross-cousin marriage is replaced by patrilineal endogamy, providing a new 'norm' for Israelite marriage which is never articulated as such in the primary literature. The goal of Steinberg's analysis still seems to be a structural principle which is then used to formulate a highly generalized account of how the patrilineal endogamy, while unknown to the agents involved, serves as a defence of community boundaries after the exile (Steinberg 1993: 142-47; cf. Mullen 1997: 95-98). Steinberg's thesis does not explain why Abram should be commanded by Yahweh in Gen. 12.1 to leave his father's house, nor does it deal adequately with all the evidence of exogamous marriage (cf. Lemche 1985: 272-75).

To be fair, it is important to recognize that there are a range of inter-pretative goals within the human sciences, and intentionalist criticism cannot be aligned with all of them. Anthropology and sociology attempt to explain large-scale social relations and processes, and such attempts can never be restricted to the evidence that comes from the discourse of individual actors. It is not just that a social scientist has to collect a large number of communicative acts before they have a statistically signifi-cant sample. The methodological issues are more complex. Some aspects of social life never come to expression in discourse, and in this respect it simply does not matter whether discourse is understood as the product of intentional action or whether discourse is understood (as in extreme versions of poststructuralism) as an anonymous intertextuality within which an individual's subjectivity is completely dissolved (so Foucault 1972: 55, 122). Even where intentional action turns out to be influential, individuals are always constrained by the conventions and institutions of their milieu, and actions regularly have consequences which are quite unintended. Intentional action is not simply the aggre-gate of psychological states. These issues are taken for granted in the recent social theory that attempts to recover a balance of structure and agency (notably Giddens 1984; 1987).

But even given that the human sciences are working with a much larger canvas than the intentionalist literary critic, it is always possible to study events and social processes in a way which highlights 'what it was like for those involved' (Runciman 1983: 42). This is a logically separable issue within the disciplines of anthropology and sociology, and it is a focus on this issue which suggests the need for cooperation between the human sciences and literary criticism (Runciman 1983: 236-42; Rogerson 1985: 255). What was the actor's point of view? Or to put the question into the plural: what were the actors' points of view, and how did they interact?

This brings us back to the earlier suggestion that we should distinguish carefully between the linguistic structuralism of Saussure and the anthropological structuralism Lévi-Strauss (cf. Thiselton 1992: 80-141). Building on an analogy with Saussure's phonology, Lévi-Strauss aimed to analyse social phenomena across various traditional societies and to reduce them to a small number of structural principles. This kind of comparative anthropology produced results which were never intended to be intelligible to the anthropologists' informants; that was not the aim. Another linguist, Kenneth Pike, built on Saussure's phonology for a quite different purpose, and Pike's work has been important in shaping another school of social theory which distinguishes between 'emic' and 'etic' goals of interpretation.

Pike (1964) derived his terms from the linguistic disciplines of phonemics and phonetics: phonetics attempts to describe systematically all the sounds of human speech, irrespective of whether native speakers of particular languages would recognize the scientific metalanguage of the linguist (it was this aspect of Saussure's work which most interested Lévi-Strauss). Phonemics, on the other hand, describes the significant differences between the sounds of speech as perceived by native speakers in their own linguistic system. Pike applied this distinction to the study of human action, suggesting that some kinds of social-scientific explanation need not be understood in 'native' categories; for example, if it seems that a society lacks the concept of economy, it does not follow that they are never influenced by economic forces (cf. Runciman 1983: 13). Emic social science, however, defines its goal in terms of describing 'native points of view'. Pike's distinction has generated a great deal of discussion, and it is now clear that any emic–etic contrast must be conceived as a continuum, rather than as a sharp dichotomy; interpreters necessarily betray the categories of their own culture (Taylor 1985). But it is still viable to distinguish between forms of social explanation which primarily seek to satisfy only scientific communities and forms of description which are actor-oriented.

A pluralist can promote both programmes of research as complementary. And a pluralist who is interested in authorial intention, such as myself, could form an alliance with emic social science, without attempting to give this interpretative interest any methodological or ethical privilege. There are, however, some problems attached to actor-oriented research which need to be drawn out at this point. The author of an ancient text can be regarded as a kind of informant from a foreign culture, but as anthropologists have made clear, it is always necessary to be aware of informant bias. For example, an actor's gender, or power, can have considerable bearing on how their discourse is to be interpreted (Ardener 1972; Keesing 1987). A woman's perspective on her society could be considerably different from the point of view of a male chief. And in the case of Genesis, it would be highly relevant to know whether the final editors oppose the ethnocentrism represented by the imperial governors; the asymmetry of power would affect strategies of communication. A comprehensive actor-oriented interpretation of a society will seek to encompass the variety of voices that make up a culture (cf. Carroll R. 1995a).

I have mentioned, uncritically up to this point, terms like 'social system', 'culture' and 'linguistic system'. These are the presumed 'wholes' of which the individual agent is seen as a part. But clearly, there are substantial questions about the extent to which these 'wholes'—whether individual societies, cultures, languages or even the individual self—can be considered a unity. Recent poststructuralist theory, both literary and social-scientific, has consistently sought to undermine the assumptions of wholeness with respect to both corporate and individual agency. Precisely how are these wholes—whether language, culture or the self—constructed?

One of the most important features of Saussure's work was his idea of 'synchronic' linguistic systems, and this idea represented an attempt to constrain the relevant context for interpreting a language. Synchronic interpretation (both in linguistics and in anthropology) began as an opposition movement to the nineteenth-century historicist idea that in order to understand any social phenomenon it is necessary to understand its place within a process of development. Saussure insisted, on the contrary, that it was necessary to understood words within the context of their contemporary linguistic system: the most relevant context was not the history of a word's usage (much of which is unknown to the average native speaker) but the range of possible options available to a speaker at any particular moment. Language, for Saussure, was like a game of chess: the semantic content of a term draws its significance from its relationship with other terms in the system; it is this system of relationships which has priority for semantics, not the ways in which language hooks on to the world, or the ways in which linguistic meanings develop through time. On analogy with these insights in linguistics, anthropologists reacted against the evolutionary doctrine of 'survivals', arguing that social phenomena should be understood as part of their contemporary social system, rather than as a barely understood 'survival' of a previous age.

My approach to reading Genesis is synchronic insofar as it focuses on the intentions of the final editors of Genesis in the Persian period, considered against the background of the cultural options of the time. This implies that wherever the editors have used pre-existing sources they have used them for purposes which need to be understood in the immediate historical context. I am not denying the probability that some of these sources were composed much earlier than the Persian period; it is just that the historicist tendency to treat the sources as survivals of an earlier period is not sufficient for our interpretative purposes.

My concern also has analogies with Saussure's programme in that I am not primarily concerned with 'referential' uses of language, in the straightforward sense of referring to events in the distant past. That is to say, even though the narratives of Genesis purport to describe events in the lives of Israel's progenitors, even before settled life in Canaan, these events are not at issue here. Rather, the primary concern is with the relationships between discourses of the Persian period. Following Slavoj Zizek, I take the texts to be ideological, or political, even if they are quite accurate or 'true' in relation to their referential claims—'if true, so much the better for the ideological effect' (Zizek 1994: 7-8). What is at issue is not the asserted content but the way in which this content is related to particular social interests. Thus, the age of the stories about Abraham or Joseph, or whether they are historically accurate, are questions which are quite separate from the social interests served by the narrative in the Persian period. And it is these social interests which are the focus of this study.

The history of the composition of Genesis is, no doubt, complex. The variation in the naming of God is just one factor which indicates the complexity of textual prehistory. Precisely this complexity means that the final form of Genesis is not a logically unified whole, a point which has been taken for granted in critical studies of the Bible for more than a century. However, historical criticism has tended to resolve these complexities by reconstructing coherent layers of literary sources and subsequent editing, assuming that these authors and editors were themselves all characterized by a coherent subjectivity. Alternatively, the 'traditio-historical' approach has attempted to identity coherent layers of oral tradition.

A great deal can be learned from this historicist style of scholarship, but it is burdened by some key assumptions which are highly questionable. First, the presumption of coherent agency has been undermined by poststructuralist theory in both literary criticism and the social sciences. Communicative interaction is commonly marked by incongruities, repetitions and contradictions, some of which may be deliberate and some not. Biblical scholars have too often credited the sources of Genesis with an extraordinary consistency (cf. Whybray 1987).

Secondly, there has been a common presumption that the key to an editor's intention is to be found in the peculiar additions made to the sources; the earlier material is merely 'traditional', and it has been left intact for reasons which are difficult to determine—either out of antiquarianism or out of some sort of religious respect for the tradition. The difficulty here is twofold: the editors were clearly not antiquarian or respectful enough to have left the material alone altogether, yet once any editorial intervention has been posited, it is impossible to know how much of the 'traditional' material has been lost. An interpreter can hardly presume to know what has be cut from the narrative by an ancient editor if what has been cut is, clearly, entirely missing. Moreover, it is no more plausible to assume that the key to an editor's intention is to be found in their additions than to assume the reverse: it would make eminently good sense for the editors of Genesis to have kept 'traditional' material because it suited their purpose; any additions to the text could simply have been designed to stitch together the sources that were most appropriate to their communicative purposes.

The presumption of the present study, on the other hand, is that the activity of the final editors can be characterized as 'intentional hybridity', a concept of agency which has been developed especially within postcolonial theory. What is envisaged here is neither an organic hybridity wherein the complex prehistory of cultural elements are entirely unknown (the characteristic assumption behind Saussure's synchronic emphasis), nor a serial addition of traditions, all equally coherent and perspicuous. Rather, intentional hybridity is a blending of two or more voices, without compositional boundaries being evident, such that the voices combine into an unstable symphony—sometimes speaking univocally but more often juxtaposing alternative points of view such that the authority of the dominant voice is put into question (Bakhtin 1981:

358-61; Young 1995: 20-26). Hybridization takes the focus off particular editorial additions and allows a more 'holistic' consideration of the texts, except that this notion of holism is poststructuralist to the extent that it expects complexity and contradiction, not unity. In the case of Genesis, the overriding ideologies have been juxtaposed with so many traces of otherness that the dominant voices can be deconstructed by audiences who have ears to hear.

This postcolonial version of deconstruction has got nothing to do with the deconstructive criticism that Terry Eagleton has caricatured as a libertarian pessimism, blessedly free from the shackles of meaning and sociality (Eagleton 1991: 38; contrast Bhabha 1994: 183; Norris 1990). There are indeed forms of literary criticism which advocate the 'free play' of textuality, but deconstruction is construed differently within postcolonial theory. My purpose in reading Genesis is to trace the patterns of incongruity in the final Hebrew text and to suggest that these patterns point to an ancient editorial agency which is contesting the privileged grasp of colonial power in the Persian period. The agency of resistance is not seen as the product of a pure, egalitarian and consistent consciousness (cf. Bhabha 1994: 187). On the contrary, the text of Genesis seems to reveal a hybrid inter-subjectivity, not necessarily perspicuous to itself, incorporating diverse cultural elements both from within Israelite tradition and from outside it. Older literary sources may well have been used without any knowledge of the origins of such sources. Against extreme forms of postmodernism that would deny hybrid subjectivity any agency at all, the present study follows Homi Bhabha (1994: 171-97) in asserting that some kind of agency is necessary in any resistance to a dominant culture.

4. *An Illustration: Genesis 17*

Having suggested that Genesis can be read as an example of such subversive and artful hybridity, I turn now to explore this hypothesis with respect to just one more example,[5] Genesis 17—a text customarily associated with the 'exclusivism' of the Priestly tradition.

Genesis 17 reiterates the divine promises in the language of 'covenant'. Although this word was first used in a patriarchal promise in 15.18 (cf. 9.8-17), there a number of important differences between chs. 15 and 17. The first difference is to be found in the divine names. The

5.   For a reading of Genesis as a whole, see Brett (2000).

narrator introduces ch. 17 speaking of 'Yahweh', as was the case in ch. 15, but the divine speech to Abram in v. 1 has Yahweh providing a different name: 'Yahweh appeared to Abram and said to him, "I am El Shaddai"'.

The meaning of 'El Shaddai' is disputed, but it is clearly associated with the Canaanite divine name 'El' (cf. Smith 1990), used previously in the combinations 'El Elyon' (14.18-22) and 'El Roi' (16.13). Unlike the latter case, the narrator does not provide an interpretation of 'Shaddai'. It seems sufficient, from a synchronic point of view, to observe that this is a trace of an archaic epithet, the origins of which have been lost. Commentators routinely draw attention to the parallel text in Exod. 6.2-3 which even denies that the name 'Yahweh' was known in this early period: 'Elohim spoke to Moses, and he said to him, "I am Yahweh. I appeared to Abraham, to Isaac and to Jacob as El Shaddai, but by my name Yahweh I did not make myself known to them."'

Accordingly, Genesis 17 belongs to the traditions of Genesis which scrupulously keep the specifically Israelite divine name in the background (contrary to 12.8; 13.4; cf. 4.26). Here it appears only in v. 1, in the narrator's discourse. Elsewhere in the chapter, the narrator speaks of 'Elohim'. It seems that the editors of Genesis may have introduced 'Yahweh' into 17.1 simply to provide a link with the immediately preceding narrative: 16.13 provides a parallel case where the narrator speaks of Yahweh whereas the main character, Hagar, knows God by another name, El Roi. In short, the editors have identified the God of Hagar with the God of Abram, in spite of the diversity of divine names known to the actors. Divine reality, one could say, exceeds nominal constructions. The final editors have not attempted to reduce the naming of God to a single coherent scheme.

Another significant feature of 17.1 is that this is the first time where Abram is exhorted to be 'blameless' (*tamîm*, also used in Gen. 6.9 to describe Noah's integrity). Moreover, this divine demand might even be construed as providing the condition of the covenant promises that follow. The conditionality is not made explicit, but it is perhaps suggested by the juxtaposition of clauses: 'Walk with me and be blameless, and I will grant my covenant between me and you, and I will multiply you very greatly' (cf. 18.19). This expansion of the basic promise is remarkable in that Abram has been represented up to this point without distinguishing features of righteousness. Even his 'belief' mentioned in 15.6 is framed by his doubts in v. 3 and v. 8. Genesis 15.6 is the 'exception that proves the rule': whatever belief Abram might have possessed was 'attributed to him as righteousness', that is, it was not itself righteousness.

While this new element of divine exhortation in ch. 17 cannot be denied altogether, it should not, however, be overestimated. First, there are no formulaic corollaries here, such as one finds in Deuteronomy 28; Genesis does not say, 'if you are blameless, then you will receive the promised goods; if you are not blameless, you will not receive them'. The implications of the divine demand in Genesis 17 are not explicated in any logical detail. Just as Abram first received divine promises without any rational grounds, so also the possibility remains that continuing divine favour is not predicated upon absolute human integrity. If absolute integrity were required, then one would think that the covenant would have been lost the second time that the patriarch attempts to pass his wife off as his sister, simply to save his own skin (20.11-12).

Even within ch. 17, the editors have rendered Abraham's obedience somewhat ambiguous. The obligation laid on Abraham by Elohim's covenant is specified in only one respect: every male of the household is to be circumcised, both those born in the household and those bought from 'any foreigner—those who are not of your seed' (17.9-14). Verses 23-27 read like a textbook fulfillment of the requirements in v. 14: Abraham circumcises every male of his household, including the foreigners, beginning with his son Ishmael.

However, between these two sections lies the most problematic part of the chapter, vv. 15-22. First, there is a parallel promise to Sarai: her name is changed (just as Abram's was in v. 5), and it is said that she will become the mother of nations and of kings, just as Abraham is to become the father of nations and kings (v. 6). An innovation here is that although Abraham was previously promised descendants as numerous as the dust of the earth (13.16) and the stars of the sky (15.5), this extraordinary fecundity could still be interpreted within the framework of the single 'great nation' mentioned in 12.2. Now that Abraham and Sarah are set to become the father and mother of many nations, it is no longer possible to restrict this covenantal promise to the people of Israel. The catch for Abraham, however, is that if Sarah's inclusion within the covenant means that she herself must have a son, then the status of Hagar's son is thrown into question. Abraham therefore intercedes on Ishmael's behalf (v. 18), only to be assured that Hagar's son will become a 'great nation', but outside the covenant with Sarah's son (vv. 19-21). This divine reassurance in vv. 19-21 is precisely what makes the conclusion of the chapter so problematic: if circumcision is the 'sign' of the covenant (v. 11), and the covenantal line is to go through Isaac—not through Ishmael—why have the editors so blithely placed the 'obedience' of vv. 23-27 at the end of the chapter? The first person circumcised is Ishmael, the son excluded from the covenant.

The standard historicist response to this kind of problem is to reconstruct the layers of the text so that the first layer of the narrative is seen to be coherent, while the clumsy additions have rendered the final text illogical (e.g. Grünwaldt 1992: 27-70).[6] This kind of interpretative response has its own legitimacy, but it leaves one of the most interesting questions unexplained: why would anyone want to add a contradiction to a text? This question can only be avoided by assuming that the editors were cognitively less gifted than the authors of the earliest traditions, an assumption which is often unjustifiable. It seems much more likely that the editors had a purpose in view, but this purpose could not conveyed by a perspicuous logic, since the issue at stake lay at the heart of a dominant ideology of the Persian period. The ostensibly simple 'obedience' of Abraham in 17.23-27 is exploiting the tensions within the final text: the circumcision of Ishmael contradicts the exclusivism of vv. 19-21 by holding to the inclusivism of vv. 9-12. If every male of the household is to be circumcised, as suggested in the first part of the chapter, then that should include Ishmael. Moreover, if Ishmael is to be the father of a 'great nation' (v. 20), then that is in some sense the fulfillment of the promise that Abraham is to be the father of many nations (v. 5). In short, the editors have smudged the edges of the covenant tradition by gently undermining its exclusivist tendency.

The rite of circumcision in Genesis 17 is therefore much more inclusive than one might have thought. Any reader familiar with the narrow interpretation of the 'holy seed' in Ezra 9.1-2, for example, would have been struck by the wording of v. 12: 'For the generations to come every male among you who is eight days old must be circumcised, including those born in your household or bought with money from a foreigner— he who is not of your seed'. If this text is implying that all slaves are to

6.   According to Grünwaldt, the first layer of P contained a circumcision of Ishmael (17.24-26) but no statement of his exclusion from the covenant. Since, however, he argues that the supplement was added in the Persian period, his thesis could be construed as support for my overall argument concerning the final editing.

be bought from foreigners, then it presumes the legal background of Lev. 25.39-46, rather than Deut. 15.12-15 (the Deuteronomic slave law permits the buying of Hebrew slaves, but the Levitical law prohibits this, permitting only the purchase of foreign slaves). But whatever the legal presumption, Genesis 17 is clearly envisaging that foreigners would be circumcised, and in this sense, the covenant is seen as broader than Israelite kinship. It would include those born outside the line of Ezra's 'holy seed'.

Indeed, in the setting of the Persian period, circumcision could no longer have the same significance as it had during the exile: the Babylonians did not practise circumcision, and therefore the rite would have been a distinctive mark of social identity for Israelites living in Babylon, but the distinctiveness of this mark of the covenant would have been lost as soon as the Israelites moved back to the Promised Land. As indicated by a text in Jeremiah, Israel's neighbours also practised circumcision, including the Egyptians, Edomites, Ammonites, Moabites and 'all who live in the desert' (Jer. 9.25-26). If we can include the Ishmaelites among these desert-dwellers (cf. Gen. 21.20-21), then the people listed in Jeremiah 9 include *not just the exclusive people of the covenant but also all peoples represented in Genesis as related to Abraham*. Ezra 9.2, we should remember, prohibits inter-marriage specifically with Egyptians, Ammonites and Moabites, three of the peoples listed in Jer. 9.25-26 as circumcised. In short, the logic of the exclusivism in Ezra 9.2 cannot be based on the sign of the covenant in Genesis 17.

To summarize: a close reading of the final form of Genesis reveals a complex editorial agency which is not reducible to a social commonplace like 'groups under threat tend to defend their identity'. For example, even if the practice of circumcision could be read simply as a defence of Israelite identity in the context of exile, and even if this purpose lies behind the original P text in Genesis 17, it does not follow that the same purpose applies to the final edition of Genesis. Read in the context of the Persian period, Genesis seems to undermine any exclusivist tendency in the construction of Jewish identity. The agency of the final editors can be illuminated by drawing on a wide range of methods, both literary and social-scientific, but the particular combination of methods and reading strategies can only be formulated with respect to the specific goals of an interpretation.

GAUGING THE GRAIN IN A MORE NUANCED
AND LITERARY MANNER:
A CAUTIONARY TALE CONCERNING THE CONTRIBUTION OF THE
SOCIAL SCIENCES TO BIBLICAL INTERPRETATION

Gerald O. West

1. *Introducing the Graininess of Texts*

'Oppressive texts cannot be totally tamed or subverted into liberative texts', argues Itumeleng Mosala (Mosala 1989a: 30). Why? Because they have grain. But, I ask in this essay, do texts have grain—do they have clearly identifiable ideologies? This is not an idle question to wile away time between the other duties of a university lecturer in biblical studies; it is question that lies at the heart of liberation hermeneutics, particularly as postmodern forms of discourse buffet and scour the familiar certainties of the liberation paradigm.

Drawing on the work of Terry Eagleton and Norman Gottwald, Mosala presents a passionate case for the graininess of texts. Mosala contends that the impotence of black theology as a weapon of struggle comes from the enslavement of black theology 'to the biblical hermeneutics of dominant ideologies' (Mosala 1989a: 4). More specifically, black theology's impotence comes from embracing 'the ideological form of the text'—'the oppressors most dangerous form' (Mosala 1989a: 28). Existential commitment to the struggle against apartheid in South Africa was no substitute 'for scientific analysis of the valence of a tradition in the class struggle' (Mosala 1989a: 34). While Mosala accepts that 'texts that are against oppressed people may be coopted by the interlocutors of the liberation struggle', he insists that

> the fact that these texts have their ideological roots in oppressive prac-
> tices means that the texts are capable of undergirding the interests of the
> oppressors even when used by the oppressed. In other words, oppressive
> texts cannot be totally tamed or subverted into liberative texts (Mosala
> 1989a: 30).

Mosala rejects what he calls a 'fundamentalism of the Left', that 'attempts to transplant biblical paradigms and situations into our world without understanding their historical circumstances'. Like Gottwald, Mosala criticizes liberation theologians who invoke biblical symbols of liberation but who 'seldom push those biblical symbols all the way back to their socio-historic foundations' and consequently are not able to 'grasp concretely the inner-biblical strands of oppression and liberation in all their stark multiplicity and contradictory interactions'. Not only does this 'picking and choosing' of biblical resources by some liberation theologians 'not carry sufficient structural analysis of biblical societies to make a proper comparison with the present possible', a lack of interest in and knowledge of social forms and ideas from biblical times to the present may mean that 'unstructural understanding of the Bible' simply reinforces and confirms 'unstructural understanding of the present' (Mosala 1989a: 31-32). It is 'a risky business', says Gottwald, 'to "summon up" powerful symbolism out of a distant past unless the symbol users are very self-conscious of their choices and applications, and fully aware of how their social struggle is both like and unlike the social struggle of the architects of the symbols' (Gottwald 1979: 703).[1] Efforts to draw 'religious inspiration' or 'biblical values' from, for example, early Israel 'will be romantic and utopian unless resolutely correlated to both the ancient and the contemporary cultural-material and social-organizational foundations' (Gottwald 1979: 706).

Mosala agrees; his fundamental objections against the biblical hermeneutics of black theology are that not only does it suffer from an 'unstructural understanding of the Bible' but, both as a consequence and as a reason, it also suffers from an 'unstructural understanding' of black experience and struggle. Central to Mosala's hermeneutics of liberation is the search for a theoretical perspective that can locate both the Bible and the black experience within appropriate socio-historical contexts. Historical-critical tools (to delimit and historically locate texts), supplemented by sociological resources (including a historical-materialist understanding of struggle) provide the theoretical perspective for Mosala's treatment of texts; historical-materialism, particularly its appropriation of 'struggle' as a key concept, provides the categories and concepts necessary to read and critically appropriate both black history and culture and the Bible. 'The category of struggle becomes an

---

1.   Gottwald gives considerable space to developing this point (1979: 703-706).

important hermeneutical factor not only in one's reading of his or her history and culture but also in one's understanding of the history, nature, ideology, and agenda of the biblical texts' (Mosala 1989: 9).

In order to undertake this kind of analysis, Mosala argues, black interpreters must be engaged in the threefold task of Terry Eagleton's 'revolutionary cultural worker': a task that is projective, polemical and appropriative. While Mosala does not doubt that black theology is 'projective' and 'appropriative' in its use of the Bible, it is 'certainly *not* polemical—in the sense of being critical—in its biblical hermeneutics' (Mosala 1989a: 32). Black theology has not interrogated the text ideologically in class, cultural, gender and age terms. Black theology has not gauged the grain or asked in what code the biblical text is cast and so has read the biblical text as an innocent and transparent container of a message or messages (Mosala 1989a: 41). By not using socio-historical modes of interpretation, black theology continues to spar 'with the ghost of the oppressor' in its most powerful form—the ideological form of the text (Mosala 1989a: 28).

The Bible, according to Mosala's analysis, is a complex text best understood as a 'signified practice'. 'It cannot be reduced to a simple socially and ideologically unmediated "Word of God". Nor can it be seen merely as a straight forward mirror of events in Ancient Israel. On the contrary it is a *production*, a remaking of those events and processes' (Mosala 1989b: 3). Using the language of redaction criticism, Mosala argues that the different 'layers' historical-critical work detects each have a particular ideological code. Some layers of the Bible are cast in 'hegemonic codes', which represent social and historical realities in ancient Israel in terms of the interests of the ruling classes. Other parts of the Bible are encoded in 'professional codes', which have a relative autonomy, but which still operate within the hegemony of the dominant code. Then there are layers that are signified through 'negotiated codes', which contain a mixture of adaptive and oppositional elements, but which still take the dominant codes as their starting point. Finally, there are a few textual sites that represent 'oppositional codes' which are grounded in the interests and religious perspectives of the underclasses of the communities of the Bible (Mosala 1989a: 41-42).

A critical and structural analysis of the biblical text requires that black theology identify the ideological reference-code in which a particular text is encoded. For it is only by recognizing the particular ideological encoding of a text that interpreters can prevent themselves from colluding with the dominant and hegemonic. Moreover, it is only by recognizing the particular encoding of a text that the interpreter can then interpret the text 'against the grain'. In other words, the polemical task of the interpreter is vital because it enables the appropriative task. A critical analysis of the biblical text ensures that black theology is able to appropriates the text against the grain. Such an approach would not be selective, nor would it engage in 'proof-texting'. Rather, a critical and structural ideological mode of reading 'advocates an analytic approach to the text of the Bible that exposes the underlying literary and ideological plurality in the text without denying the hegemonic totality or shall we say unity of the final product' (Mosala 1989a: 4).[2]

This phrase of Eagleton's, 'against the grain', seeks to remind us, Mosala argues, 'that the appropriation of works and events is always a contradictory process embodying in some form a "struggle"'. The interpretive struggle consists of, depending on the class forces involved, 'either to harmonize the contradictions inherent in the works and events or to highlight them with a view to allowing social class choices in their appropriation' (Mosala 1989a: 32).[3] The concern of Mosala is not that black theologians *cannot* read any text, no matter what its encoding, against the grain, but that they *ought not* to do this without *recognizing* what they are doing.

Mosala acknowledges that the black interpreters he criticizes are clearly correct 'in detecting glimpses of liberation and of a determinate social movement galvanized by a powerful religious ideology in the biblical text'. His point, however, is that while the 'existence of this phenomenon is not in question', the problem 'is one of developing an adequate hermeneutical framework that can rescue those liberative

---

2. Elisabeth Schüssler Fiorenza makes a similar point when she argues that 'The failure to bring a critical evaluation to bear upon the biblical texts and upon the process of interpretation within Scripture and tradition is one of the reasons why the use of the Bible by liberation theologians often comes close to "proof texting"'. Later she adds, 'a critical hermeneutic must be applied to *all* biblical texts and their historical contexts' (Schüssler Fiorenza 1981: 101-102, 108).

3. David Tracy notes that 'the particular form of "correlation" [between the tradition and contemporary situation] that liberation and political theologies take will ordinarily prove to be a form not of liberal identity nor one of the several forms of analogy or similarity but rather one of sheer confrontation'. 'The confrontations will be demanded by both the retrieval of the prophetic tradition's stand for the oppressed and by the suspicions released by the prophetic ideology-critique embedded in that retrieval' (Tracy 1981: 2–3).

themes from the biblical text'. 'One cannot', Mosala maintains, 'successfully perform this task by denying the oppressive structures that frame what liberating themes the texts encode' (Mosala 1989a: 41).

The social sciences provide the resources for this task—the task of identifying, unmasking and demystifying the ideological agenda of particular biblical texts. The social sciences are the preferred tools for ideological criticism.

2. *Do Texts Have Grain?*

But do texts have ideologies? The discussion thus far assumes so, but does it move too quickly and is there some sleight of hand? In a carefully argued article Stephen Fowl considers such questions. Recognizing that 'ideological criticism' has become an accepted practice within biblical studies, he sets out to problematize the claim that the Bible or a biblical passage has an ideology (Fowl 1995: 15). He begins by demonstrating that those who make such claims usually make two moves. Their initial move is to argue that 'those who produced the biblical texts shaped them in the light of their own economic, ethnic, social or gender based interests'. They then go on to say that 'the racism, androcentrism or elitism of the people who produced the text is a property of it. Hence, the text has an ideology.' In support of his argument Fowl cites Mosala's work: biblical texts, 'as products, records and sites of social, historical, cultural gender racial and ideological struggles ... radically and indelibly bear the marks of their origins and history. The ideological aura of the Bible as the Word of God conceals this reality' (Mosala 1989a: 20, cited in Fowl 1995: 15 n. 2).[4]

Fowl's article takes issue with these claims, 'arguing that speaking of the Bible (or any text) as having an ideology introduces a whole range of conceptual confusions and fails to take seriously the varied history of Bible interpretation' (Fowl 1995: 16). He immediately qualifies this statement by noting that he cannot 'demonstrate that texts do not have ideologies'; his assignment in this article is more modest. What he hopes to show, and he succeeds in doing this, is that

> if one insists on talking as if texts have ideologies, then one also has to
> hold a whole range of other inelegant, awkward or incoherent positions.

4.   Fowl then cites my work: 'The growing recognition of the ideological nature of all interpretation has led inevitably to the acknowledgement of the ideological nature of *the biblical text*'' (West 1992: 4).

> Furthermore, dropping the idea that texts have ideologies will allow us to
> think in clearer more productive ways about particular texts, about the
> relationships between texts and social practices and about how one might
> alter the social practices underwritten by particular texts (especially
> biblical texts) (Fowl 1995: 16).

Drawing on an earlier article in which he examines what it means to
speak of a text having 'meaning' (Fowl 1990), Fowl asks whether it
makes sense to speak of ideology as *a property* of a text. Such thinking,
he argues, assumes that the text 'is viewed as a relatively stable element
into which an author inserts, hides or dissolves (choose your metaphor)
ideologies and meanings, and the task of the critic or reader is to dig
out, uncover or distill these properties from it' (Fowl 1995: 16). But
there are a number of problems with this way of thinking. First, there
has to be some agreement on what we are looking for when we look for
ideologies. This is not a substantial problem, as 'ideology' is less slip-
pery than 'meaning'. Fowl's working definition of 'ideology', for example, would be quite acceptable to Mosala: ideology 'as a consensual
collection of beliefs, attitudes, and convictions that is related in certain
specifiable ways to a whole range of social, political, and material artifacts and practices' (Fowl 1995: 17; see also West 1995a: 251 n. 7). But
agreement on what we understand by 'ideology' 'does not entail that
texts *have* ideologies' (Fowl 1995: 17).

A second, more serious, problem is that 'over its life a text can be
pressed into the service of so many varied and potentially conflicting
ideologies that talk about a text having an ideology will become
increasingly strained' (Fowl 1995: 18). Fowl carefully illustrates this
point by providing a history of interpretation of the story of Abraham.
As the Abraham story is read in a range of different socio-historical
contexts, so the ideological interests that shape and are shaped by each
reading shift. Philo puts the story of Abraham to quite different ideological purposes to those of tribal Israel; Paul's reading reflects and is
related to a whole range of ideological interests in his context; and
when we compare Justin Martyr's interpretation with that of Paul's we
find a different set of socio-political and theological interests. Clearly
(Fowl 1995: 28), the question that persists as we reflect on these various
ideological interpretations is this: which is the ideology of the text?

Mosala would respond quite quickly, I think, stating that it is the
ideological interests and aims at work in the production of a text that
constitute the ideology of the text. Texts get their grain from the

ideological sites that produced them.[5] Fowl anticipates such a response, and counters by asking why one would want to privilege this particular moment in a text's history (Fowl 1995: 29). This is a good question, and posing it is one of Fowl's considerable contributions to clarifying what is going on in biblical interpretation. Biblical scholars do not, and need not, have the same interpretive interests. This does not, of course, prevent biblical scholars from insisting on, and in some cases arguing for, particular sets of interpretive interests. Mosala is in good company with, among others, Norman Gottwald and Elisabeth Schüssler Fiorenza in arguing for particular interpretive interests. I have discussed these arguments at length elsewhere (West 1995a: 131-73), so here I will briefly allude to their main concerns.

First, Mosala and others are concerned that liberation theologies develop hermeneutical procedures that work with the whole Bible and not only with selective bits and pieces; they want to avoid a fundamentalism of the Left. Second, and Mosala is especially insistent on this, they are concerned that the poor and marginalized acquire forms of analysis that will enable them to interpret critically both biblical texts *and their own social context*; and socio-historical resources are particularly useful for this dual task. There is not doubt that there is some significant transfer between a socio-historical analysis of the Bible and a socio-historical analysis of the reader's context, and so Mosala has a point. However, on the first score their case is overstated. Literary and metaphoric/symbolic modes of interpretation can provide a systematic, structured and theoretically well-grounded hermeneutics of liberation.[6] They can also supply useful resources for 'reading' one's context.

But there is something more going on in the claims of those who use the social sciences. Something else is at stake. The social sciences provide useful resources for establishing lines of connection between our present locations and the socio-historical originary events that we believe partially constitute our present locations.

5. As my discussion of Mosala's work indicates, Mosala would accept the plurality of ideologies in a text; while what Mosala means by this is primarily a series of layers of differing ideologies, a more nuanced analysis would insist on there always being more than one ideology within any particular layer.

6. See above note.

3. *Locating Lines of Connection*

The socio-historical work of Carol Meyers is a good example of the importance of establishing lines of connection between past and present. Meyers offers a detailed historical and sociological reconstruction of the life of ordinary women in early Israelite society (Meyers 1988). In order to accomplish this task an interdisciplinary approach including feminist scholarship and social scientific (mainly sociological, anthropological and archaeological) research is used.[7] Beginning with social interests rooted in the experienced reality and identities of particular women, Meyers recognizes that the Bible

> as a source presents problems of omission in its treatment of women as individuals or as a group. Its androcentric bias and also its urban, elite orientation mean that even the information it contains may be a distortion or misrepresentation of the lives of women removed from urban centers and bureaucratic families.

However, socio-historical resources recover the average Israelite woman, who is neither named nor described in the biblical text (Meyers 1988: 13-14).

Meyers argues that because gender relationships 'are the consequence of complex influences, involving specific social and economic arrangements', reconstructing the internal dynamics of a society 'is the only legitimate way to dispel the "myth" and to increase the visibility of Eve'—'a figure no less powerful than her male counterpart' (Meyers 1988: 181). Understanding the contextual reality of the early Israelites, particularly the social reality of Israelite women, is thus 'central to interpreting the original message and function' of biblical texts (Meyers 1988: 93, 120). However, while Meyers continually makes the point that understanding biblical texts requires that we interpret them from the perspective of their ancient context and not from the perspective of our modern context, she is concerned to ask, overtly, what her reconstructions and readings might mean for women's struggles in her own context.

Her response to this question demonstrates the importance both of her reading process and the particular texts she chooses to read:

7.   This does not mean that Meyers pays no attention to literary aspects of the text; to the contrary, Meyers demonstrates considerable sensitivity to the literary dimensions of the text.

> If the egalitarian values and patterns that prevailed during those prestate
> centuries are to have any meaning for later generations, including our
> own, this recovery of Everywoman Eve's life and context should make
> the nonhierarchical position of women a visible and enduring model, as
> are the other widely acclaimed theological and social innovations and
> accomplishments, of early Israel (Meyers 1988: 14).

Socio-historical modes of reading are what make the recovery of the
social reality of women in prestate Israel possible; concentrating on
prestate Israel is important because it is the formative era in the long
story of the biblical people (Meyers 1988:14).[8]

As the quotation above indicates, other scholars too have found 'visible and enduring models' for present communities in the 'theological
and social innovations and accomplishments' of early Israel. Norman
Gottwald is one such scholar, who, from a slightly different angle,
argues that as socio-historical study of the origins of Israel

> penetrates more and more deeply to the circumstances and dynamics of
> Yahwism's emergence, the integral social-revolutionary character of
> Yahwism comes more clearly to light and thereby once again challenges
> the synagogues and churches with the disturbing implications and conse-
> quences of claiming continuity with a religion sprung from such roots
> (Gottwald 1979: 597).

We can now see what is at stake. The (re)construction of the past, in
Keith Whitelam's words, 'is a struggle over the definition of historical
and social identity', particularly when we are dealing with originary
events. As the work of Meyers and Gottwald demonstrates, and as
V. Dharwadker has pointed out, the 'first moment of true civilization' is
especially significant in the history of any people (cited in Whitelam
1996: 234). Such moments—and the periods of the 'emergence' of
Israel in Palestine and the development of an Israelite state are good
examples of such moments—provide 'the basis for understanding all
subsequent history' (Whitelam 1996: 234), which is why there is so
much at stake in reconstructing them and finding lines of connection
with them.

It is precisely because so much is at stake that Meyers can ignore the

---

8.   Another reason she gives for her focus on this period is that it is the period
of Israelite existence which is best known in terms of its social configurations;
recent developments in the reconstruction of ancient 'Israel' would undermine
Meyers' confidence at this point (see below).

cautionary words of Gottwald concerning the presence of feminist impulses in early Israel. While arguing that

> women and men who care about the future of feminism in our religious
> communities should be examining the techno-environmental and socio-
> political conditions of ancient Israel to see what parameters actually
> existed for a feminist movement and to assess the extent to which
> Israelite women benefitted or lost from the transition between elitist hier-
> archical Canaan and a generally much more egalitarian intertribal Israel

he is not particularly confident that such socio-historical research will
contribute very much to the feminist cause.

> A careful calculus of these gains and losses [of women in early Israel]
> will ultimately be of far more significance to the contemporary religious
> feminist movement than attempts to make ancient Israel religion look
> more feminist than it actually was. I personally estimate that Israelite
> women gained much from their break with Canaanite society, but I do
> not for a moment think that they achieved—or could have achieved
> under ancient technological and social conditions—what women today
> are capable of achieving. I would not like to see contemporary religious
> feminists, and I include myself among them, led into the trap of pinning
> many hopes on dubious arguments about an ancient Israelite feminism
> which to this point is more a chimera than a demonstrated reality. For
> feminists who wish to keep in continuity with their religious heritage, I
> believe it is sufficient to assert that contemporary feminism in church
> and synagogue is a logical and necessary extension of the social egalitar-
> ian principle of early Israel, which itself did not exhibit any appreciable
> independent feminist consciousness or praxis (Gottwald 1979: 797
> n. 628).

That Meyers believes it is not 'sufficient to assert that contemporary
feminism in church and synagogue is a logical and necessary extension
of the social egalitarian principle of early Israel', and that she goes on
to pursue signs of an 'appreciable independent feminist consciousness
or praxis' demonstrates just how much is at stake!

Mainstream biblical scholarship has tended to monopolize the originary moments of early Israel for its own purposes, as Whitelam's recent
book *The Invention of Ancient Israel* amply articulates. Whitelam makes
a persuasive case for an intricate and intimate link between biblical
criticism and the cultural and political agendas of contemporary developed states such as Western Europe, Israel and North America. His
study, which is based on a careful analysis of all the major histories of
Israel, concentrates on two of the 'originary' periods of Israelite history:

the period of the so-called 'emergence' or 'origins' of Israel in Palestine during the Late Bronze–Iron Age transition and the subsequent period of the founding of an Israelite state in the Iron Age (Whitelam 1996: 5).

Whitelam focuses on these 'two defining moments' because 'it is these two periods which have represented Israel's control of the past'; they are the key moments that 'define the essential nature of Israel, its sense of national identity, which is portrayed as unchanging throughout subsequent periods of history *connecting* the past with the present' (Whitelam 1996: 234, my emphasis). Driven by the desire of Western nation states to find and found themselves historically, biblical scholars forged lines of connection with the past that fitted their political agendas.

> Biblical scholars accepting, in broad outline, the construction of the past offered by biblical traditions began the search for Israel's physical presence among the monuments and ruins of the land. What they found, or were predisposed to find, was an Israel which resembled their own nation states: Israel was presented as an incipient nation state in search of a national homeland in which to express its national consciousness. Throughout the present century, this projection of ancient Israel has come to dominate and control the Late Bronze and Iron Ages. It is a representation of the past which was given added urgency and authority with the rise of the Zionist movement, an essentially European enterprise, whose own history was seen to mirror ancient Israel's conquest of the land followed by the founding of a nation state which soon dominated the region (Whitelam 1996: 223).

This in broad outline is the master narrative that mainstream biblical studies has constructed from the defining moments of Israel's past.

The power of such narratives lies in their ability to create

> not only knowledge but also the very reality they appear to describe. In time such knowledge and reality produce a tradition, or what Michel Foucault calls a discourse, whose material presence or weight, not the originality of a given author, is really responsible for the texts produced out of it (Said 1985: 94, cited in Whitelam 1996: 4).

By claiming the right to represent the origins of 'ancient Israel' mainstream biblical studies has, according to Whitelam, 'collaborated in an act of dispossession, or at the very least, to use Said's phrase, "passive collaboration" in that act of dispossession'. The construction of ancient Israel (retrospectively) in the images and likenesses of European visions of itself 'has silenced the history of the indigenous peoples of Palestine in the early Iron Age' (Whitelam 1996: 222), and has contributed to the marginalization of the Palestinian people in Israel today (Whitelam 1996: 225-27).

This is not all; more can be laid at the door of the dominant discourse in biblical studies. Not only have Palestinians been dispossessed; others too have been dispossessed. By controlling the originary moments of early Israel through their representations, the dominant sectors of biblical scholarship have participated in dispossessing others of their place in these defining moments. Representing the past is a social and political act that has important ramifications for present 'because personal or social identity is either confirmed by or denied by these representations' (Whitelam 1996: 12; see also Tonkin 1992: 6). It is not surprising, therefore, that the formative periods of Israel's past, the period of the so-called 'emergence' or 'origins' of Israel in Palestine during the Late Bronze–Iron Age transition and the subsequent period of the founding of an Israelite state in the Iron Age, have predominated and preoccupied biblical scholarship. Much is at stake in staking a claim to this territory, and the preferred tools for this task have been those of the social sciences.

For those who stand in some form of continuity with the biblical traditions it is important to believe that there are lines of connection between their particular stance and the founding moments of the tradition. It matters whether early Israel emerged from among the marginalized classes of Palestine; it matters whether women in early Israel were part of a nonhierarchical society; it matters whether Jesus was an organic intellectual working among the poor and marginalized; it matters whether women were an integral part of early Christianity. For the previously dispossessed it matters whether they too have a place in the founding moments of a tradition that is meaningful, powerful and true for them, but who do not find themselves represented in its dominant discourse (see West 1999). Rosemary Radford Ruether says it well when she argues that to express contemporary experience in a cultural and historical vacuum is both 'self-deluding and unsatisfying'.

> It is self-deluding because to communicate at all to oneself and others, one makes use of patterns of thought, however transformed by new experience, that have a history. It is unsatisfactory because, however much one discards large historical periods of dominant traditions, one still seeks to encompass this 'fallen history' within a larger context of authentic and truthful life. To look back to some original base of meaning and truth before corruption is to know that truth is more basic than

falsehood and hence able, ultimately, to root out falsehood in a new
future that is dawning in contemporary experience. To find glimmers of
this truth in submerged and alternative traditions through history is to
assure oneself that one is not mad or duped. Only by finding an alternative historical community and tradition more deeply rooted than those
that have become corrupted can one feel sure that in criticizing the dominant tradition one is not just subjectively criticizing the dominant tradition but is, rather, touching a deeper bedrock of authentic Being upon
which to ground the self. One cannot wield the lever of criticism without
a place to stand (Ruether 1983: 18).

So while Fowl is right to remind us that an interest in the origins of a
text is just that—*an* interest, he perhaps underestimates the power of
this particular interest in the struggle of various sectors of society for a
place in the formative moments of their faith. What complicates this
struggle for marginalized sectors of society, as Whitelam's study estab-
lishes, is not only that the dominant discourses have already coopted the
originary moments for their own ends, but that the alleged objectivity of
this master story masks the political subjectivity of the biblical narratives themselves, and colludes with, for example, the literate elite of the
Second Temple period to silence competing pasts (see Whitelam 1996:
28, 232). Consequently, marginalized sectors of society have a legitimate interest in both the ideological uses to which a text is and has been
put and the ideological aims of the text's author or of its production.[9]
Fowl is right, we must pay more attention to the interpretive history of
biblical texts—'to show how specific social, political, material and theological influences and conflicts shaped and were shaped by the interpretation of particular biblical texts at particular points in time', but
because for professional biblical scholars the most important phases of
a particular text's interpretive life 'are those initial phases associated
with the production and first reception of biblical texts' (Fowl 1995: 32-
33), we who work with the poor and marginalized cannot permit these
initial phases to remain uncontested.

4. *Getting to the Grain by Going behind the Text*

While it is extremely difficult to determine the socio-historical origins
of many biblical texts, with the consequence that their ideological

9. These two senses of 'the ideology of a text' are both acceptable senses in
Fowl's analysis.

agendas must remain a matter of some speculation, and while it is 'often very difficult to read back from an ancient textual artifact to the ideological interests behind its production' (Fowl 1995: 29), these difficulties have not deterred marginalized sectors and those who read with them from the task of attempting to detect the grain of biblical texts.

The favoured route in gauging the grain of a biblical text has been to go behind the text by means of socio-historical tools. With some variations, the moves scholars make follow a fairly familiar framework. First, historical-critical tools are used to determine the text, its limits and its historical period. Second, a range of tools from the social sciences, including archaeological, geographical, anthropological and sociological, are then used to provide a description and analysis of the text's production. Third, the reconstructed context of production is used to correlated the text with a particular ideology. Fourth, the text is appropriated, either with or (consciously) against the grain.[10]

Social scientific reconstructions assist in recovering the grain of a particular text, and in doing so enable appropriate appropriations of that text. This is significant, as we have seen; misappropriating a biblical text by failing to detect its ideological grain can be dangerous, as Mosala, Gottwald, and Schüssler Fiorenza contend.[11] And, as I have argued, such appropriations are potentially important for poor and marginalized sectors who are contesting for lines of connection with a tradition that is meaningful, powerful and true for them, but in which the dominant discourse has the loudest voice and provides little space or place for them.

So the social sciences have a significant part to play in a process of gauging the ideological grain of a particular text and in its appropriate appropriation. But do they always have the opening part in the play; do they always make up the first act? My question, and the literary allusion is deliberate, arises from recent reflections within the social sciences themselves.

10. The work of Meyers and Gottwald mentioned earlier in the essay are good examples of such procedures; see also Gottwald 1993b; Mosala 1993; and Mosala 1989a: 101-53.

11. See above; Schüssler Fiorenza is critical of Phyllis Trible's literary approach because she abstracts the text 'from its cultural-historical context' (Schüssler Fiorenza 1983: 20). See my discussion of these issues in West 1995a: 140-46.

5. *Theorizing the 'Silences' in a Text*

Much of the analysis of the social sciences proceeds from the perspective that the biblical text in its final form is the product of the dominant sectors of society in any particular period. However, while there is consensus that the biblical text exhibits a ruling class and patriarchal 'ideological unity' (Mosala 1993: 265; Mosala 1989a: 102), it is recognized that there are enough contradictions to 'enable eyes hermeneutically trained in the struggle for liberation today to observe the kindred struggles of the oppressed and exploited of the biblical communities in the very absence of those struggles in the text' (Mosala 1993: 269-70; Mosala 1989a: 121). Actually, however, and this is an important point, the struggles of the oppressed and exploited are not entirely absent.

In Mosala's analysis of Micah (Mosala 1989a: 101-53; Mosala 1993), which draws on a similar analysis by Robert Coote of Amos (Coote 1981), the voices of the marginalized do find some form of representation. While the text in its final form is cast in the dominant code of the priestly ruling elite, it contains traces of the social struggles that produced it, which can be detected by socio-historical analysis in the hands of the socially committed biblical scholar (Mosala 1993: 265; Mosala 1989a: 102). The ideologically astute and discerning reader can thus find (redactional) layers of representation, including some signs of the poor and marginalized. So, for example, in the book of Micah, while the oppressed and exploited peasants, artisans, day labourers and underclasses of Micah's Judah 'are entirely absent in the signifying practice' of the ruling class formulation that constitutes the final form of the text, 'something of their project and voice has almost accidentally survived' in the respective representations of the scribal and/or prophetic sectors who have respectively negotiated and/or mediated the struggles of the poor and exploited peasants, but whose representations have in turn been coopted and appropriated—re-represented—by the ruling classes (Mosala 1993: 291; Mosala 1989a: 151).

The socio-historical dimensions of this type of interpretation are well documented, and Mosala's sources and his own study of Micah provide examples of this type of interpretation in practice.[12] But it is his attempt to *theorize* the silences/absences of the text—'to explain the ideological necessity of those "not-saids" which constitute the very principle of its

---

12. Even if Mosala's own analysis is somewhat muddled at times.

[the text's] identity' (Eagleton 1978: 89, cited by Mosala 1993: 268 and Mosala 1989a: 119)—that particularly interests me in this essay. Here there appears to be something of a tension in Mosala's work (and those who share his assumptions). On the one hand, Mosala works with a strong notion of ideological hegemony in which ideology is 'a harmonization of contradictions in such a way that the class interests of one group are universalized and made acceptable to other classes' (Mosala 1993: 268; Mosala 1989a: 119);[13] on the other hand, Mosala wants to foreground the struggles of the poor and marginalized and to give them some form of presence in the text. There is a tension here. If the class interests of the dominant group are universalized and *made acceptable* to other classes, then what does it mean to speak of *the struggles* of the poor and marginalized and what type of presence do they have in texts? Is the resistance of the poor and oppressed, as Mosala asserts, 'present only by its absence'? (Mosala 1993: 283; Mosala 1989a: 141).

The problem with, and hence the tension within, Mosala's form of ideological analysis is that it does not allow for a sufficiently nuanced understanding of the relationship between domination and resistance. Mosala is not alone here. Informed by forms of Marxist analysis and aspects of our experience, many of us, including myself, believed that forms of critical consciousness are necessary so that the poor and marginalized can 'create their own language' (Frostin 1988: 10). Forms of critical consciousness, we argued, break 'the culture of silence' created by the accommodation of the poor and marginalized to the logic of domination. This was certainly my own understanding in the early days of my work with local communities of the poor and marginalized in South Africa. But now I am not so sure that this understanding is the whole story.

When it comes to understanding the alleged silence of the poor and marginalized we find thick and thin accounts of ideological hegemony. The thick version emphasizes the role of ideological state apparatuses, such as education systems, the church and government structures, in controlling the symbolic means of production, just as factory owners monopolize the material means of production. 'Their ideological work secures the active consent of subordinate groups to the social arrangements that reproduce their subordination' (Scott 1990: 73). The thin theory of hegemony makes less grand claims for the ideological control

13. See also Per Frostin's discussion of Mosala's use of 'ideology' in Frostin 1988: 164-65.

of the ruling class. What ideological domination does accomplish, according to this version,

> is to define for subordinate groups what is realistic and what is not realistic and to drive certain aspirations and grievances into the realm of the impossible, of idle dreams. By persuading underclasses that their position, their life-chances, their tribulations are unalterable and inevitable, such a limited hegemony can produce the behavioral results of consent without necessarily changing people's values. Convinced that nothing can possibly be done to improve their situation and that it will always remain so, it is even conceivable that idle criticisms and hopeless aspirations would be eventually extinguished (Scott 1990: 74).

But because 'the logic of domination represents a combination of historical and contemporary ideological and material practices that are never completely successful, always embody contradictions, and are constantly being fought over within asymmetrical relations of power' (Giroux 1985: xii), organic intellectuals, who are able to learn from the poor and marginalized while simultaneously helping them to foster modes of self-education and struggle against various forms of oppression, are able to point to the spaces, contradictions and forms of resistance that raise the possibility for social struggle. However, and this is a key element of this analysis, oppressed people's accommodation to the logic of domination may mean that they actively resist emancipatory forms of knowledge offered by organic intellectuals (Giroux 1985: xviii-xxiii). Such accounts of ideological hegemony argue that 'when oppressed people live in silence, they use the words of their oppressors to describe their experience of oppression'. It is only within the praxis of liberation and in dialogue with organic intellectuals that it is possible for the poor and marginalized 'to break this silence and create their own language' (Frostin 1988: 10).

Working with a thinner theory of hegemony, Jean and John Comaroff nuance the kind of accounts discussed above by emphasizing the instability and vulnerability of hegemony (Comaroff and Comaroff 1991: 19-32). Drawing substantially on Antonio Gramsci, the Comaroffs pose a triangular relationship between culture, ideology, hegemony. Culture, they suggest, can be viewed as the shared repertoire of practices, symbols and meanings in which and with which the dialetics of domination and resistance operate. Hegemony and ideology are the two dominant forms in which power is entailed in culture. Placing power at the center of their analysis of hegemony and ideology, the Comaroffs characterize hegemony and ideology as the two faces of power.

Hegemony is the nonagentive face of power that hides itself in the forms of everyday life; it is a form of power that is not always overtly felt in that 'it may not be experienced as power at all, since its effects are rarely wrought by overt compulsion'.

> They are internalized, in their negative guise, as constraints; in their neutral guise, as conventions; and, in their positive guise, as values. Yet the silent power of the sign, the unspoken authority of habit, may be as effective as the most violent coercion in shaping, directing, even domi-nating social thought and action (Comaroff and Comaroff 1991: 22).

'Hegemony is that order of signs and practices, relations and distinc-tions, images and epistemologies—drawn from a historically situated cultural field—that come to be taken-for-granted as the natural and received shape of the world and everything that inhabits it'; its power lies in what it silences—what it prevents people from thinking and say-ing (Comaroff and Comaroff 1991: 22).

Ideology is the agentive face of power that refers to the (relative) capacity of humans being to command and exercise control over the production, circulation and consumption of signs and objects in specific historical contexts. Ideology articulates and owns systems of meanings, values and beliefs for any group with a communal identity, whether dominant or subordinate, within a historically situated cultural field. While hegemony homogenizes, ideology articulates (Comaroff and Comaroff 1991: 22).

The particularly creative and insightful contribution of the Comaroffs to this discussion is their suggestion that hegemony exists in reciprocal interdependence with ideology in that 'it is that part of a dominant worldview which has been naturalized' (Comaroff and Comaroff 1991: 25). According to this account, hegemony and ideology are related along a continuum, with the hegemonic proportion of any dominant ideology being greater or lesser depending on the context and the con-trol of the dominant. Typically, the making of hegemony requires the exercise of control over various modes of symbolic production, includ-ing educational and ritual processes, patterns of socialization, political and legal procedures, canons of style and self-representation, public policy and communication, health and bodily discipline, and so on. Hegemony is made when control is so sustained that it becomes deeply inscribed in the signs and practices of everyday life, becoming, to all intents and purposes, invisible. However, because the ideology of the dominant never occupies non-ideological terrain, while it might establish itself at the expense of prior ideologies, it seldom succeeds in totally subjecting what was there before. Hegemony 'is always threatened by the vitality that remains in the forms of life it thwarts' (Comaroff and Comaroff 1991: 25). Consequently, along the hegemony/ideology continuum, the hegemonic is constantly being made—and, by the same token, may be unmade. Hegemony, then, 'is always intrinsically unstable, always vulnerable' (Comaroff and Comaroff 1991: 27).

There remains a final element in the Comaroffs construction. What differentiates one face of power from the other—hegemony from ideology—is the factor of human consciousness and the modes of representation that bear it. Rejecting 'the unspecified Cartesian assumptions about personhood, cognition, and social being that persist in mainstream Western thought, both orthodox and critical' (Comaroff and Comaroff 1991: 28), the Comaroffs suggest that it is much more plausible to see social knowledge and experience as situated along a chain of consciousness that is akin to the hegemony/ideology continuum. Consciousness, therefore, is a continuum 'whose two extremes are the unseen and the seen, the submerged and the apprehended, the unrecognized and the cognized' (Comaroff and Comaroff 1991: 29). And so just as hegemonies and ideologies shift in relation to one another, so too consciousness may shift between these poles.

> On the one hand, the submerged, the unseen, the unrecognized may under certain conditions be called to awareness; on the other, things once perceived and explicitly marked may slip below the level of discourse into the unremarked recesses of the collective unconscious [that] is the implicit structure of shared meaning that human beings absorb as they learn to be members of a particular social world (Comaroff and Comaroff 1991: 29).

Along the continuum between the conscious and the unconscious, the Comaroffs argue, 'lies the most critical domain of all' for the analysis of domination and resistance.

> It is the realm of partial recognition, of inchoate awareness, of ambiguous perception, and, sometimes, of creative tension; that liminal space of human experience in which people discern acts and facts but cannot or do not order them into narrative descriptions or even into articulate conceptions of the world; in which signs and events are observed, but in a hazy, translucent light; in which individuals or groups know that something is happening to them but find it difficult to put their fingers on quite what it is. It is from this realm ... that silent signifiers and unmarked practices may rise to the level of consciousness, of ideological assertion,

and become the subject of overt political and social contestation—or from which they may recede into the hegemonic, to languish there unremarked for the time being (Comaroff and Comaroff 1991: 29).

This is also the realm from which the poets and organic intellectuals draw the innovative impulses that give voice to the struggles of the people (Comaroff and Comaroff 1991: 29).

But, what if this analysis is inadequate and the poor and marginalized have not accommodated themselves to the logic of domination? What if they already have a language and already speak? What if the hegemonic/ideological continuum is *always* contested? What if the hegemonic is constantly having to be made *because* it is always being unmade? What if we take out the 'but cannot' in the quote immediately above this paragraph? Without denying the richness of the Comaroffs contribution, which I will continue to draw from, such moves as my questions contemplate would seriously undermine even a thin version of hegemony. These are questions that reflection on the contextual Bible-study process in South Africa has begun to generate. James Scott's work on 'domination and the arts of resistance' has been particularly useful in helping us to reflect more deeply and carefully on our experience and practice.[14]

Scott problematizes both thick and thin versions of ideological hegemony. In his detailed study of domination and resistance we find a more nuanced analysis, which argues that theories of hegemony and false consciousness do not take account of what he calls 'the hidden transcript'. 'The hidden transcript' is the discourse, including speech acts and a whole range of other practices,[15] that subordinate groups create in response to their ordeal of domination—a discourse 'that represents a critique of power spoken behind the back of the dominant' (Scott 1990: xii). Behind the scenes, subordinate groups 'create and defend a social space in which offstage dissent to the official transcript of power relations may be voiced' (Scott 1990: xi). The practices and rituals of denigration and domination routinely generated by slavery,

14. In what follows I lean towards Scott's work; for a South African analysis that leans more towards the Comaroffs see Petersen 1995. For an account of the dynamics of domination and resistance which is quite close to that of Scott's see de Certeau 1985.

15. Among these other practices are activities such as poaching, pilfering, clandestine tax evasion, intentionally shabby work, and so on (Scott 1990: 14, 118, 189-94).

serfdom, the caste system, colonialism, patriarchy and racism usually deny subordinates the ordinary response of asserting their dignity through negative reciprocity: a slap for a slap, an insult for an insult (Scott 1990: xi-xii). Instead, subordinates establish their dignity, register their resistance, and elaborate their hidden transcript, a restricted 'public' or social circle that excludes—that is hidden from—certain specified others.[16] In this relatively safe space subordinates find a partial refuge from the humiliations of domination. Suffering from the same humiliations and subject to the same terms of domination, subordinates for whom survival is the primary objective

> have a shared interest in jointly creating a discourse of dignity, of negation, and of justice. They have, in addition, a shared interest in concealing a social site apart from domination where such a hidden transcript can be elaborated in comparative safety (Scott 1990: 114).

The hidden transcript represents the safe articulation and acting out of forms of resistance and defiance that is usually thwarted in contexts where the exercise of power is nearly constant. 'Discretion in the face of power requires that a part of the "self" that would reply or strike back must lie low. It is this self that finds expression in the safer realm of the hidden transcript' (Scott 1990: 114). The hidden transcript speaks what must normally be choked back and takes back the speech or behaviour that seemed unavoidable and was required for survival in power-laden encounters with the dominant (Scott 1990: 18, 114-15).

The crucial point of Scott's detailed argument is that 'the hidden transcript is a self-disclosure that power relations normally exclude from the official transcript' (Scott 1990: 115). The public transcript—the open interaction between subordinates and those who dominate—where it is not positively misleading, is unlikely to tell the whole story about power relations, because it is frequently in the interest of both parties to tacitly conspire in misrepresentation (Scott 1990: 2).

It would be a mistake, Scott argues, to see the discourse of deference and subordination merely as performances extracted by power; such discourse also serves as a barrier and a veil that the dominant find

16. In instances those excluded may include members of a subordinate community that have voluntarily embraced the dominant ideology in order to occupy positions of power (see Scott 1990: 82) or sectors of the community that dominate other sectors, for example men over women or the not-yet-disabled over the disabled. In other words, there are for any particular actor several public and hidden transcripts, depending on the context and the audience addressed (Scott 1990: 14 n. 24).

difficult or impossible to penetrate. The appearances that power requires are, to be sure, forcefully imposed, but this does not preclude 'their active use as a means of resistance and evasion' (Scott 1990: 32). While evasion comes at the considerable cost of contributing to the production of a public transcript that *apparently* ratifies the social ideology of the dominant, where the script for survival is rigid and the consequences of a mistake severe, the appearance of conformity is a necessary tactic (Scott 1990: 32-33). Within the normal constraints of domination subordinates have both 'a vested interest in avoiding any *explicit* display of subordination' and 'a practical interest in resistance'. 'The reconciliation of these two objectives that seem at cross-purposes is typically achieved by pursuing precisely those forms of resistance that avoid any open confrontation with the structures of authority being resisted'. 'The greater the power exerted over them and the closer the surveillance, the more incentive subordinates have to foster the impression of compliance, agreement, deference' (Scott 1990: 89-90). The goal of subordinate groups, as they conduct their ideological and material resistance, is precisely to escape detection, and to the extent that they achieve their goal, such activities do not appear in the archives. 'In this respect, subordinate groups are complicitious in contributing to a sanitized official transcript, for that is one way they cover their tracks' (Scott 1990: 87).

The dominant, for their part, also play a role in maintaining the appearance of a public transcript of deference and compliance. To call attention to detected forms of resistance and defiance might expose the fissures in their power and erode their authority and perhaps encourage other acts of insubordination. Elites, in other words, 'have their own compelling reasons to preserve a public facade of unity, willing compliance, and respect' and so to keep conflict out of the public record (Scott 1990: 90).

So 'unless one can penetrate the official transcript of both subordinates and elites, a reading of the social evidence will almost always represent a confirmation of the status quo in hegemonic terms' (Scott 1990: 90). The strategic appearances that elites and subordinates alike ordinarily insert into the public transcript make it a very unreliable vehicle for social analysis. 'The official transcript of power relations *is* a sphere in which power appears naturalized because that is what elites exert their influence to produce and because it ordinarily serves the immediate interests of subordinates to avoid discrediting these appearances' (Scott 1990: 87). You cannot believe all you read in the public transcript! A comparison of the hidden transcript of the weak with that of the powerful, who also develop a hidden transcript representing the practices and claims of their rule that cannot be openly avowed, and of *both* hidden transcripts to the public transcript of power relations offers a substantially new way of understanding resistance to domination (Scott 1990: xii).

But is there still not a case for Gramsci's notion of the dominated consciousness of subordinate groups? For Gramsci hegemony works primarily at the level of thought as distinct from the level of action (Gramsci 1971: 333). Scott turns this around. He considers

> subordinate classes *less* constrained at the level of thought and ideology, since they can in secluded settings speak with comparative safety, and *more* constrained at the level of political action and struggle, where the daily exercise of power sharply limits the options available to them (Scott 1990: 91).

So, Scott argues, subordinate groups have typically learned, in situations short of those rare all-or-nothing struggles, 'to clothe their resistance and defiance in ritualisms of subordination that serve both to disguise their purposes and to provide them with a ready route of retreat that may soften the consequences of a possible failure' (Scott 1990: 96). This is because most protests and challenges—even quite violent ones—'are made in the realistic expectation that the central features of the form of domination will remain intact'. Consequently, '[m]ost acts of power from below, even when they are protests—implicitly or explicitly—will largely observe the "rules" even if their objective is to undermine them' (Scott 1990: 93).

Scott believes that 'the historical evidence clearly shows that subordinate groups have been capable of revolutionary *thought* that repudiates existing forms of domination' (Scott 1990: 101). However, because the occasions on which subordinate groups have been able to act openly and fully on that thought are rare, the conflict will usually take 'a dialogic form in which the language of the dialogue will invariably borrow heavily from the terms of the dominant ideology prevailing in the public transcript' (Scott 1990: 102). The dominant discourse becomes, then, 'a plastic idiom or dialect that is capable of carrying an enormous variety of meanings, including those that are subversive of their use as intended by the dominant', for in most contexts of domination 'the terrain of dominant discourse is the only plausible arena of struggle' (Scott 1990: 103). So by recognizing that adopting and adapting the dominant discourse is a guise induced by power relations that is necessary outside of the safety of the hidden transcript, and by learning to read the dialects and codes generated by the techniques and arts of resistance, we can discern a dialogue with power in the public transcript (Scott 1990: 101-103, 138).

So instead of focusing on the public transcript, which represents the formal relations between the powerful and weak, as most social analysis does, we should attempt to 'read, interpret, and understand the often fugitive political conduct of subordinate groups' (Scott 1990: xii; see also Comaroff 1985: 261). A focus on 'a partly sanitized, ambiguous, and coded version of the hidden transcript' that is always present in the public discourse of subordinate groups in the form of rumours, gossip, folktales, songs, gestures, jokes, theatre and other forms of popular culture, reveals forms of resistance, defiance and critical consciousness (Scott 1990: 19). In the words of the Ethiopian proverb with which Scott opens his study, 'When the great lord passes the wise peasant bows deeply and silently farts'. Theories of ideological hegemony look at the stage, the public transcript of the bowing peasant. Scott draws our attention to what is hidden, offstage, the silent fart.

Mosala would, I suspect, want to agree with Scott's stress that instead of focusing on the public transcript we ought to attempt to 'read, interpret, and understand the often fugitive political conduct of subordinate groups'. But his account of ideology leaves little space for a real presence of such forms of discourse in the public transcript. Scott's analysis not only recognizes that the poor and oppressed are already engaged in forms of resistance, but he also provides a more concrete presence to their resistance, albeit it that we usually have access to this presence only via the public transcript. Furthermore, Scott offers those of us who would read, interpret and understand the disguised discourses of the dominated some important advice, advice that biblical scholars with socio-historical interpretive interests would do well to heed. Reading the discourse of subordinate groups from the public transcript, which is all we have access to in the case of the biblical text if we accept the arguments of Mosala, Gottwald, Meyers, Schüssler Fiorenza, Radford Ruether and others, 'requires a more nuanced and literary reading' (Scott 1990: 165). Unfortunately, Scott does not go on to elaborate on the contours of what he implies by 'a more nuanced and literary reading'. But his phrase is suggestive and, I would argue, offers a word of caution concerning the limits of the social sciences.

6. *Nuancing Socio-Historical Modes of Reading*

Before I come to this final phase in my argument it may be useful to briefly restate the outline of the argument so far. Those of us who work within a liberation paradigm, which grants an epistemological privilege to the discourses of the poor and marginalized, refuse to accept the final form of the biblical text, the public transcript, as the last word. The text as we have it, we believe, is an ideological product, usually of the ruling classes. The text has grain. While we accept that determining, or even talking about, the ideology of a text is problematic, we persist because we hope to find lines of connection between our present faith and struggles and the faith and struggles of communities similar to ours in the originary movements of our tradition. In order to read against the grain we have generally taken up socio-historical resources, beginning with historical-critical forms of analysis and then going on to sociological (including the socio-anthropological, socio-cultural, socio-geographical, socio-archaeological, etc.) tools and trajectories. However, there have been a number of contradictions, tensions and inconsistences in our accounts of ideological hegemony that have prevented us from recognizing just how much of the resistance of subordinate groups is present in the public transcript,[17] and consequently we have not paid enough attention to what Scott refers to as 'a more nuanced and literary reading' of the biblical text.

I have chosen to draw and dwell on Scott's phrase because it seems appropriately apt to the current situation in biblical studies. Until very recently, and perhaps I am already overstating matters, socio-historical, with an emphasis on the historical end of this alliance, interests have dominated academic biblical studies. But gradually this hegemony is disintegrating, and we can now discern a shift of emphasis. While we are still a long way from declaring that there is a new literary orthodoxy, literary (in the broadest sense) interpretive interests certainly do demand respect within the corridors of the academy.

17. Mosala's tendency to emphasize just how much of the biblical text is the product of the ruling classes of any particular period is a common one among those who adopt socio-historical forms of analysis; see, for example, Coote and Coote 1990.

But this is only part of the picture. Alongside the arrival of literary modes of reading, various manifestations of postmodernism(s) have gradually gripped the discipline (The Bible and Culture Collective 1995). While postmodern impulses have generally been enthusiastically embraced by those preferring literary modes of reading, the allusion of certainty that has usually accompanied socio-historical modes of reading has been challenged. Postmodern probings—'always problematize', being the constant cry—have made those with socio-historical interests somewhat skittish. Witness, for example, the relocation of emphasis in the work of Walter Brueggemann. In his early work on Old Testament theology he was prepared to situate theological trajectories in clearly delineated socio-historical contexts (Brueggemann 1993). With both literary and postmodern means of interpretation asserting their place in Brueggeman's readings of the Hebrew Bible, the emphasis in his most recent book moves quite dramatically into the intratextual world of the Old Testament (Brueggemann 1997).

Those of us on the margins of the discipline, particularly those of us who work with the poor and marginalized, have not been too disturbed by this concurrence and convergence of the literary and the postmodern. Briefly (for more detail see West 1999), as Cornel West remarks, a postmodern form of discourse 'can lend itself to emancipatory ends' in that the allegedly stable structures and symbols of the dominant discourse become central objects of criticism, which is particularly significant for 'those on the underside of history' because 'oppressed people have more at stake than others in focusing on the tenuous and provisional vocabularies which have had and do have hegemonic status in past and present societies' (1985: 270-71). Furthermore, and this makes a nice connection between postmodern impulses and an affirmation of the literary dimensions of text, West points out that with advent of the former 'the distinction between the "soft" human sciences and the "hard" natural sciences collapses'. This 'rudimentary demythologizing of the natural sciences is of immense importance for literary critics, artists, and religious thinkers who have been in retreat and on the defensive since the Enlightenment' (1985: 265).

In my work with ordinary 'readers' (whether literate or not) of the Bible from poor and marginalized communities (West 1996), the confluence of postmodernism(s) and literary modes of reading have been used to good effect. An emancipatory appropriation of postmodernism, which avoids both the genial play of pluralism and the nihilistic abyss of meaningless (see Jobling 1990; Tracy 1987: 90), not only allows postmodern readers such as myself genuinely to believe that ordinary 'readers' can make as much meaning of the Bible as I can (even though they will do so differently), but also enables postmodern socially engaged biblical scholars and premodern poor and marginalized 'readers' to collaborate as we transact with modernity, albeit from different ends. Furthermore, by breaking the hegemonic hold of social scientific biblical interpretation and giving space and a place to literary forms of interpretation, socially engaged biblical scholars and poor and marginalized 'readers' can begin their collaborative readings with the text. The tendency in liberation theologies until fairly recently has been to start with the social sciences (and so to begin behind the text; see Segundo 1985), largely because of their understanding of domination and resistance. However, with a revised and more nuanced analysis, such as that indicated above, the role of the social sciences in conscientizing subordinate groups must be reconsidered too (West 1999). An alternative analysis accepts that the poor and marginalized already are already engaged in forms of resistance and already have a language. The culture of silence is a strategy and not the whole story. What is hidden is hidden for good reason, so any attempt to penetrate the disguise is dangerous. And when dignity and autonomy demand an irruption or an articulation, this is done in ways determined by the dominated. There does not appear to be a silence to break or a language to create. The social sciences do still have an role, but it is not the traditional role (of conscientizing) they have been assigned.

So instead of starting behind the text—the domain of the social sciences—we can begin with what both socially engaged biblical scholar and ordinary poor and marginalized 'reader' of the Bible have in common—the text (see West 1993). By reading the text carefully and closely together,[18] we not only have a similar, though not the same, starting point, but the socio-historical questions that do emerge in the interpretative process are those of the reading group and not the imported questions of white, male, First World (and usually, dead) scholars.[19] When, and only when, socio-historical questions are asked,

18. I realize that ordinary 'readers' do not usually read like this, but facilitating such a literary form of reading may be one of the creative and critical contributions of the socially engaged biblical scholar in the collaborative task (see West 1999).

19. This point has important pedagogical implications; see Clines 1995: 273 n. 83.

and they usually are, the socially engaged biblical scholar in the group may share the resources of their training with the group. To restate the argument, by beginning with the text the contextual Bible-study process minimizes ordinary 'readers' becoming dependent on the 'expert' social scientific knowledge of the trained reader; furthermore, by beginning with the text, the move behind the text to socio-historical forces and factors that produced the text becomes a move that ordinary 'readers' themselves make, for reasons that are apparent to them. This in itself is an emancipatory and empowering move; the social sciences now become useful resources because they are serving to address the questions particular communities of real readers raise.[20]

Implicit in the above paragraph is the refusal of ordinary 'readers' from poor and marginalized communities to remain with the text 'as is'. There is usually a deep desire on the part of subordinate groups to locate themselves with respect to the biblical tradition, and while finding lines of connection between their lived faith and working theologies is important and empowering, they yearn too to know that there are lines of connection between their socio-historical reality and the socio-historical of sectors of the society that produced the text. For them the commonsense distinction between text and world holds. In their experience, texts are the product of an elite, and so are always ambiguous.

Their readiness to embrace the resources offered by the socially engaged biblical scholar who reads the Bible with them, resides in both the usefulness of their resources to provide a more nuanced and literary reading of the public, final form, transcript that is the Bible, and the usefulness of their resources to probe behind the text to the social struggles that produced the text. To uncover lines of connection between their lived faith and working theologies and the lived faith and working theologies of others like them, both in the text and in the socio-historical world behind the text, is empowering, particularly as their daily experience is often that of being alienated from the dominant forms of Christianity, even those in their churches.

The extensive elaborations that are taking place in the social sciences, including new forms of archaeological, geographical, demographic,

20. Lest we forget; the origins of biblical studies as a critical discipline lie precisely here! The social sciences, preceded by the historical-critical array of resources, developed out of the attempts by readers to make sense of their close and careful reading of the biblical text.

economic and technological analysis, together with theoretical shifts in historiography away from a focus on great individuals as the shapers of historical destiny to the struggles of ordinary Palestinians (or Galileans),[21] have much to offer to ordinary 'readers' in poor and marginalized communities. But they are not always the starting point. I would therefore answer the question I posed several pages ago by saying that yes, the social sciences do have a significant part to play in a process of gauging the ideological grain of a particular text and in its appropriate appropriation, but they do not always have the opening part in the play; they do not always make up the first act. My experience in reading the Bible with poor and marginalized 'readers' of the Bible in South Africa suggests that these others usually find it more empowering to read otherwise!

7. *Coming Back to Biblical Studies (Proper)*

None of what I have said concerning the ordinary poor and marginalized 'reader' of the Bible in South Africa has any necessary repercussions for biblical scholarship. I realize this. As Fowl so compellingly shows, biblical scholars have their own particular interpretative interests, and all of them are legitimate. What my (somewhat wide-ranging) analysis does suggest, I would venture, is that biblical scholars with socio-historical interests might benefit by making a place for a more nuanced and literary reading of the biblical text. Perhaps the well-worn ruts we are accustomed to working within have become so deep that we cannot any longer see out of them. But maybe there is enough ground for forms of rapprochement between literary and socio-historical interests.

For those of us working on the margins, in collaboration with poor and marginalized 'readers' of the Bible, matters of survival, liberation and life drive us to find resources that are useful, that work. So we are not perturbed about crossing disciplinary boundaries. We are prepared to take whatever tools are at hand to do the job. This is why most of the attempts at integrating literary and socio-historical modes of criticism are to be found outside the mainstream of biblical studies, in the work

21. Most of my examples have been taken from the Old Testament/Hebrew Bible; for a glimpse of the exciting (and useful) work being done with the social sciences in the New Testament see Horsley 1995, 1996; Horsley and Silberman 1997, 1989.

of socially engaged biblical scholars (see, for example, Meyers 1988, and the various essays in Segovia and Tolbert 1995a; 1995b; 1998; Sugirtharajah 1991). As the references above indicate, there are plenty of scholars who provide models for a more integrated form of scholarship. My purpose here is not to provide another model. My ambition is more modest. My aim is to provide a cautionary tale, to ask the social sciences to nuance, and so enhance, their interpretative practices and products by finding a place for a more literary reading of biblical texts.

I would not prescribe what place literary readings might occupy for those with socio-historical interpretative interests. The work of Carol Meyers, mentioned above, demonstrates a variety of creative and illuminating exchanges between a close and careful reading of the text and a vast array of social scientific tools (see also Carter and Meyers 1996). The largely literary readings I have done among and with ordinary poor and marginalized readers of Genesis 27, probably a trickster tale which has become embedded in genealogical material, and 2 Sam. 21.1-14, an excellent example of the struggle within a text of dominating and resisting discourses (West 1999), usually arouse intense interest in the socio-historical contexts that may have generated them, a task that remains to be done.[22] My contribution here is more theoretical, and is to encourage those who use the social sciences to find some place for a close and careful reading of the text, because by so doing they may avoid falling into the ruts of those whose wagons, laden with 'the accepted consensus' of a particular time and agenda, have gone before them. I share Mosala's conviction that determining the grain of Micah is important. Our experience in South Africa and what we know of ancient Palestine suggests that there may well be layers of discourse within a text, with each layer representing the ideological position of a particular social sector. But the reservation that continually recurs as I reflect on Mosala's reconstructed layers, and this goes for most of the source critical reconstructions I read, concerns the scarcity of literary resources used. Most scholars with socio-historical interpretative interests do not read the research of those with literary interpretative interests, so this is not surprising. What is worrying, though, is that while their delimiting of texts, their determining of sources, and their socio-

22. The task will require biblical scholars with socio-historical interests to take up a range of less familiar tools; see the work of Finnegan 1988; Foley 1995; Gee 1994; Niditch 1996; Ong 1987.

historical reconstructions do make some appeal to the text,[23] their sense of text is usually shaped by somewhat ad hoc and dated forms of literary analysis.[24] Literary modes of reading have come a long way since the days of Martin Noth! By keeping an eye on the enormous creativity that currently constitute literary studies of the Bible, the social sciences may discover a useful dialogue partner.

By now the careful reader will have noted the emphasis I give to the adjective 'useful'. The social sciences are useful for gauging the grain of biblical texts and in enabling those who read the Bible on the margins to find lines of connection between their lived faith and working theologies and a Bible that is usually used against them, but they would be more useful still if they were prepared to engage in a more nuanced and literary reading of the Bible.

23. That is if they do not unquestioningly follow the demarcations and determinations of the prevailing consensus.

24. Mosala's work on Micah demonstrates little feeling for the texture of texts; fortunately, in the work of Meyers we have a good example of the kind of textual touch I am calling for in those who lean towards the social sciences.

Part II

THE SOCIAL SCIENCES AND BIBLICAL INTERPRETATION:
CASE STUDIES

A MAP OF IDEOLOGY FOR BIBLICAL CRITICS*

Jonathan E. Dyck

1. *Introduction*

The concept of ideology has surfaced in biblical studies in recent decades in the wake of sociological approaches to biblical interpretation,
and ideological criticism is being placed alongside established critical
methods as one more methodological option for biblical critics. We
have yet to see a volume entitled 'What is Ideological Criticism?' to
add to our collection of other 'do-it-yourself' manuals on source, form,
redaction, literary, reader-response, social scientific criticisms, but the
appearance of such a book is, no doubt, simply a question of time. One
has to wonder, however, whether or not ideological criticism lends
itself to methodological domestication within biblical studies. The
conceptual territory covered by the term 'ideology' and presupposed in
the practice of critique is broad, uneven and highly contested by social
theorists themselves, all of which stands in the way of standardization
within biblical studies. Simply put, ideology and ideological criticism
does and will continue to mean different things to different people both
inside and outside the guild.

Instead of putting forward one particular theory of ideology or
approach to ideological criticism, I will focus my attention on the concept of ideology itself. My principle objective in this essay is to map
out the way in which ideology is actually used in sociological contexts
(broadly understood). Using this map, the biblical critic should be able
to differentiate more clearly between uses of the term 'ideology' in contemporary biblical studies and critically evaluate the appropriateness of
its use in terms of the interpretive context within which it is employed.
In order to give some depth to this treatment of ideology, I will also

*   Adapted from J.E. Dyck, *The Theocratic Ideology of the Chronicler* (Biblical Interpretation Series; Leiden: E.J. Brill, 1998), chapters 1 and 2.

discuss Ricoeur's theory of ideology with special regard to its role in the construction and maintenance of power. Ricoeur's approach draws equally on sociological and hermeneutical traditions in formulating a 'critical hermeneutic'. I conclude with some reflections on the implications of the above for biblical interpretation.

2. A Map of Ideology

The first and last problem with ideology is its definition. Terry Eagleton begins and ends his introductory chapter on ideology with a list of definitions of ideology. The opening list (Eagleton 1991: 1-2) is a random sampling of definitions of the term 'currently in circulation', which clearly indicates just how wide the 'semantic range' of ideology is:

(a) the process of production of meanings, signs and values in social life;

(b) a body of ideas characteristic of a particular social group or class;

(c) ideas which help to legitimate a dominant political power;

(d) false ideas which help to legitimate a dominant political power;

(e) systematically distorted communication;

(f) that which offers a position for a subject;

(g) forms of thought motivated by social interests;

(h) identity thinking;

(i) socially necessary illusion;

(j) the conjuncture of discourse and power;

(k) the medium in which conscious social actors make sense of their world;

(l) action-oriented sets of beliefs;

(m) the confusion of linguistic and phenomenal reality;

(n) semiotic closure;

(o) the indispensable medium in which individuals live out their relations to a social structure;

(p) the process whereby social life is converted to a natural reality.

The concluding list (Eagleton 1991: 28-31) is Eagleton's own narrower set of definitions. They are arranged according to the degree of specificity of the social location and/or function of ideology:

1. the general material process of production of ideas, beliefs and values in social life;

2.   ideas and beliefs (whether true or false) which symbolize the conditions and life-experiences of a specific, socially significant group or class;

3.   the promotion and legitimation of the interests of such social groups in the face of opposing interests;

4.   the promotion and legitimation of the interests of the dominant group;

5.   ideas and beliefs which help to legitimate the interests of a ruling group or class specifically by distortion and dissimulation;

6.   false or deceptive ideas which arise from the material structure of society as a whole.

The first four definitions are increasingly specific in terms of the social group involved, moving from society as a whole, to socially significant groups within society, to the dominant social group. The function of ideology in each of these contexts is also increasingly specific. The last two definitions are not any more specific in either of these two ways but rather involve a different (and some would say more specialized) theoretical perspective, one which calls for critical judgment to be passed. The line between definitions four and five is crucial to the theory of ideology. That which distinguishes definitions one to four from five and six is not so much the object of study—this social phenomenon as opposed to that social phenomenon—as the research contexts within which these definitions makes sense. It makes sense, therefore, to map the different meanings of ideology according to the sociological projects (broadly understood) of which they are a part.

Raymond Geuss (Geuss 1981) presents this sort of analysis of the concept of ideology, and the map of ideology that follows is an adaptation of his analysis of the term. The basic distinction, as he sees it, is between ideology in the context of social science and ideology in the context of social criticism. In the former ideology is used in a descriptive sense to denote the ideas, beliefs and attitudes of a social group, while in the latter ideology is used in the pejorative sense to denote false or distorted ideas, beliefs or attitudes. A third research context is an interpretive sociology. In this context ideology is used in a positive sense to denote the symbolic universe by means of which social life is meaningfully structured. It should be noted at the outset that there is some overlap between research contexts and definitions of ideology. The lines drawn between the three research contexts are there for the sake of analysis and are not intended to represent fully the complexity of the situation on the ground.

3. *Ideology in the Context of Social Science*

The research agenda of the social sciences is defined here as 'the empirical study of human groups' (Geuss 1981: 4). Geuss himself uses the term 'anthropology' to designate this research context, but I would argue that 'social science' more accurately reflects the basic orientation of research, that it is a science on the model of the natural sciences. That which makes for a successful science is objectivity. On the one hand, objectivity refers to the accuracy with which a science apprehends the object of study; its methods are to be judged on the basis of how well they are suited to the objective phenomena. On the other hand, objectivity means that the subjective position of the scientist is at best irrelevant and at the worst detrimental to scientific progress. The aim of the scientist is to observe and describe social phenomena from a value-neutral perspective and explain cause and effect from an etic perspective.

Social science takes as its object of study the social and cultural features of human groups, which collectively Geuss calls the 'socio-cultural system'. He describes the tasks of social science as follows:

> for any given human group we can undertake to describe the salient features of its cultural system and how they change over time. If we have at our disposal descriptions of several human groups, we may begin to look for universal or invariant features which all cultures exhibit or for relations of concomitance among apparently distinct socio-cultural features; we may try to elaborate a typology of human cultures, classifying them according to their similarities and differences; if we are bold, we may hazard hypotheses about why certain features are found in certain societies or why certain historical changes take place (Geuss 1981: 4-5).

According to Geuss, ideology in the context of a social science is something that is 'out there' waiting to be discovered by empirical investigation. In the context of pursuing this social scientific agenda, ideology

> will refer to one of the 'parts' into which the socio-cultural system of a human group can be divided for convenient study. Depending on how the particular division is made, the 'ideology' of the group will be more or less extensive, but typically it will include such things as the beliefs the members of the group hold, the concepts they use, the attitudes and psychological dispositions they exhibit, their motives, desires, values,

predilections, works of art, religious rituals, gestures, etc. I will call 'ideology' in this very broad sense (including at least all of the above listed
elements) 'ideology in the purely descriptive sense' (Geuss 1981: 5).

This definition of ideology corresponds to Eagleton's first and broadest
definition of ideology: 'the general material process of production of
ideas, beliefs and values in social life' (Eagleton 1991: 28). Ideology is
not something about which one has to make a value judgment—that it
is objectionable, false or distorted—but is rather something that is found
out there in the object field of social science; ideology is something that
every social group has.

Key issues that differentiate one social scientific definition of ideology from another is the way in which the socio-cultural system is
divided into its constituent 'parts' and the way in which the relationship
between the 'ideological part' and the 'other part' is conceptualized.

The most important model of the socio-cultural system, historically
speaking, is Marx's base-superstructure model. According to this model,
the economic base determines the ideological superstructure. 'Life is
not determined by consciousness, but consciousness by life' (Marx and
Engels 1959: 247). This most famous of Marx's propositions is also the
mother of all social theories of ideology. It is found in *The German Ideology*, the aim of which is to make the case for historical materialism in
terms of a critique of German idealism. The basic premise of *The German Ideology* is that all thought, all consciousness, is socially determined. Thus, 'what men say, imagine, conceive', all the products of
consciousness, are but the 'ideological reflexes and echoes of this life
process'. These 'ideological reflexes' can be defined as but 'one part of
the socio-cultural system' (to use Geuss's terms), though not the 'basic'
or 'determinative' part. That is to say (and continuing in this vein), the
definition of ideology we find here is, in the first instance, a social-scientific definition of ideology and not a social-critical definition as one
would expect.

But this understanding of ideology is not what is meant in the phrase
'the German ideology'. Here ideology is being used in a critical sense,
not a social-scientific sense. The specifically *German* ideology is the
idealism of early nineteenth-century German philosophy, particularly
that of Hegel and Feuerbach. This idealism is, according to Marx, a
form of consciousness which doesn't recognize its own historicity, that
it is determined by the social context of early nineteenth-century Germany and is powerless to change society and the course of history: 'In

politics the Germans have thought what other nations have done' (Marx 1970: 137). German idealism is false consciousness in that it inverts the base-superstructure model and denies social determinism. It is considered false from the point of view of a particular theory of how society works, namely, historical materialism.

Marx's critique of the 'German ideology' was in the first instance a historical analysis of a particular historical situation, but in the history of Marxism this doctrine and the base-superstructure model have been understood universally as applying to all societies past and present. But if we leave orthodox Marxist dogma to one side, we are left with what has become a central tenet of sociology—the social-determination of consciousness—and the central problem of social theory—the nature of social-determination. All social theories of ideology are in this sense either neo-Marxist or post-Marxist.

There are, of course, a host of other social theoretical models of society and in these other models the relationship between the 'ideological part' of the socio-cultural system and 'the other part'—the social, economic and political structures, and so on—is conceived of in much more complex terms. The fundamental problem with the analytical distinction between economic base and ideological superstructure has to do with its view of language. In keeping with the philosophy of consciousness, language is viewed as a recepticle for our ideas, beliefs, attitudes—our ideology—and the means by which conscious minds interact. More recent accounts of language, such as discourse theory, emphasize that language is itself a social activity: we do things when we say things and our 'saying' is embedded in social discourse. Looking at the same thing from the point of view of social activity, one could say that social activity, as opposed to social behaviour, is always already meaningful activity. This account of language as discourse undermines a strictly etic perspective and brings us to the very edge of what is possible within the framework of a social science as defined above. What it requires is, of course, an interpretive sociology, but before moving on to discuss this approach there are a number of more specific definitions or subsets of 'ideology in the purely descriptive sense'.

There are various ways of classifying *subsets of ideology* in the descriptive sense. Subsets can be identified on the basis of their 'manifest content' or on the basis of their 'functional properties' (Geuss 1981: 8). Intuitively, we tend to identify ideologies on the basis of their content: a religious ideology is the set of beliefs a group holds about religion, and so forth. To identify ideologies on the basis of functional properties is to classify beliefs in terms of the kind of behaviour they give rise to or influence. A religious ideology in this sense would be a set of beliefs which influences religious behaviour, whether or not the manifest content of the ideology has anything to do with religion. As a rule one might expect the manifest content of an ideology and its functional properties to mesh, but a religious ideology (in terms of manifest content) may also serve to influence political behaviour or a political ideology may serve to influence economic behaviour. The way in which the participants classify the manifest contents and functional properties of their ideologies and the way outsiders classify them might differ sharply. Perceived clashes between content and function will be of particular interest to the ideological theorists. Hence, functional classifications will tend to be counter-intuitive from the point of view of participants. But in keeping with the descriptive task of social science, '[i]t will in general be an important fact about a given society how the various kinds of acts and institutions are individuated, how large a class of acts are considered to be "purely economic transactions" or what acts to which religious beliefs are directly relevant' (Geuss 1981: 9).

A more common way of delineating subsets of ideology is to speak of the ideology of one particular group within a larger socio-cultural system. Eagleton's second definition (from the second list above)— ideas and beliefs (whether true or false) which symbolize the conditions and life experiences of a specific, socially significant group or class—is a straightforward delineation of ideology according to its social location. The next two definitions on Eagleton's list (again, from the second list) are examples of classification according to a combination of social location *and* function:

3. the promotion and legitimation of the interests of such social groups in the face of opposing interests;
4. the promotion and legitimation of the interests of the dominant group.

These last two definitions are more specialized in that the ideology of a social group is defined in terms of its functional properties. Ideologies of this sort exist only when there are two or more groups with conflicting interests. Ideas, beliefs and attitudes of social groups which do not function to promote their interests are not included in this definition. What these interests are can vary depending on one's social theory. A

Marxist will speak in terms of class interest, whereas a Weberian will speak in terms of status groups and their interests. A political scientist might use the term ideology to denote the program or plan of action of a political party.

4. *Ideology in the Context of an Interpretive Sociology*

In an interpretive sociology the emphasis is on the hermeneutical understanding of the socio-cultural system. The posture of the sociologist or anthropologist engaged in this sort of work is that of the conversation partner in dialogue with the participants with the aim of 'gaining access to the conceptual world in which our subjects live' (Geertz 1973: 24). In an interpretive sociology participants are subjects in their own right. The participants' understanding of their social world and the way they conceive of the relationship between their ideas, beliefs, and attitudes and their social activity is all important. In contrast to a social science, the relationship between different parts of the socio-cultural system is not apprehended in causal terms but rather in terms of the interaction between them. From the point of view of an interpretive sociology, 'participating in a culture is a way of satisfying certain deep-seated human needs. Humans have a vital need for "meaningful" life and the kind of identity which is possible only for an agent who stands in relation to a culture' (Geuss 1981: 22).

In the context of an interpretive science, ideology is used in a positive sense to denote the socially constructed worldview, or 'symbolic universe' of the group; that is to say, ideology is positive in the sense of being good (or at least indispensable for the good life) and positive in the sense of having a particular positive content. It is not simply something that one observes as 'a neutral fact about human groups' (Geuss 1981: 22). Ideology as in symbolic universe is a *central feature* of the socio-cultural system in that it

> provides a comprehensive integration of all discrete institutional processes. The entire society now makes sense. Particular institutions and roles are legitimated by locating them in a comprehensively meaningful world (Berger and Luckman 1967: 103).

In a similar vein is Geertz's understanding of the role of ideology. In the context of social crisis 'a loss of orientation…gives rise to ideological activity' (Geertz 1973: 219), for it is the role of ideology

No Identity?
displa

to render otherwise incomprehensible social situations meaningful, to so construe them as to make it possible to act purposefully within them... Whatever else ideologies may be—projections of unacknowledged fears, disguises for ulterior motives, phatic expressions of group solidarity— they are, most distinctively, maps of problematic social reality and matrices for the creation of collective conscience (Geertz 1973: 220).

5. *Ideology in the Context of Social Criticism*

Social criticism involves making value judgments about ideology where it is used in a pejorative sense to denote a false or distorted consciousness. The main question to be asked is this: 'In what sense or in virtue of what properties can a form of consciousness be ideologically false; i.e. can it be an ideology in the pejorative sense?' (Geuss 1981: 11-12). In the context of social science one is describing and explaining a group's ideology in a non-evaluative way, whereas in social criticism one is evaluating the ideology of a group in light of one's own social theory. The overall objective of social science is to explain, while the final aim of social criticism is 'to free the agents from a particular kind of delusion' (Geuss 1981: 12).

Me

In social criticism the subjective position of the critic is all important. As a sociological project, social criticism is a second order research agenda in that it presupposes a theory of how society works. The social scientist practises social criticism from the subjective position of having an objective knowledge of how societies work or should work if they were working properly. To use an analogy from medicine: social science is to social criticism what anatomy is to pathology. In the former, ideology is a 'normal' part of social life, while in the latter it is a distortion, a pathology, within social life. The trouble with these ideological distortions (and indeed with this analogy) is that ideological distortions do not have the objectivity of an physical ailment. There are bound to be as many diagnoses as there are social theories and, even if social critics agree on the diagnosis, one cannot expect an unambiguous 'cure'.

There are other less-than-scientific accounts of critique. One approach is simply to argue that critique need not imply some unequivocally correct way of viewing society. It need not first seek to ground itself in a 'scientific' theory of society but can and does operate in an intuitive way (Eagleton 1991: 11-13). But whatever the approach taken to social criticism, the demand is the same, namely, that one is able to account for the subjective position from which one is practising critique. In other words, Geuss's question should actually read, 'In what sense or in virtue of what properties *and from what perspective* can a form of consciousness be ideologically false?'

The significance of this point can be illustrated by considering the kinds of things that have been labeled ideologically false. Geuss identifies three forms of false consciousness: (1) epistemologically false consciousness; (2) functionally false consciousness; and (3) genetically false consciousness.

By 'epistemologically false consciousness' Geuss means a type of thinking which contains an element of faulty logic with a particular social force. These errors are not to be construed as simple logical errors on the part of any individual but are errors that are built into the discourse of the community itself. Geuss cites four epistemological errors, none of which presuppose a systematic social theory. The first error is thinking which is dependent on mistaking the epistemological status of its beliefs. An example of this would be when statements of belief are mistaken for statements of fact. A second error is thinking which contains an objectification mistake in that social phenomena are treated as if they are natural phenomena. The classic example of this is Marx's analysis of the fetishism of commodities, whereby the social character of exchange value is mistaken for the objective value of a thing. A third error is thinking in which the particular interest of a subgroup is mistaken for the general interests of the group as a whole. A fourth error is thinking which does not recognize the self-fulfilling/self-validating character of its beliefs. 'If we think that the members of a subgroup G are lazy, unreliable, and unintelligent, and hence act toward them in ways which make them become lazy, unreliable and unintelligent, the belief that the members of G are lazy etc. is self-fulfilling' (Geuss 1981: 14). This example also contains an objectification mistake.

Genetically false consciousness is false in virtue of its origin. This is a distinctly Marxist definition and the most problematic of the three, given that it seems to involve the genetic fallacy. Geuss attempts to reconstruct the logic of this definition of ideology by defining ideology of this sort as 'systems of beliefs and attitudes accepted by the agents for reasons which they could not acknowledge', though he wonders whether or not there have ever been cases like this. A possible example of this might be implied in Engel's description of bourgeois consciousness, when he states that 'the real motive forces impelling him remain unknown to him', which seems to suggest that were these 'real motive forces' known to the bourgeoisie there would no longer be a bourgeoisie. The use of 'motive' implies consciousness, but the use of 'forces' points to the origin of this consciousness in external processes, an origin that must of necessity remain unrecognized by the participants (Geuss 1981: 19-22).

More important for our purposes is ideology as functionally false consciousness. Functionally false forms of consciousness are false, 'because my retaining it depends in some way on my being in ignorance of or having false beliefs about its functional properties' (Geuss 1981: 19). This definition of ideology builds on the distinction between manifest content and functional properties noted above. An ideology may be true in what it says but false in what it does not say; true as a piece of language but false as a piece of discourse; true in its empirical content but deceptive in its force (Eagleton 1991: 16).

Geuss discusses the example of an ideology which may be criticized as functionally false in virtue of its role in supporting, fostering or stabilizing domination or *Herrschaft*. To say that a form of consciousness is false in this sense presupposes either that no forms of domination are legitimate or that there are legitimate and illegitimate forms of domination. If the social critic believes that all forms of domination are illegitimate, then the practice of critique is relatively simple. If, on the other hand, one accepts some forms of domination as legitimate, the critical task becomes more complicated. The ideology may or may not directly address the question of legitimacy, nor is it the case that only dominant groups produce ideologies which support, foster or stabilize domination. For example,

> a belief that a given ruling class is strong and ruthless, so that any resistance to the dominant social order is futile, may well be a belief, the acceptance of which by large segments of the population will have the effect of stablizing the existing relations of dominance, but is unlikely that such a belief could be used to justify these relations (Geuss 1981: 15).

The belief is true in terms of its manifest content and the group holding such a belief need not intend to support this system of domination, but a functional consequence of holding such a belief actually contributes to the ongoing stability of an illegitimate form of domination. This example presupposes that the dominated group does not accept the legitimacy of the dominant group's claim to and exercise of power, which makes the critique of this belief an immanent critique. The supposition on the part of the social critic is that, if the dominated group were made to realize the functional error in their thinking, they may choose to resist the ruling class and change their circumstances for the better.

A more difficult case is when the dominated group accepts the system of rule as legitimate, even though it appears to be distorted in the interests of the ruling class and against the interests of the ruled. As Geuss observes,

> the major way in which ideologies (in the pejorative sense) have tradi-tionally maintained themselves is by harnessing what are in themselves perfectly human aspirations, such as the desire for a sense of collective identity, so as to create a situation in which the agents can satisfy legit-imate existential needs only on condition of accepting the repression the ideological worldview imposes (Geuss 1981: 25).

Critiquing ideological distortion of this sort requires a vantage point that transcends the socio-cultural system within which it is found, for the participants do not seem to know what their own interests are. And, because there is no internal lever with which to prise open the distor-tion, the subjective position of the critic is of crucial importance. Against what standard is ideological distortion to be judged? The clas-sic analysis of distortion is, of course, a Marxist critique. A Marxist would define human interests in terms of class interests, which in turn are defined in historical material terms, and critique would proceed via a causal dismantling of the ideology which supports or maintains the interests of the ruling class. The ruling ideology is linked in causal terms with the ruling interests of the ruling class. In other words, the perspective from which a form of consciousness is judged to be false is a Marxist social science working with a base-superstructure model. Other more complex analyses of the problem of ideological distortion and sophisticated theoretical approaches to critique could be cited here, but the one I have chosen to look at is Ricoeur's 'critical hermeneutic'. Ricoeur's approach contrasts sharply with a 'scientific' Marxism, yet still recognizes the problem of systemic distortion as first analysed by Marx.

6. *Ideology in Ricoeur's Critical Hermeneutic*

Instead of trying to do justice to Ricoeur's 'critical hermeneutic' in a few short pages, I will focus on his analysis of the problem of domination and the role of ideology within it. The relevant text is found in Ricoeur's *Lectures on Ideology and Utopia*. In this study Ricoeur notes significant interconnections between the different functions of ideology relating to distortion, legitimation and integration. He uncovers these interconnections via a 'regressive phenomenology', beginning with Marx's understanding of ideology as systematically distorted conscious-ness and ending with a discussion of the integrative function of ideol-ogy, which he believes is the fundamental function of ideology. The task Ricoeur sets himself is not only to explain the inner workings of ideological distortion—how it happens and why—but also and at the same time to identify the point of view from which distortion is cri-tiqued. As he sees it, materialistic explanations do not to tackle distor-tion in its own symbolic terms but rather resort to the scientific lan-guage of economic cause and ideological effect.

Ricoeur develops his theory of ideology against the backdrop of a critique of Althusser's account of ideological distortion. Althusser's theory of ideology (which builds on Marx's analysis of ideology) con-tains two central propositions. The first proposition is that *ideology has a material existence*. By 'materiality' Althusser means that 'the "ideas" of a human subject exist in his actions' (Althusser 1994: 105), which are inserted into practices which in turn are inscribed within the mate-rial existence of the institutional apparatuses of the state. 'This exis-tence is material' (Althusser 1994: 104). Although the modality of this material existence is not the same as that of a stone, it can nonetheless be described as 'material' at the level of social structure.

This understanding of ideology applies specifically to the capitalist mode of production. Following Marxist–Leninist theory, Althusser sees the modern state as an instrument of repression which contains two bodies: the *Repressive State Apparatus* or RSAs (government, army, police and courts), which ultimately function by violence, and the *Ideo-logical State Apparatuses* or ISAs (religious, educational, family, legal, political, trade union, communications, cultural institutions), which function by ideology (Althusser 1994: 110-11). That which unites these ISAs is that beneath them all is the ruling ideology of the ruling class. Since ideologies always express class position, 'a theory of ideologies depends...on the history of social formations, and thus of the modes of production combined in social formations, and of the class struggles which develop in them' (Althusser 1994: 99). Thus, the materiality of ideology is cast in terms of a Marxist economic determinism referring 'in the last instance to the relations of production' (Althusser 1994: 104).

The second proposition, that *ideology interpellates or summons individuals as subjects* specifies the main task of ideology at this higher level. By this Althusser means that ideology is a particular organization of signifying practices which constitute us as social subjects. Just as we are named by our parents and called by name a thousand times over so too are we 'named' by society and made subjects of the state. Like our own name, we take our status as subjects for granted; to be a subject is to immediately recognize oneself and be recognized without considering how recognition is possible. According to Althusser, the 'taken-for-grantedness' of our subjectivity is but an effect of an ideological process. Ideology is a reality insofar as it is embodied in social practices, but it is nevertheless the reality of something which is illusory: 'What is represented in ideology is...not the system of real relations which govern the existence of individuals, but the imaginary relations of those individuals to the real relations in which they live' (Althusser 1994: 103). Thus, the fundamental illusion of ideology is the illusion of subjectivity. For Althusser, to recognize oneself as subject is to be recognized by the State as subject to and as object of the State: *all recognition is miscognition.*

Unlike Althusser, Ricoeur pursues a humanistic interpretation of Marx, retaining the dialectical tension between individual and society, consciousness and discourse, autonomy and determinism. What he recovers from Marx is a sense of 'individuals living in definite conditions' as opposed to the notion of 'the individual as simply contingent with regard to its conditions' (Ricoeur 1986: 100). According to Ricoeur, Marx seems to allow for a 'basic' pre-distorted level of consciousness and communication when he states that '[t]he production of ideas, of conceptions, of consciousness is at first directly interwoven with the material activity and the material intercourse of men, the language of real life' (Marx and Engels 1959: 247). This consciousness, and indeed one could say this level of ideology, is an intrinsic aspect of the socio-cultural system as distinct from but also intertwined with productive activity and not simply a 'reflex' or 'echo' of this activity. To use the base-superstructure model against itself, if human existence is irreducibly linguistic, even as it relates directly to material activity, then language and indeed ideology belong to the base.

It is here that Althusser and Ricoeur part company. Althusser turns away from humanistic concepts such as consciousness and representation and turns instead to the 'science' of the forces of production—reality in terms of autonomous forces. Ricoeur is critical of this move. To say, for example, that everything is distorted, that all recognition is miscognition, is to say that nothing is distorted. If there is no symbolic structure *from the start*, then there is nothing to distort. There is no fundamental reality behind ideology that is not already symbolically structured.

The practical implication of this insight as it relates to the relationship between ideology and power is that one cannot simply correlate ruling ideology and ruling class with an economic interest providing the causal link. If one wants to understand systems of domination and the role of ideology within them, one has to look at the way ideologies of legitimation work on the inside seeking to determine where distortion is 'anchored' in the symbolic universe of the group. The link between ruling ideology and ruling class, between power structures and economic interests, is in the first instance the individual self-conscious ruler and the self-conscious work of legitimation that the ruler performs. Ricoeur, therefore, turns to Weber's motivational model as an alternative way of modelling systems of domination or authority and attendant modes of legitimation (Ricoeur 1986: 184). In keeping with an interpretive sociology, a motivational model is concerned with the participants' own understandings and motives for acting in the way they do.

Weber identifies three different systems of domination (or *Herrschaft*): bureaucratic, charismatic and traditional, each with its own motivational framework. According to Weber, domination or *Herrschaft* has to do with the probability that a command with a specific content will be obeyed by a given group. Other than using or threatening to use force, those in authority can claim legitimacy in various ways with the hope of motivating individuals to act in a certain way. Because all claims to *legitimate* authority presuppose a legitimate order, an ideology that legitimates must not only speak to the issue of who rules but also to the issue of who we are (as in the unity which embraces both ruler and ruled). In other words, ideologies of legitimacy must not only address the question of the ruler's identity as established on the basis of certain legitimate *claims* but must also address the *beliefs* people already have about who they are. An ideology of legitimation must incorporate an ideology of identity, which integrates the group and provides for the mutual orientation of action for the members of the group.

One can see this most clearly perhaps in traditional forms of authority, where the most important issue is the continuity of the social order through time. Social relationships are ordered according to the idea that what comes from the past has more legitimacy than that which has come about in the present. But the same thing can be said of any kind of authority. A political body like the modern democratic state is governed not only via the instrumental criteria of bureaucratic efficiency but also by the way in which it identifies itself among other groups. The first function of ideology is to preserve the group's identity through time ... to connect past, present and future (Ricoeur 1986: 210). In traditional authority the gap between claim and belief is small. Recognition of who rules is tightly bound up with recognition of who we are, which is all but taken for granted. But in other forms of domination where legitimation requires a more conscious effort on the part of the ruling class, the gap between claim and belief is more significant.

Ricoeur's main thesis with regard to the role of ideology in legitimation is that ideology fills this gap between claim and belief. There is always more in the claim to legitimacy of a given system of authority than the normal course of legitimation can satisfy; that is to say, there is a supplement of belief provided by an ideological system (Ricoeur 1986: 201-202). Charismatic authority is a good example of this. Recognition of who rules is decisive in this system of authority, for if people did not believe in the claims of the charismatic leader, their leadership would not even begin. In this form of authority the leader is completely dependent on the belief of the people, yet the leader cannot make their claim to authority in these terms (i.e. that they need belief) but rather has to state them in ideological terms, that is, in terms of their exceptional qualities. Claims of this sort are the ideological investment made by the charismatic leader and, when successful, pay a dividend in terms of what Ricoeur calls a surplus of belief. Charismatic leaders seek out, via ideology, this surplus of belief, but they can never admit that they rely on this belief. This is the point at which recognition (beliefs concerning who we are and who should rule) becomes miscognition. One is encouraged to believe, but can one disbelieve? The danger with the ideology of legitimation is that recognition becomes a duty. In this way the true origin of power is stolen, for once belief is given one cannot get it back. In other words, the ideas and beliefs that the participants hold about who they are and who should rule, when taken on aggregate, have functional consequences of a systemic nature.

Applying this to the larger question of domination, Ricoeur argues that the lack of reciprocity between claim and belief is a potential source of distortion within all ideologies of legitimation (Ricoeur 1986: 211-12). Ideological distortion is not something that comes from the outside—like an economic interest—but is something that happens within a system of symbols. A political ideology is not an economic interest in disguise. It is a discursive formation that is generated by and generative of social structures and systems that remain irreducibly symbolic. That is to say, 'what is really going on' cannot be got at by an appeal to 'reality' or 'science'; it has to be got at hermeneutically. What is required is a hermeneutic with attitude, an attitude that recognizes that the 'function of ideology is to make a politics possible by providing the authoritative concepts that render it meaningful, the suasive images by means of which it can be sensibly grasped' (Geertz 1973: 218). This attitude of suspicion is, according to Ricoeur, ultimately grounded in a different vision of human life:

> we must assume that the judgment on ideology is always the judgment from a utopia. This is my conviction: the only way to get out of the circularity in which ideologies engulf us is to assume a utopia, declare it, and judge an ideology on this basis. Because the absolute onlooker is impossible, then it is someone within the process itself who takes the responsibility for judgment... It is to the extent finally that the correlation ideology-utopia replaces the impossible correlation ideology–science that a certain solution to the problem of judgment may be found. (Ricoeur 1986: 172-73).

At the level of integration, ideology functions to preserve the order, whereas utopia puts into question what presently exists and represents an awareness of the contingency of social order. At the level of legitimation, ideology serves to maintain systems of domination, whereas utopia challenges authority, providing an imaginative variation on the nature of power and represents an awareness of the credibility gap that exists in all systems of legitimation. And at the level of distortion, ideology reifies and alienates, whereas utopia is mere escapist fancy with no link between the future and the present. Thus, one 'breaks' with ideology by exploiting the critical self-reflective and distantiating potential within social imagination. The task of ideological criticism is to disentangle recognition from miscognition or, as Taylor puts it, 'to distinguish between objectification—the positive transformation of values into discourses, practices and institutions—and alienation—the distortion of these values, the reification of discourses, practices and institutions' (Taylor 1986: xxvii). This task is carried out from the point of view of a utopia of total recognition and from a 'deep-rooted interest in the plenitude of individual existence' (Ricoeur 1986: 153).

7. *Implications for Biblical Criticism*

The concepts of ideology generated by social science and interpretive sociology as described above would have little impact on a biblical criticism oriented in accordance with the project of understanding that is aimed at 'a fair-minded, patient and sympathetic re-creation of the meaning and significance and intentions of the ancient text in its own time' (Clines 1995: 18-19). These definitions of ideology are fairly innocuous additions to the biblical critical lexicon. Gottwald, for example, uses the word ideology to refer to 'the consensual constitutive concepts and attitudes of early Israel…[which] are more commonly in biblical studies called "religious ideas or beliefs", "religious thoughts or symbols", or "theology"' (Gottwald 1979: 65). The reason he uses 'ideology' instead of these other terms is to distance his 'sociological inquiry into Israel's religion and the more familiar historical and theological approaches' (Gottwald 1979: 65), but at the end of the day 'ideology' and 'theology' are used to refer to the same thing.

One would, of course, want to differentiate between an approach which draws on social-scientific models and one informed by an interpretive sociology. Gottwald's sociological approach, for example, is social-scientific in its orientation and is concerned with exploring 'the systematic relationship between the religion of Israel [the ideological part of a socio-cultural system] and the wider social system [the other part of the socio-cultural system]' (Gottwald 1979: 65). A more recent example is Yee, who breaks down ideological criticism into two distinctive tasks: extrinsic criticism (the text as product of a social context) and intrinsic criticism (the text as reproductive of a social context). 'Extrinsic analysis makes use of the social sciences and historical criticism to understand the complex social structures of specific historical groups and their relationships with other parts of the society' (Yee 1995: 150).

By contrast an interpretive sociology underlies Dutcher-Walls's approach to 'ideological analysis'. She defines ideology as 'a particular definition of reality with its own symbolic universe and accompanying ideas about knowledge, institutions, and roles' (Dutcher-Walls 1996: 106). This positive definition (in both senses of that term) is contrasted to 'the negative overtones of "ideology" as a narrow, doctrinaire view of a marginal political group' (Dutcher-Walls 1996: 106). The goal of ideological analysis is 'to gain access to the conceptual world of the author' (Dutcher-Walls 1996: 107).

The real watershed for biblical criticism occurs with the appropriation of definitions of ideology thrown up by social criticism. I say 'watershed', because taking distortion into account involves a completely different attitude in approaching the biblical text. On one side of the divide you have social science that by definition *does not* inquire about ideological distortion and the hermeneutical project of understanding that *cannot* deal with it. On the other side you have a critique which says, 'Distortion happens'. On one side of the divide you have descriptive or positive definitions of ideology, and on the other you have pejorative definitions. An awareness that distortion happens means that one approaches the text with an attitude of suspicion, an attitude biblical scholars are not, generally speaking, conditioned to have. Without putting to fine a point on it, the hermeneutics of understanding and retrieval—the characteristic posture of much of biblical scholarship— 'is animated by faith, by a willingness to listen, and it is characterised by a respect for the object as a revelation of the sacred' (Thompson 1981: 46). A critical hermeneutic, on the other hand, is 'wide awake to the designs that texts have on them' (Clines 1995: 21) and 'animated by suspicion, by a scepticism towards the given, and it is characterised by a rejection of that respect for the object granted by the hermeneutics of faith' (Thompson 1981: 46).

But critique is really more involved than just adopting a suspicious attitude as opposed to a credulous one. The basic ingredient of social criticism is the emphasis on the subjective position of the interpreter. Clines makes this point with characteristic clarity:

> It is a measure of our commitment to our own standards and values that we register disappointment, dismay or disgust when we encounter in the texts of ancient Israel ideologies that we judge to be inferior to ours. And it is a measure of our open-mindedness and eagerness to learn and do better that we remark with pleasure, respect and envy values and ideologies within the biblical texts that we judge to be superior to our own. 'Critique' does not of course imply negative evaluation, but it does imply evaluation of the texts by a standard of reference outside themselves— which usually means, for practical purposes, by the standards to which

we ourselves are committed. For the task of critique, it is not distance
between the ideology of the text and our own that we want (as for the
project of understanding), but a close confrontation (Clines 1995: 19-20).

Assuming that one approaches biblical interpretation in this way and
with the presupposition that distortion happens, how does one draw the
line between distortion and non-distortion? What sort of lever does one
use to prise it open? What sort of subjective position does one adopt?
What sort of external 'standard of reference' should one employ? Clines
suggests we begin with the default standard of reference, that is, our
own personal standards. In practice, however, most ideological critics
of biblical texts also adopt scientific or humanistic standards or some
combination of the two. I say 'also', because it is unlikely that a critic is
not also personally committed to the truth or superiority of the critical
standard employed.

The standard by which some biblical critics judge the text are 'biblical' standards; that is to say, ideological criticism of biblical texts can
be an immanent critique. This is, in fact, a quite common mode of critique in Old Testament studies especially in treatments of the so-called
'royal ideology'. For example, when Brueggemann describes the royal
ideology as 'vested self interest which is passed off as truth, partial
truth which counterfeits as whole truth, theological claim functioning as
a mode of social control' (Brueggemann 1988: 111; cited in Clines
1995: 13), he is evaluating it on the basis of not only his own standards
but also on the basis of the 'biblical' prophetic critique of kingship. In
this mode, the critic acts as a virtual participant in the palaces of ancient
Israel standing alongside the prophets in their denunciation of monarchy (see also Whitelam 1989).

A more sophisticated, and at the same time explicitly transcendental,
critique of the royal ideology is Jobling's analysis of Psalm 72 (Jobling
1992). He adopts a neo-Marxist Jamesonian approach to texts which

> aligns their failure to 'make sense' (to close their internal semantic sys-
> tem) with the contradictions (in the Marxist sense) in the social forma-
> tions generating them. The contradictions in the text are accessible to
> literary analysis, while those in the social formation are accessible to an
> analysis of the unstable coexistence of incompatible historical modes of
> production (Jobling 1992: 95).

In other words, the lever employed to uncover the distortion is a Marxist social science which, presumably, is a better account of the underlying social 'realities' than that on offer (potentially at least) in the text

itself. This is not to say that Jobling is a positivist, but rather that he is employing a particular account of society that (elsewhere) claims to be a true account in historical and scientific terms.

Ricoeur's account of social reality disputes the possibility of a 'scientific' critique but at the same time claims to offer a superior analysis of distortion. In sociological terms this means a better account of the ideological and utopian tendencies at work in the social imagination. But in the last instance, the standard by which Ricoeur judges ideologies is a superior view of what it means to be human … a better account of what it is that makes for the good life. And, insofar as the good life has not been fully realized, one would have to say that this standard is utopian.

There is one final turn in the road that needs to be negotiated. This account of ideological criticism has focused on the ideology of the writers of the biblical text, not the ideology of the readers of biblical texts. According to the Bible and Culture Collective, 'all readings of a text are ideological' and the 'ideological criticism of the Bible entails the twin effort (1) to read the ancient biblical stories for their ideological content and mode of production and (2) to grasp the ideological character of contemporary reading strategies' (Bible and Culture Collective 1995: 277). The aim of this paper was to analyse the former task from the point of view of different sociological agendas and social theories and, while due emphasis was given to the standpoint from which the reader as critic engages the text, I did not explore the implications of ideological criticism for a reader-oriented approach. The concern in the examples of ideological criticism just cited above was to show that there was something at stake—politically, socially, economically—in the writing of the text. There is, however, also something at stake in the interpretation of the text. The reader is not an innocent bystander but an active participant with particular interests, whether or not these are articulated in terms of a specific agenda. A thoroughly self-conscious ideological criticism would admit that we are all subject to distortion— we all have ideologies.

EZRA 2 IN IDEOLOGICAL CRITICAL PERSPECTIVE*

Jonathan E. Dyck

1. *Introduction*

Ezra 2 is an inconspicuous document from the point of view of some-one interested in practicing ideological criticism. It is merely a list of the names of the 'people of the province who came from those captive exiles whom King Nebuchadnezzar of Babylon had carried captive to Babylonia; they returned to Jerusalem and Judah, all to their own towns' (Ezra 2.1). To be sure, there are one or two aspects of this list that draw the critics attention, such as the case of persons without proper Israelite pedigree, but it appears to have little else that is re-motely suspicious to an eye trained to spot royal or priestly ideologies. The list is repeated in Nehemiah 7 and described as 'the book of the genealogy of those who were first to come back' (Neh. 7.5), but even from the point of view of 'genealogy' this list is disappointing. It is well known that biblical genealogies are ideological creations of one sort or another, but this 'genealogy' is much less ambitious—and hence less obviously ideological—than the genealogies in other parts of the Old Testament. Missing is the panoramic depiction of Israel among the nations (Gen. 10; 1 Chron. 1), the twelve tribe schema (1 Chron. 2–8), or the multi-generational sweep of time (Gen. 5 and 11). This geneal-ogy appears to perform a very simple task, namely, the listing of retur-nees according to 'family' beginning with 'the sons of Parosh, two thousand one hundred seventy two' (Ezra 2.3). True, this list is now part of a narrative with a very clear ideological line on the identity of the community (ideological as in representing the viewpoint of a par-ticular group), but most commentators imagine that in its original form it served a more mundane purpose.

---

* An earlier version of this paper was presented to the 'Constructs of the Social and Cultural Worlds of Antiquity Group' at the Society of Biblical Literature annual meeting in November, 1997, in New Orleans.

The purpose of this article is to re-examine the function of this list from an ideological critical perspective. Against the notion of a benign original purpose I want to show how this text was reproductive of the ideological tensions within the postexilic community relating to the construction of group identity and the articulation of internal hierarchy. Although this text is not a clear-cut illustration of the function of ideology in relation to power, it is nevertheless a good example of the central problem of ideology, which is the way ideology purports to describe social reality when in fact it is part of the construction of that reality.

In exploring the ideological dimensions of this construction of reality, I will draw on my previous article on ideology in an eclectic way. My point of departure is Geertz's comment that 'Whatever else ideologies may be...they are, most distinctively, maps of problematic social realities and matrices for the creation of collective conscience' (Geertz 1973: 220). What was problematic in this particular context was the identity of the Jewish community in Persian Yehud; there was no single agreed 'map' of this territory. Ezra 2 is, in my view, an attempt to establish some clear lines, some sort of bottom line, by means of which a particular collective consciousness could emerge and the fact that this 'map' takes the form of a concrete list of names is not an indication that an incontestable bottom line was found. The concreteness of the 2172 sons of Parosh is one thing, the stability of the community's identity another. This sense of a stable genealogically defined line separating the clean from the unclean is just that, a *sense* of stability; it is not the reality of stability. Indeed, the fact that a list of names such as this was put forward is itself of ideological critical interest. As Zizek puts it,

> one of the fundamental strategems of ideology is the reference to some self-evidence—'Look, you can see for yourself how things are!' 'Let the facts speak for themselves' is perhaps the arch-statement of ideology—the point being, precisely, that facts never 'speak for themselves' but are always made to speak by a network of discursive devices (Zizek 1994: 11).

What I want to do in this paper is to expose this ideological strategem for what it is, an ideological move that not only masks (intentionally or unintentionally) the problematic nature of Jewish identity in this period but also reproduces the struggle for identity and control. I begin with the facts and then move on to ask how they are made to speak, and why.

2. *An Overview of Contents and Historical Critical Questions*

The list in Ezra 2 (and Nehemiah 7) is one of the many so-called 'documents' which make up the historiographical pastiche known as Ezra–Nehemiah. The pastiche-like character of the work has meant that two separate sets of questions have been asked: one set concerned with the authenticity and setting of the documents in their original form and the other with the ideology (as in religio-political agenda) of the editor who stitched them all together. Assuming that the reader is familiar with the narrative of Ezra–Nehemiah as a whole, I will give but a brief overview of the contents of the list found in Ezra 2 and survey the historical critical questions raised.

a. *Contents of the List*
The list found in Ezra 2 appears at first glance to be a straightforward list of returnees but on closer inspection reveals considerable variety. It has the following subdivisions:

1. Introduction (2.1-2a)
2. Main list of 'returnees' organized into lay and clerical groups (2.2b-58)
3. List of those not able to prove their Israelite genealogy (2.59-63)
4. Sum totals for the 'whole assembly' (2.64-67)
5. Note on donations given to the building fund (2.68-69)
6. Conclusion (2.70)

1. The introduction, which identifies this list as comprised of 'the sons of the province who came up out of captivity', fits reasonably well in both contexts and is used on both occasions as the list of the earliest returnees. In Ezra it continues the story of the return showing that there was an enthusiastic and unified response to Cyrus's 'edict' (Ezra 1.2-4). Just as the departure from Babylon is reminiscent of the Exodus, so too is the return to the land reminiscent of the conquest account in Joshua. They return 'each to his own town' led by twelve men (following Neh. 7.7), representing perhaps the 12 tribes of Israel. They are led by Zerubbabel and Jeshua, just as the conquering Israelites were led by Joshua and Eleazar. The only difficulty with the sequence of Ezra 1 and 2 is the fact that whereas Sheshbazzar is the leader of the community in ch. 1, Zerubbabel is the one named in the list of ch. 2.

2. The main list of returnees is organized as follows into a number of categories subdivided into groups with the number of people in each group:

2.2-35   'the men of the people of Israel' (31 groups; 25,406)
vv. 36-39   'the priests' (4 groups; 4289)
vv. 40   'the Levites' (1 group; 74)
v. 41   'the singers' (1 group; 148)
v. 42   'the gatekeepers' (6 groups; 138)
vv. 43-54   'the temple slaves [נתינים]' (35 groups)
vv. 55-58   'the sons of Solomon's servants' (10 groups; a com-
            bined total of 392 is given for this and the previous
            group)

The groups within each subdivision are for the most part identified as 'the sons of so and so', but a significant proportion are identified according to place name as either 'the men of such and such a place' or 'the inhabitants (lit. sons) of such and such a place'. Most of the places named are in the territory of Benjamin.

3. The third section of the list is of special interest. It enumerates those who 'could not prove their ancestral house [בית אבות] or their descent [זרע], whether they belonged to Israel' (2.59). Within this final group of 'returnees' are three lay groups (v. 62: of 652 men) and three priestly groups (v. 63: no number given). The consequence of this lack of demonstrable Israelite pedigree is only spelled out with reference to the priests. Because they are unclean, 'the governor told them that they were not to partake of the most holy food, until a priest with Urim and Thummim should come' (2.65). Included among the priestly families are the sons of Hakkoz who seems to have been reinstated later on (cf. Neh. 3.4, 21; 7.63).

4. The returnees as a whole are referred to as 'the assembly' (הקהל), which is a significant term in Ezra–Nehemiah as a whole. The number given for the assembly is greater than the sum of the parts. Excluded from this assembly are the slaves.

5. The return to the land is closely linked with the restoration of the sanctuary in Ezra–Nehemiah as a whole, and in this list we encounter this same interest in terms of a note on donations given to the temple. This section of the list is the only section in which there is substantial disagreement between Ezra 2 and Nehemiah 7. In Ezra 2 it is simply the 'heads' of the fathers' houses who give generously to the building fund,

whereas in Nehemiah the 'heads', the governor and the rest of the people are named as donors. The sums given also vary, but in either case they are large (61,000 drachmas of gold in Ezra 2.69 and 20,000 in Neh. 7.70 [71]).

6. The list concludes with the notice that 'all Israel dwelt in their towns', which is again reminiscent of Joshua and the lists of cities assigned to the various tribes.

b. *Historical Critical Issues*
Historical critical study of this list has focused on three questions:

1. Which is the original form? Ezra 2 or Nehemiah 7?
2. What is the date of the list? Sixth or fifth century?
3. What was the original purpose of the list? Tattenai's visit, a Nehemianic census or something else?

1. The first question concerns both the content of the list and the relationship between the list and the two contexts in which it is found. Most would argue that the Nehemianic version is the original, or closer to the original and that it was subsequently taken over and incorporated by the editor of Ezra 1–6 (Rudolph 1947: 13; Clines 1984: 44-45; and Williamson 1985: 29-30). The main features cited in favour of Nehemiah 7 are the account of donations to the temple fund[1] and the transition from the list to the subsequent narrative.[2] Nehemiah 7.72b (73b); 'When the seventh month came...') serves to introduce a new narrative section about the reading of the law which began 'on the first day of the seventh month' (8.2). Ezra 2 has this same introductory verse, 'When the seventh month came...' but uses it to introduce the story of the restoration of sacrifice on the altar. It is argued that the narrative sequence in Nehemiah 7 is more likely to be original.

More recently, however, Blenkinsopp has argued that Ezra 2 is original citing the narrative continuity between the list and Ezra 1 and 3, especially as it relates to the restoration of the temple. These details are out of place in the narrative context of Nehemiah. Regarding the reference to the seventh month, Blenkinsopp notes that Ezra 3.6 also refers

---

1.   Ezra 2.68-69 appears to be a summary of Neh. 7.69-70 [70-71], specifically as it relates to the numbers. Furthermore, Ezra 2.68 contains a plus over against Neh. 7.70, tying it in with Ezra 1 and 3–6 in terms of content and vocabulary. For a summary of these arguments, see Williamson (1985: 34).

2.   As noted earlier, Neh. 7.7 names twelve leaders in versus Ezra 2.2.

to 'the first day of the seventh month' (Blenkinsopp 1988: 83). Whatever the merits of these two positions are, it goes without saying that
larger composition-historical issues are at stake. For my purposes, these
larger issues are irrelevant: I am interested in the purpose of this list as
a 'document' in its own right on the one hand (assuming for now that
this is possible) and with the purpose of this list as an integral part of
the narrative of Ezra–Nehemiah on the other; not with how this
document became part of the larger work.

2. There are only two serious options as to the date of this list, neither
of which is 538 BCE or the time of the first return under Cyrus as
implied by the narrative context in Ezra. A number of factors speak
against this view, not least of which is the leader with the Persian name
Bigvai. The groups named according to place (presumably of residence)
also suggests a list which postdates the return by a good margin. The
numbers given for the returnees (c. 50,000) are large compared to those
given for the exile (c. 20,000). Thus, the earliest plausible date is the
time of Zerubbabel who is in fact mentioned in the text. On this reading
the list could be construed as a record of all the returnees from the time
of Cyrus to Darius and not just a single return.

Another option is to date the list closer to the time of Nehemiah,
using the same arguments about the inclusion of residential groups and
the large numbers (Batton 1913: 71-73; and Mowinckel 1964: 75).
There is, however, some difficulty with a later date as noted by Rudolph
and others. Rudolph points out that the lack of the title of high priest for
Jeshua seems to indicate a time before the temple is complete. Also,
Meremoth son of Uriah son of Hakkoz does not seem in any way dis-
advantaged in the days of Ezra (Ezra 8.33) and Nehemiah (Neh. 3.4),
even though the sons of Hakkoz are banned from priestly activity in this
text (2.61) (Rudolph 1947: 16-20; see also Williamson 1985: 30-32).
Again, the composite nature of the list makes it difficult to reach any
certainty on these matters, though on balance an earlier date seems
more likely.

3. Finally, regarding the purpose of this list, a number of explanations
have been advanced, but as with the question of date no firm solution is
likely. One reason suggested for the drawing up of this list is that it
occurred in connection with Tattenai's visit (Ezra 5.3-4, 10) or some
such visit by an official. In this case the list would be a record of those
who were granted permission to return and rebuild the sanctuary
(Galling 1964: 89-108; see also Schultz 1980). The other main alterna-

tive is suggested by the association of the list with Nehemiah. In Nehemiah 7 this list is found as a result of Nehemiah's request to have a new census taken, and the phrase 'all the congregation' (Ezra 2.64 // Neh. 7.66) may reflect such a census (Blenkinsopp 1988: 83). Other less plausible suggestions (because they fail to take into account the composite nature of the list) are that it was made for taxation purposes (Alt 1953: 316-37) or that it is connected with land rights (Hoelscher 1923).

c. *Evaluation*

I describe the approach taken in these accounts of the setting and purpose of the list as the 'documentary approach'. The documentary approach gets its name from the tendency in historical critical circles to treat this and other texts in Ezra–Nehemiah as (originally) independent documents with their own setting and purpose. One of the supposed benefits of this approach is that it has the (perhaps desired) effect of bracketing out the 'ideological' purpose of the list in the narrative in favour of more specific administrative purposes, perhaps on the assumption that only bureaucrats make lists and they do so for practical, as opposed to ideological, reasons only. Another feature of the 'documentary approach' to these lists is that it attempts to explain why the community is enumerated quite apart from the question of who exactly is identified in this list and how they have been identified.

An ideological critical approach to this list, on the other hand, is sensitive to the constructed and contested nature of social identity and attune to the possibility that a list such as this may be deeply implicated in the ideological struggles for identity and legitimacy. In other words, instead of approaching the text as a source document, it treats the list and the making of such lists as itself part of the social fabric of the postexilic community. That this is the case should become clear as I examine whom this list identifies and how.

2. *Whom Does this List Identify?*

According to Ezra 2.59 each of the groups recorded in the list was a בית אבות or 'house of the fathers', the groups identified according to locale notwithstanding. The בית אבות thus appears to be the basic social unit within the postexilic community (Weinberg 1992: 49).[3] In asking

3.   Weinberg (1992: 49) cites the following lexical statistics in support of this

about the 'who' of this list, the first order of business is to take a closer look at the nature of this social unit.

Following Meyer (1896: 134-35), Kippenberg asserts that the בית אבות was a 'clan' (*Geschlecht*) comparable to the pre-exilic משפחה (Kippenberg 1982: 23-41). Because the משפחה is, in Kippenberg's view, a classic kinship group, the structure, function and ethos of post-exilic Judean society can be illuminated with reference to pre-exilic texts concerning the משפחה.[4] The assumption here is that there is an essential continuity at the level of kinship groups between the pre-exilic and postexilic periods. The 'tribe–clan (משפחה)–extended family (בית אבות)' sequence (as operative for example in Josh. 7) is essentially intact in the postexilic period; it is only that the tribe is no longer all that significant and the name for the middle group has changed changed from משפחה to בית אבות. In this view the בית אבות continues to be a sub-division of the 'clan' in the postexilic period which goes by the name בית אבות.

Another approach, first put forward by Weinberg in conjunction with his Bürger-Tempel Gemeinde hypothesis (Weinberg 1992: 49-62), is to see the בית אבות as a new exilic structure and not simply the continuation of the משפחה under another name or the rising to prominence in the exile of the smaller בית אב following the demise of the משפחה. The size of the בית אבות, reaching in some cases into the thousands (Ezra 2.6), suggests a radical departure from the pre-exilic בית אב which cannot be attributed simply to natural growth within a kinship group. In line with this, Smith would argue that the most likely scenario is that the בית אבות is an exilic conglomerate of a number of בתי אב under the fiction of a common ancestor (Smith 1989: 102). It resembles the משפחה in size, the בית אב in name, but its origin and function have more to do with structural adaptation in exile than with the tribal-kinship system of pre-exilic Israel (Smith 1989: 101-102).[5]

view: the terms בית אבות and אבות (a shortened form of בית אבות) occur six times in Joshua to 2 Kings, 46 times in Chronicles and 19 times in Ezra–Nehemiah. בית אב, on the other hand, occurs 35 times in Joshua to 2 Kings and 10 times in Chronicles and once in Ezra–Nehemiah.

4.   According to Kippenberg's typology (Kippenberg 1982: 25-28), the משפחה had the following characteristics: patrilineal descent; corporate ownership of the land; militia unit; common residence; right of possession passed on as inheritance; sub-divided into בית אב; mutual support; endogamous marriage; maintains religious customs and the collective memory; a unit of the tribe.

5.   The textual evidence outside of Ezra–Nehemiah which supports this argu-

The differences between these groups can be defined further with reference to the anthropological study of kinship. According to Rogerson,
the מִשְׁפָּחָה was 'probably a maximal lineage—that is, a descent group
which established ties of kinship between families through a common
ancestor who was no longer living' (Rogerson and Davies 1989: 57).
The actual distance between the living descendants of this common
ancestor varies, and hence size of the group thus designated, varies with
the result that the term מִשְׁפָּחָה is used variously to designate a group
within an Israelite tribe (e.g. Num. 27.1-11; 36.1-9), a tribe (e.g. Judah
in Judg. 17.7) and even Israel (Amos 3.1). בֵּית אָב, on the other hand, is
used to designate (among other things) an ordinary lineage or residential group consisting of a living head (i.e. the grandfather or father) and
his sons together with wives and children (Gen. 50.8). The מִשְׁפָּחָה could
thus contain a number of smaller, ordinary lineages or בָּתֵּי אָב. Assuming that the בֵּית אָבוֹת is a kinship group on this model, this difference
between ordinary and maximal lineages might account for the large size
of many of the בָּתֵּי אָבוֹת. On this reading, a small group like the 'sons
of Ater' (Ezra 2.16) is a smaller lineage within the larger בֵּית אָבוֹת
of Hezekiah, making the full name of the group 'the sons of Ater,
namely of Hezekiah (לְחִזְקִיָּה)'.[6]

ment is found in Numbers (P) and Chronicles where the term בֵּית אָבוֹת is confused
with larger social units. In Num. 1.4 and 17.2 the בֵּית אָבוֹת is used as a synonym of
מַטֶּה, 'tribe'. This confusion may stem from the failure of the writer to differentiate
between the smaller pre-exilic בֵּית אָבוֹת and the larger postexilic בֵּית אָבוֹת; in other
words, it may be nothing more than the unintended consequence of a poor choice of
name. In 1 Chron. 15.12 the leaders (שָׂרִים) of the secondary sub-divisions within
the tribe of Levi are called the 'heads of the fathers' [houses]' of Levi, whereas in
1 Chron. 6.4 the secondary subdivisions are called מִשְׁפָּחָה while the tertiary units
are בֵּית אָבוֹת (cf. 1 Chron. 23.7-11). These 'mistakes' on the part of the postexilic
writers may be no more than just a question of confusing nomenclature, to be sorted
out with reference to less-confused/confusing social realities, but they also may be
indicative of more substantial social ambiguities. It is true, of course, that the
difference between kinship terms used before and after the exile raises the question
of what happened in the exile, but it may be that the post-exilic realities, within
which this nomenclature was used, are more relevant to our inquiries, especially in
view of the fact that the most important texts concerning the בֵּית אָבוֹת are
postexilic.

6.   There are other examples of subgroupings within the list: 'the sons of
Pahath-moab of the sons of Jeshua and Joab' (v. 11), 'the sons of Jedaiah of the
house of Jeshua' (v. 39), and 'the sons of Jeshu, namely of Kadmiel of the sons of
Hodevah' (v. 43). Another view is to see the returnees as only part of exilic groups.

The lack of a category name for these smaller groups and the fact that
only one such group is mentioned suggests a weak kinship structure in
the postexilic community. I say 'weak' because the 'strength' of a kin-
ship-based society rests in its being based upon the pre-given family
unit. Smaller groups obviously existed at the time but they did not have
a well-defined status. This would mean that the בית אבות is some sort of
hybrid quasi-kinship social unit and not an 'ordinary' maximal lineage.
Thus, in line with Smith, the comparison between the משפחה and the
בית אבות only takes us so far.

It would appear also that the בית אבות was not as flexible as the
משפחה. The eponym of the בית אבות is used like a surname, much like
the Scottish clan names. Though members of a Scottish clan claim
descent from the founder of the group, they are not necessarily able (or
required) to demonstrate the genealogical link to this ancestor. Indeed
the clan system, whereby people took the clan name as a surname, was
an eighteenth-century development. The important element at the time
was the surname itself, which marked out one clan from the next for
social and political purposes. This system of nomenclature transformed
the once more fluid genealogical relationships into more rigid kinship
groups. There are only as many Scottish clans as there are clan names—
the MacGregors, the MacDonalds and Macleods, etc.—and, since surnames cannot be divided, these clans cannot split up to form new clans.
Hence, the clans simply grow in size over time.[7] The משפחה, on the
other hand, takes its name from the given name of the ancestor. The
משפחה, unlike the surname-clan, was thus an inherently flexible kinship
grouping in that it could more easily absorb new members via the
amalgamation of two small kinship groups into a new משפחה (taking
the name of a more distant 'common' ancestor as eponym). If the
growth was internal, occurring say at the level of the בית אב, a large

7.   'The Gaels of Scotland and the Jews of Poland were two ancient communities who long escaped surnames. Both had enjoyed communal autonomy, surviving
for centuries with traditional name forms using either patronymics (such as the
Jewish "Abraham Ben Isaac", i.e. Abraham, son of Isaac) or personal epithets. The
famous Highland outlaw, whom English-speaking Lowlanders called Rob Roy
MacGregor, c. 660–1732, was known to his own as Rob Ruadh (Red Robert) of
Inversnaid. Both Gaelic and Jewish nomenclatures fell victim to state bureaucracies
in the late eighteenth century. After the Jacobite defeat, the Scottish Highlanders
were registered according to clan names which they had previously rarely used,
thereby giving rise to thousands upon thousands of MacGregors, MacDonalds, and
MacLeods' (Davies 1996: 169).

משפחה could split into two taking the name of a more recent 'common' ancestor.[8]

The large size of the בית אבות, on the one hand, and the absence of any socially significant group at the extended family level, on the other, suggests that the בית אבות did not have the flexibility of the משפחה. As an exilic formation the בית אבות was not 'designed' to accommodate that kind of growth and expansion. One could well imagine that in the immediate aftermath of deportation the exiled Jews residing in various locations in Babylonia formed new social groups (i.e. בתי אבות probably named after the first leader or head) using a combination of real and fictive kinship ties in order to maintain their identity as an ethnic minority. Having regrouped in this way there was no need for a mechanism to incorporate new members or groups. Boundary maintenance was probably the order of the day. The number of בתי אבות so formed and named would have stayed the same and all those who belonged to a בית אבות would have used the name of the founding leader in a manner analogous to the use of the Scottish clan name; that is, as a surname. This is at any rate one way of explaining the origin, size and apparent indivisibility of the eponymic בתי אבות. Only the 'sons of Ater, of Hezekiah' suggests a significant sub-division. The sons of Ater seem to have established themselves as a significant social group in their own right though continuing to identify themselves as related to another (larger?) group.

3. *How Does this List Identify?*

There are, of course, some subtle and some not so subtle variations in the list of returnees which draw our attention to how this list identifies. The first significant variation one encounters is the groups named after a locality. The members of the majority of these groups (in Neh. 7) are described as 'the men of [place name]', all of which are located in and around the Persian province of Yehud. This suggests both a postexilic setting and an expanding community, if one accepts the hypothesis presented above regarding the exilic origin of the eponymic בית אבות. But why not simply create new בתי אבות named after an eponym? If it was done in the exile, why not in the postexilic setting? Why maintain this

---

8. Thus, the term משפחה as used in the Old Testament can refer to a subdivision within a tribe, a tribe or even all Israel. In the story of Achan, the tribe of Judah is called שבט and a משפחה (Josh. 7.14-17).

subtle distinction between exilic and non-exilic groups (a distinction that would still obtain even if they were both considered בתי אבות) and yet cover up this distinction at a higher level in claiming that all these groups came from the exile?[9]

Another more serious anomaly, and one which takes us closer to the heart of the matter, is the separate section that lists those unable to prove their Israelite pedigree. Why do these groups not have genealogical records which link them to Israel via a בית אבות, when the בית אבות is itself somewhat of a fiction? Were they Babylonian converts to Judaism? If not (and the fact that some of them were priests suggests that they were not converts), why was it so important to have a particular type of kinship connection when, according to the main criterion (being a returnee), one was considered to be an acceptable member of the assembly (as opposed to the slaves and the 'remainees')? The priestly families without the right connections were not allowed to partake of the most holy food, but they were free to partake of the lesser holy food. In other words, they were not excluded outright but merely had to wait for the time when the high priest would consult the Urim and Thummim.[10] All these groups did belong to a kinship group of one description or another but, apparently, not of a socially-significant kind. Is it possible that they had no memory of their grandparents or great grandparents who were taken into exile? I venture they did. It appears, therefore, that the בית אבות (or at least this particular list of בתי אבות) was also a mechanism of social discrimination within the community as well as a vehicle for identity maintenance. In other words, more is involved in this list than 'the determination of *true Israelites*' (Smith 1989: 105; and Japhet 1981: 113-14).

9.   If one were to take the view that the groups named after locality were also exilic, one would still have to ask why they were not organised into eponymic בתי אבות. Why the distinction?

10.   Exod. 28.30; Lev. 8.8; Num. 27.21. Williamson (1985: 34) argues that they were waiting for their status to be confirmed. The relationship between descent (fictional or otherwise) and cultic purity is not spelled out, though one finds an echo of this in the intermarriage 'crisis' of Ezra 9, which also concerns the 'seed' (the 'holy seed' no less: 9.2) and cultic concerns as indicated by the use of 'separate' and 'abomination' (9.1). According to Smith (1989: 145-48), the priestly concerns for pure categories reflects the concerns of a minority community which is seeking to maintain its distinct identity, ethnic and religious, via ritual *and* social practices which emphasize separation (בדל).

While the overall and overt concern is to distinguish between the community of returnees and the 'people of the land' or 'remainees' (and even this was not a watertight distinction)[11] in terms of descent from Israel, the means by which this is done—that is using the בית אבות as the fundamental building block—seems to serve other and perhaps conflicting purposes. It was important to be a returnee, but it was not the only important issue. While those unable to prove their descent are clearly marked off in this list, the בתי אבות named after a place are not distinguished in any way except by being put at the end of the list of 'the Israelites'. Both groups had kinship relations but, presumably, not of the right kind. Being able to trace one's ancestry back to *the right type of group*—the eponymic בית־אבות—was clearly as important as the larger issue of being of exilic and 'Israelite' descent. In other words, the ostensible function of this list (to identify the returnees group) stands in tension with another function (to mark off the eponymic בתי אבות), the latter undermining the former. We are now at the point of showing how this list is reproductive of the struggle for identity and control in the postexilic community.

4. *Why Identify in this Way?*

In a recent monograph on Numbers, Mary Douglas has proposed a cultural typology which she uses to contrast the ideology of Ezra–Nehemiah with that of Numbers (Douglas 1994: 42-82). According to Douglas, the postexilic community was marked by tension between two cultural biases: enclavist and hierarchist. The enclave is a minority community that does not have in its power the coercive resources of the state. The enclave is characteristically egalitarian and has weak authority structures. Its primary concern is the maintenance of boundaries between itself and the outside world, both in terms of maintaining a distinctive ethos and in terms of preventing the loss of members. Because it cannot enforce conformity via authoritarian structures, it has to resort to moral persuasion as its only means of social control. It is governed, ideally-speaking, by consensus but more often than not is torn by internal strife and factional disputes. A hierarchical culture also has definite boundaries but is more concerned with the articulation of a

11. By positive terms I mean those texts which speak of those 'who had joined them and separated themselves from the pollutions of the peoples of the land' (Ezra 6.21).

hierarchical structure within an all-encompassing well-differentiated whole. The greatest fear of the hierarchist is disaffection of the lower ranks. The solution is to create buffer zones, special spaces and discourses that underline the incommensurability of roles and expectations between the various segments of the community. Because a hierarchical system cannot expel dissenting members, it tends to be both more tolerant of difference and more assimilationist in its stance, so long as this does not threaten the position of the leading group.

According to Douglas, Ezra–Nehemiah represents an enclavist ideology put forward by a party (Ezra, Nehemiah and allies) taking advantage of a populist enclavist cultural bias for their own agenda. Numbers, on the other hand, is a hierarchical ideology put forward by a priestly hierarchy in opposition to the Ezra–Nehemiah party. On this reading of the situation, the list in Ezra 2 (if taken at face value) would have to be construed as a document of the enclavist party. Elsewhere in Ezra–Nehemiah the line between returnee and remainee is put forward as the all-important distinction, which, though under threat, is not in itself disputed. And why is this so? This is so because the facts have already spoken for themselves and the evidence (in the form of a concrete list) is plain to see. When the narrative speaks of 'the sons of the *golah*' ('exile') (Ezra 2.1), the people in this list and their descendants is what is meant. Also in keeping with the enclavist mentality is the lack of emphasis on internal differentiation; yes, there are leaders but the community of the 'first returnees' is a community that thinks and acts as one. This list clearly distinguishes between lay and clerical families and those who have no proper genealogical claim to being 'Israelite', but other than that it points firmly in the enclavist direction.

But the above analysis of the list suggests that to read the text in this way—as an enclavist document—is to succumb to a bit of misdirection. I do not challenge the view that this text (and Ezra–Nehemiah as a whole for that matter) takes an overtly enclavist line, but it does not do so in an entirely consistent way, even at the point at which it makes the case in objective terms. Something else is going on in this text which undermines or stands in tension with its 'documentary' meaning. I would argue that the tension between the enclavist and hierarchical tendencies within the community is inscribed in this text as well. Not that this list is equally a product of the two parties in the community, the one headed by Ezra and Nehemiah and the other by the aristocratic priesthood, but rather that it is a product of a community at odds with

itself. Its fundamental principles were enclavist, but within this community a not-yet-fully-articulated hierarchical structure was emerging
that only later in the Second Temple period formed an aristocratic class.
In the absense of a native king and attendant ruling class, the issue of
group identity (who we are) takes centre stage. This means that the
question of legitimate authority (who rules) is not dealt with, institu-
tionally and ideologically, in an obvious manner (except in regard to
imperial authority) and in this void other, less obvious, forms of authority were operative. It is my view that the eponymic בית אבות filled that
void in the form of a patriarchal authority concentrated in the hands of a
limited number of leading families. And these families were as divided
over the issue of boundary definitions as the community at large and did
not, therefore, fit as a whole into any one party.

This view is confirmed when we consider the only other context in
Ezra–Nehemiah in which the בית אבות is mentioned, namely, in connection with the 'heads of (the houses of) the fathers' (ראשׁי [בתי] האבות). It
is my view that these 'heads' are the patriarchs of these leading families.
The following list of texts illustrates the degree to which these 'heads'
are involved in (or are portrayed as involved in) the central events and
leading affairs of the community.

Ezra 1.5	The *heads* are the leaders of those who respond to Cyrus's edict.
Ezra 2.68-69	The *heads* donate large sums of money towards the construction of the temple (parallel in Neh. 7.70-72).
Ezra 3.12	The *heads* are among those who remember the first temple.
Ezra 4.3	The *heads* respond to the charges of the 'adversaries of Judah and Benjamin'.
Ezra 8.1	Ezra gathers leaders 'from Israel to go up with him... These are the *heads* of the בות and this is the genealogy of those who went up with me from Babylonia...' The list generally follows the pattern: 'from the sons of [eponym], x'. Eleven of the seventeen eponyms found in Ezra 2.3-19.
Ezra 10.16	Ezra selects *heads* to examine the matter of mixed marriage and those who agree to divorce their foreign wives are listed according to בתי אבות. Again, the pattern is 'from the sons of (eponym)'. Six of the seventeen eponyms from Ezra 2.3-19 are included here.
Neh. 8.13	The *heads*, the priests and the Levites come to Ezra to study the Law.
Neh. 10.1-27	Fourteen of the signatories to the covenant have eponymic names (!) from Ezra 2.3-19.

Neh. 11.3-24   The list of inhabitants who live in Jerusalem is but of the heads
               who live in Jerusalem are named as 'x son of y son of z'.
Neh. 12.12-26 Lists the *heads* of the priestly and Levitical בתי אבות.

These examples illustrate quite clearly that the 'heads' had a prominent
role within the postexilic community and (as the writer of Ezra–Nehemiah would have it) worked closely with representatives of the imperial
administration, namely Ezra and Nehemiah.[12] The only exception to this
pattern is the role played by the 'elders of the Jews' in negotiating with
Tattenai in the time of Darius (Ezra 5.5, 9; 6.7). Smith suggests that the
elders were the leaders of the exilic community who retained some of
their leadership functions in the postexilic period. The 'heads' are
simply the most prominent members of the larger group of elders
(Smith 1989: 97).[13]

The 'heads' performed what could be described as legitimate community functions as the representatives of the community at a higher
level. The 'heads' act and speak on behalf of the community they represent; their actions are the community's actions, and their interests are
the interests of the community. This sort of representation is not, however, representation on the parliamentary model. This mode of 'representation' serves a system of power and authority which is built right
into the kinship structure. This hierarchical structure may indeed have
been integral to the בתי אבות, but it was also potentially repressive—
that is, capable of exploiting the community it represented and against
its interests. The scenario described in Nehemiah 5, where destitute

12. Their prominent position is also confirmed in Chronicles if Jehoshaphat's
judicial reforms reflect postexilic realities, for the heads are said to have given judicial duties (2. Chron. 19.8). Indeed, the genealogy of Levi is reduced to the genealogy of heads (1 Chron. 6) which indicated for Meyer the increasing prominence of
certain families between Nehemiah and the Chronicler's time (Meyer 1896: 163-
65).

13. The list of functions would be expanded if the heads were among the סגנים
and חרים (Kippenberg 1982: 37-39). The former filled local administrative positions relating to the province, including district governorships (Neh. 4.13). See Ezra
9.2; Neh. 2.16; 12.40 for references to סגנים; and Neh. 2.16; 4.8[14], 13[19]; 5.7;
7.5; 13.11, 17 for סגנים and חרים. Blenkinsopp (1988: 223 and 252) suggests that
the former were hereditary nobility (Jer. 27.20; 39.6; Isa. 34.12), whereas the latter
were probably regional administrators (Jer. 51.23, 28, 57; Ezek. 23.6, 12, 23).
According to Williamson (1985: 191) the סגנים are indistinguishable from the חרים
(cf. the last five references), and he concludes merely that they are leaders of the
community.

women bring a complaint against their fellow Jews, does not mention the 'heads' as such but is testimony to the potential for exploitation within the Jewish community.

5. *Conclusion*

What this closer look at the list of Ezra 2 has disclosed is that social structures and ideologies which relate ostensibly to the interests of the community as a whole also contain hierarchical structures, which may distort the community and its discourses from the inside. The function of this list is ambivalent. On the one hand, it served to identify the community as a whole as an assembly of returnees, a literally postexilic community. On the other hand, it served to distinguish between those within the community who had the right sort of exilic connection and those who did not. What mattered was not exilic descent as such, but descent from the right exilic family. And then there are the enigmatic groups named after locale. If these groups represent remainees, then the exilic-descent claim is a front for a community dominated by exilic בתי אבות, that is those named after an eponym. If these 'residential' groups are long-established settlers, the same sort of hierarchical arrangement would obtain: a community dominated by a select group of 'heads' of eponymic בית אבות (and the evidence from the rest of Ezra–Nehemiah seems to bear this out). It is my view, therefore, that the complexity of this list mirrors the internal differentiations within this community and indeed was an integral part of its discourses of identity and legitimacy. It is not so much a retrospective justification of certain social relations, but rather a 'map' that merges seemlessly with the social practices of a deeply divided community.

RE-EXAMINING 'POPULAR RELIGION':
ISSUES OF DEFINITION AND SOURCES.
INSIGHTS FROM INTERPRETIVE ANTHROPOLOGY

M. Daniel Carroll R.

1. *Introduction*

Scholarly interest in the popular religion of ancient Israel is not new. It
is possible to trace chronologically from the last century until the present day the elaboration of a variety of scholarly theories about Israelite
popular religion dealing with such topics as its origins, nature and the
extent of participation by different social groups. These developments
also can be placed within the broader context of the general concerns
and trends in Old Testament studies in any given time period (see
Dever 1987: 210-19; 1995: 37-52; Gnuse 1997: 62-128; Toorn 1998).
The recent explosion of research in the field, however, does attest to an
impressive increase in relevant archaeological data over the last two to
three decades with its attendant implications.

My interest, though, does not lie in offering yet another comprehensive survey of these many and diverse approaches. Rather, my focus
will be directed at two fundamental methodological issues that inescap-
ably, and increasingly more self-consciously, form part of any discussion of Israel's popular religion. The first of these is the utilization and
appraisal of the available sources, specifically the evaluation of the biblical text by scholars vis-à-vis the possible depiction of religious life
gleaned from the archaeological data. The second key point involves an
examination of the stated or implied definition of 'popular religion' that
undergirds such studies.

The first major section of this essay presents how these two issues
have been dealt with by several Old Testament scholars, both past and
present, who have contributed to the field. That brief overview will
serve to highlight the pertinent matters connected with those two issues
that will be addressed in the second part. There I appeal to the disci-

pline of interpretive anthropology, coupled with illustrations drawn from certain elements of Roman Catholic popular religion within Latin America, in order to establish the theoretical framework which will inform my own textual study in the prophetic book of Amos in the following essay.

2. *Sources and Definitions in the Study of Popular Religion*

a. *Examples of Early Approaches*

John Skinner's work on the book of Jeremiah, which was published in 1930, is a helpful starting point for surfacing my methodological questions.[1] In relationship to the issue of sources, Skinner's presentation of Canaanite beliefs and practices and of its impact on the 'public' religion of Israel and Judah is grounded exclusively in what might be reconstructed from the biblical literature (1930: 53-73). No reference, whether in the body of the argument or the footnotes, is made to any archaeological findings that might inform his point of view. In addition, he assumes as correct the text's assessment of the heterodox. He lauds the perspective of the prophet:

> There is no one who has analysed the diverse and successive currents of spiritual influence in the society around him with such penetrating and sympathetic insight as Jeremiah. There is none, either, whose whole thinking is so permeated by the experience of direct personal fellowship with God, which is the ultimate basis and secret of religious life (1930: 57).

Alluding to the syncretism of the larger populace, Skinner speaks of the 'crude notions and half-heathen ritual of the rural population around his [Jeremiah's] home' (1930: 57), which had succumbed to the 'danger of contamination from this impure [Canaanite] religion' (1930: 60). He formulates his estimation of Israel's popular religion according to the description offered in Jeremiah, ch. 2: it is a degeneration from the purer faith of an earlier time, sensual, double-minded in its contradictory embrace of both Yahweh and Baal, and unrealistic in its inefficacious efforts to achieve a relationship with Yahweh (1930: 64-72). For Skinner, therefore, the biblical text is the sole basis of information and the only arbitrator of religious worth.

---

1. Skinner was chosen over other worthy possibilities of the first decades of this century, because of my interest in the prophetic literature.

The title of his chapter ('The Two Religions of Israel') communicates the juxtaposition and opposition between the two kinds of faith and illuminates Skinner's own understanding of the realities of religious life in ancient Israel. On the one hand, in his mind, there is the 'official religion' of the Jerusalem Temple with its cult and theology; on the other, stands the 'popular (or, "public") religion' of the common, especially rural, people. The latter, reflective of the 'national mind', finds at least some of its roots in the 'nature-religion of the Canaanites', which responded to day-to-day needs dealing with crops and fertility and ultimately was combined with Yahweh worship (1930: 57-60). Skinner admits that his characterization of the religious situation is more of a generalization than what probably actually was the case, as some individuals surely did respond in more appropriate ways to the god of Jeremiah (1930: 72-73).

This cursory summary demonstrates that Skinner does indeed reflect my twin interest in the source(s) for study and in the definition of 'popular religion'. In tune with much of the scholarship of that day, his reconstruction, which is circumscribed by the material within the biblical text, provides no place for archaeological data to have any input in his reconstruction. On the basis of his reading of the biblical text, popular religion is set over against official theology and practice and stands condemned.

Two decades later, and in contrast to Skinner, W.F. Albright consciously attempted to incorporate archaeological material into his research in the religion of Israel. By that time the winds within scholarship had shifted, and Albright himself had been a pioneer in the attempt to interface the new discoveries with the study of Israelite religion. His was an effort to coordinate these findings with the biblical presentation of Israelite belief and practice. Such a procedure, he felt, was the only means by which to describe objectively and scientifically the development of that faith (on through to the birth of Christianity). Today some scholars, although appreciative of his monumental achievements, criticize Albright's method as overly and overtly apologetic: in his publications extrabiblical data is brought to bear, but apparently always under the authority of certain Christian convictions about God and Scripture (see, e.g., Long 1996).

In other words, even if his work does have more breadth than that of earlier scholars like Skinner, the Bible continues in some fashion to be considered the ultimate source for producing a history of the rise of

Israelite monotheism and for assessing the spiritual and ethical sub-stance of the religious tenets of surrounding cultures. Such a predeter-mined primacy, for instance, is revealed in the subtitle to his *Yahweh and the Gods of Canaan*: this was a book designed to be *A Historical Analysis of Two Contrasting Faiths*—one (Israelite) positive, the other (Canaanite) obviously not. In Albright's view, anything of value of non-Yahwistic origin now found within the acceptable faith of the Israel of the Bible had passed through a process of 'archaic demythologizing'—that is, the eradication of unwanted polytheistic elements (1968: 183-207).

b. *Some Recent Developments*

The direction and interests of much contemporary research into Israelite popular religion have dramatically changed since the days of Albright and his disciples. The discovery of several significant worship struc-tures and thousands of artifacts now provide a gamut of information far exceeding what preceding generations of scholars might have ever imagined (Smith 1990; Dever 1987: 222-37; 1997; Holladay 1987; Keel and Uehlinger 1998). Seals, standing stones, terracotta figurines, altars, cult stands and all sorts of vessels and utensils have been uncovered at such geographically diverse sites as Tel Dan, Tirzah, Megiddo, Ta'anach, Jerusalem, Arad and Beersheba. Two particular spectacular finds have come from Kuntillet 'Ajrud in the eastern Sinai and Khirbet el-Qôm, which is near Hebron in Judah. These data have greatly enriched scholarly appreciation of the complexity of the religious life of ancient Israel, and some scholars now would chastise those who would try to reconstruct the religion of ancient Israel without this input (Dever 1995; Keel and Uehlinger 1998: 9-12, 395-96).[2]

This new situation has generated a different orientation to Israelite popular religion. Today many, while suggesting different hypothetical historical reconstructions of the process by which monotheism in Israel emerged,[3] would posit a greater continuity than earlier scholars did

---

2. Even those who champion the use of this material can be critical of one another for not having taken into account enough of the data. Note, for example, Dever's critique of Toorn (Dever 1995: 47-48) and Keel and Uehlinger's dissatis-faction with Dever and Holladay (Keel and Uehlinger 1998: 4, 8 and 4, 349 n. 87, respectively).

3. For example, Smith proposes a process of 'convergence' and 'differentia-tion' with other beliefs and practices (Smith 1990), whereas Gnuse suggests an

between the religion of Israel and that of the surrounding areas and thus a complex pluralistic religious environment. In addition, more attention, for example, is being devoted to investigating various practices, such as the veneration of the dead, and the presence and role of goddesses. A majority of scholars now believe that monotheism (or at least its wide-spread acceptance) was a late development in the history of Israel, al-though it is important to note that a few dissenting voices have offered significant counterarguments (e.g. Tigay 1986; Hess 1992; de Moor 1997).[4]

These developments have gone hand-in-hand with the two issues of sources and definitions that are the concern of this essay. To begin with, this orientation has had an impact on how the Bible is appreciated and utilized in research. For many the question no longer is simply how the archaeological data might be arranged alongside the biblical representa-tion, but rather whether the Bible even can be considered any longer to be a credible source to take into consideration. The Bible, it is claimed, should be recognized as a jaundiced text written from a hegemonic theological, gender and ideological perspective. The text has an ideol-ogy. This ideology is tagged as that of some sector of the national reli-gious elite or of a specific religious group (such as the 'Yahweh alone' party). Accordingly, earlier scholarship is faulted for too readily assum-ing its point of view.[5] In contradistinction,

> The current study of the history of Israelite religion dismisses the theo-logical constructions of the past as unreal and heavily biased. Its practi-tioners are especially eager to salvage those aspects and elements of Israelite religion that have suffered neglect or even denial by earlier scholars (Toorn 1998: 13).

evolutionary pattern with certain moments of significant developments coinciding with important changes in the broader context of the Near East (Gnuse 1997).

4.   Note Keel and Uehlinger's rather positive evaluation of Tigay's work (1998: 204-207, 279-80). Yet their interpretation of a more complete spectrum of data leads them to add: 'The evidence would indeed be misunderstood if we were to impute strictly monolatrous or directly monotheistic tendencies to the male and female inhabitants of Israel and Judah during the ninth and eighth centuries' (1998: 280).

5.   Though not dealing with the issue of popular religion, Clines in 'Meta-commentating Amos' decries that scholars are beyond excuse in accepting and repeating the social and religious critique of that prophetic text (Clines 1993).

One can detect that, for some scholars of this persuasion, research is connected with a commitment beyond a purely academic inquiry into antiquity; it is tied to the desire to allow the voices of the marginalized to find expression, both in the distant past of the ancient world and today. In other words, the new estimation of the Bible is coupled with a sense of mission and certain ethical concerns. Some feminist and liberationist scholars believe the task of identifying and unmasking the ideology of the biblical texts is a positive one, in that by so doing traces of redeemable material can be transferred to constructive efforts at achieving equality and liberation today (e.g. West 1995a: 131-73; cf. 'socio-pragmatic hermeneutics' in Thistleton 1992: 379-470). Keel and Uehlinger, for example (cf. Dever 1995: 45-48; Berlinerblau 1993; 1996; Toorn 1998:16-19),[6] close their monumental *Gods, Goddesses, and Images of God in Ancient Israel* with these words:

> Such work [i.e. research into the icongraphic] will not only expose the buried feminine aspects of the Judeo-Christian image of God, with their salvific power, it can also open our eyes to the theological dignity of many images and concepts that can nourish us from the thriving Christian groups and from the encultured theologies of Asia, Africa, and Latin America. Through openness to the traditions of these peoples, the European-North American culture of subjugation, which is threatening to drive the world to destruction, can hope not only for critique and reevaluation but also for enrichment and perhaps healing. As we look at a picture of *Pachamama* ('mother earth') from the Andean Indians, can we not distinguish the features of the Bronze Age Asherah once again? (1998: 409).

A second pertinent characteristic of many recent studies of ancient Israelite religion is the attention given to elaborating more nuanced definitions of 'popular religion'. Whereas past studies often exhibited the tendency to divide the 'official religion' of the national cult and 'popular religion' into two coherent and homogeneous entities, today the latter is especially seen as much more variegated. Scholars are attempting to ascertain with greater clarity the relationship between the official and the popular. All would hold, however, to some level of antithesis between the two.

---

6.   This criticism of the biblical text is sometimes accompanied by the claim that greater objectivity is possible by focusing on material artifacts. Note, for instance, Dever 1995: 52-53.

Several different understandings of 'popular religion' have surfaced in the literature. There are those scholars who associate the popular with the religious practices of the majority, practices which might very well cut across class and gender boundaries (e.g. Ackerman 1992: 2, 216-17; Bloch-Smith 1992: 151). The idea is that most people of ancient Israel would be involved in a number of shared religious activities beyond the reach and approval of the official theology and cult. One could say that here the focus is *demographic*.[7]

Others define popular religion according to a specific locus: the popular would refer to the religious practices and beliefs particularly within the domestic sphere and in villages and towns, as over against the national shrines (Holladay 1987: 266-82; Albertz 1994: 17-21; Toorn 1996, 1998). The popular, therefore, would be more private, familial and spontaneous in contrast to official religion. In this perspective the focus is primarily on *social settings*.[8]

Perhaps the most extensive theoretical discussion of popular religion has been provided by Berlinerblau, whose approach is explicitly *sociological*. In several publications he surveys and critiques the lack of clarity and sophistication in much biblical research on popular religion (1993, 1995, 1996: 17-41). Berlinerblau observes that within sociology there has been much disagreement as to what the terms 'official' and 'popular' religion actually mean. He builds his own particular theoretical framework by drawing on and interacting with insights from classical studies of the past, such as those by Weber (1952; cf. 1993) and Gramsci (1971, 1985; cf. Fulton 1987), as well as on more recent research (e.g. Towler 1974; Vrijhof and Waardenburg 1979; Williams 1980; Lanternari 1982). These approaches, although offering distinct configurations and explanations, consider that any analysis of the official and the popular must take into account the dynamics and tensions of economic and social class, gender, and theological institutionalization and legitimation—all of which would bring into play strategies and mechanisms of power. On the one hand, Berlinerblau therefore defines 'official religion' as:

---

7.   This position has not been developed on the basis of any significant theoretical discussion.

8.   This is not to suggest, however, that the official religion did not reach into smaller communities. It, of course, could be represented in shrines and through personnel at more local levels, not only at the primary national cult centers.

the religion of an association of male-dominated and interconnected social groups which exercises the greatest power (via coercion and/or consent) in its relations with other religious groups and thus comes to stand as the 'orthodoxy' of a particular society (1996: 29).

'Popular religion', on the other hand, would be the inverse. Thus, within ancient Israel, the term would refer to the religious expressions of women and various non-privileged groups, which had been marginalized in some way by the official religion (cf. Dever 1994: 158-60; 1997: 53-54). The biblical text, in his view, often echoes that harsh theological condemnation of the heterodoxy of these groups:

> I would define a 'popular religious group' as *any association of individuals living within the borders of ancient Israel who by dint of their religious beliefs, political beliefs, rituals, symbols and so on, are denigrated by the authors of the Old Testament* (1993: 18).

This view of 'popular religion' is linked to a specific valorization of the Bible as a source of information. Berlinerblau's position (1993: 9-15; 1996: 35-40, 166-74), which is informed by the sociology of literature, holds that scholars should consider two categories of misrepresentation—intentional and unintentional—both of which he believes are evident in the Bible's description and evaluation of popular religion. This textual misrepresentation is not innocent, as it would reflect the unequal relationships of socio-religious power between Yahwists and other groups. Accordingly, a reliable picture of popular religion can be discerned only indirectly from the Bible by looking with a critical eye at these texts written by the hegemonic 'literati', while at the same time searching for 'implicit details' that might reveal some of the realities of quotidian life but which escaped the ideological scalpel.[9] Nevertheless, Berlinerblau also recognizes that the Yahwistic perspective of the Old Testament at times can be critical of the official religion of the monarchy and the economic elite, so scholars are warned not to make too simplistic an equation between the two (1996: 29-33).

In sum, I have attempted to highlight two important issues that are relevant to a discussion of the popular religion of ancient Israel: the definition of popular religion and the significance of the Bible as a source for analyzing those religious phenomena. This very cursory look at some of the research demonstrates that scholars more and more are

---

9.   The religious practice he investigates as a test case is the vow (Berlinerblau 1996).

seeking theoretical clarity in regards to these two points. What might be the best, or at least another, manner in which to comprehend that popular religion? How might the perspective of the biblical text appropriately be employed in the endeavor to visualize more fully those practices and beliefs? The next section will appeal to some insights from interpretive anthropology and Latin America to help respond to these concerns.

3. *Interpretive Anthropology and Popular Religion*

a. *Defining Popular Religion*

An anthropological approach situates the study of popular religion within the study of culture. The several schools within the discipline of anthropology, however, propose different understandings of what 'culture' actually means (e.g. Keesing 1974; Schreiter 1985: 39-74). The option chosen here has come to be labeled 'interpretive anthropology' (Marcus and Fischer 1986: 25-110; Barfield 1997: 263-65).

The most well-known exponent of interpretive anthropology is Clifford Geertz. In several classic essays, such as 'Thick Description: Toward an Interpretive Theory of Culture' (1973: 3-30), and '"From the Native's Point of View": On the Nature of Anthropological Understanding' (1983: 55-70), he sets out his theory of culture (cf. Rice 1980; Carroll R. 1992: 49-52). Geertz proposes a paradigm shift away from deterministic analysis and positivistic explanations:

> The concept of culture I espouse...is essentially a semiotic one. Believing with Max Weber, that man is an animal suspended in webs of significance he himself has spun, I take culture to be those webs and the analysis of it to be therefore not an experimental science in search of law but an interpretive one in search of meaning (1973: 5).

This is not simply a cognitive approach to culture, but rather a hermeneutical effort to decode, as it were, the private and social symbols, mores, values and activities within the complex tapestry that is a human culture. To study culture is to investigate how groups and societies organize, experience and understand their world.

> I want to propose two ideas. The first is that culture is best seen not as complexes of concrete behavior patterns—customs, usages, traditions, habit clusters...but as a set of control mechanisms—plans, recipes, rules, instructions...for the governing of behavior. The second idea is that man is precisely the animal most desperately dependent upon such

extragenetic, outside the skin mechanisms, such cultural programs, for ordering his behavior (1973: 44).

The concern for meaning requires that anthropologists attempt to get at what Geertz calls the 'native point of view'. That is, even though anthropologists do come to a culture with their own categories and analytical agendas, ideally they should also try to comprehend how the social actors themselves structure and explain their culturally constructed reality. Some critics of the interpretive position claim that historical changes and issues of power that are manifest in the creation, legitimation and control of meaning are ignored by this perspective, but nothing could be farther from the truth. From the very beginning of his career Geertz has been interested in the interrelationship, for instance, of economics and ideologies to cultural meanings (see Handler 1983).[10] Each of these factors is integral to the construal of meaning in any culture in whatever context.

In a manner consonant with this view of culture, in another oft-cited essay entitled 'Religion as a Cultural System' (1973: 87-125), Geertz defines religion as:

> (1) a system of symbols which acts to (2) establish powerful, pervasive, and long-lasting moods and motivations in men by (3) formulating conceptions of a general order of existence and (4) clothing these conceptions with such an aura of factuality that (5) the moods and motivations seem uniquely realistic (1973: 90).

Religion weds a certain social construction and its ethos with a particular world view: attitudes, behavioral patterns, social roles and an explanation of reality now cohere with divine sanction and are grounded in transcendent 'truth'. Through religion, a cultural world has an order and rhythm, whose significance is communicated and celebrated by means of sacred images and rituals at various levels, whether formally through a whole set of institutions at specified cult centers and pilgrimage sites or more informally on a smaller scale at local shrines by various groupings, such as families or religious fraternities. Issues of survival and prosperity, health and fertility are given an accounting for and significance. Rites of passage are transcribed in particular ways, and so those crossroad moments of life are encountered within a comprehen-

10. For a recent example of this criticism, note Wolf 1999: 59–60. For a survey of critiques of Geertz from various points of view with a response based on several of his works, see Carroll R. 1992: 52-63.

sible set of meanings. What is important to grasp is that through religion a culture achieves a powerful and pervasive facticity and an interpretability. Metaphysics, in other words, makes life seem so much common sense. This shared religious appreciation of everyday life and society in all of its multiple dimensions cuts across class, ethnic and gender lines.

Yet the coherence offered by religion should not be equated with a monolithic religious homogeneity. While individuals and groups from the broad spectrum can and do share symbols and participate in the same rituals, at the same time they also can embrace different facets of religious experience or give these symbols and rituals somewhat distinct explications or emphases according to their particular social station, gender, ideological commitment or economic status. What is more, not all the observants of the religion are equally able to articulate or are completely conscious of all (the actual or possible) meanings which are being transmitted by the religious symbols or rituals. At this point, the criticisms of Geertz mentioned earlier concerning historical change and power again surface (e.g. Asad 1983; Munson 1986), but now in relation to religious meanings. Once more, Geertz does not disregard or mystify these realities, but instead places them within a dynamic matrix (1960: 355-81; 1973: 142-69, 311-41; 1983: 121-46; cf. Carroll R. 1992: 56-57). The coherence and commonalities (whether behavioral, attitudinal, ideational or existential), in other words, coexist with complexity. Religion is part and parcel of a wider cultural system of meanings, where much is shared, even as there are some dissonance and variations.

To speak of 'popular religion' within the framework of interpretive anthropology, accordingly, requires rethinking the paradigms which currently inform many of the current studies of ancient Israelite religion. From this perspective 'popular religion' would refer to the religion of the general population and would not be limited to certain subgroups. It is not to be reduced to religious phenomena which are in opposition to 'official religion', nor is the latter simply defined as the ideological weapon of the dominant classes. There is a recognition that what is professed and practiced by the people as a whole includes elements of both official religion and what lies beyond its purview. It bears repeating that interpretive anthropology does not dismiss struggles over meanings or diversity in rituals and religious perspective within this broader agreement.

Some might suggest that this more phenomenological take on 'popular religion' is sociologically imprecise, but I am persuaded that it is *culturally realistic*. This understanding of popular religion, I feel, can help clarify some of the descriptions of religious realities that are found in the biblical material. I would quickly add that it is my hope that the insights gained from interpretive anthropology in an investigation of the same biblical data handled from other methodological starting points might complement other reconstructions and assist current scholarship in attaining a more comprehensive picture of the religion of ancient Israel.

One scholar who has utilized Geertz's view of culture as 'webs of significance' is Thomas Overholt (1996a: 3-23; cf. Keel and Uehlinger 1998: 7-9, 405-407). His discussion of the usefulness of anthropology for explicating the social realities that are the backdrop of the textual world of the prophets is pertinent in two respects. First, against sceptics who see little historical value in the biblical representations of Israelite life (e.g. Carroll 1990), Overholt claims that cross-cultural comparisons can help the reader to discern consistent and well-known patterns of behavior that are visible in the text—that is, broad cultural experiences and institutions which inform a text's representation. However one might judge the accuracy of certain textual particulars, the comparative data makes it possible to say that the text is reflecting actual social realites (1990, 1996a:1-23).[11] This stance will inform my use of anthropological theory in my work in the book of Amos.

Second, Overholt uses an interpretive approach in his study of Israelite religion. He offers, for instance, extended analyses of the Elijah and Elisha narratives, which he examines in light of shamanism (1996a: 24-68) and in relationship to popular religion (1996b). Citing our own work (Carroll R. 1992) as a helpful orientation to appreciate more fully the shamanism which he discovers in the text, he says:

> it [i.e. shamanism] was not the property of a special group or groups, but pervaded the whole of society. Still it was not entirely independent of the other threads of belief and practice with which it was woven. It was,

11. Within prophetic studies different scholars defend the plausibility of the representations of the text in several manners. Whereas Overholt utilizes cross-cultural comparisons from the study of more modern societies and the insights from anthropology, others are responding to the overly skeptical by presenting comparisons with ancient materials (e.g. Barstad 1993). Laato combines some of this data with a proposal coupled with semiotic theory (Laato 1996).

rather, an integral part of a multifaceted Israelite religion during the
period of the monarchy (1996b: 111).

The key issue here is that Overholt detects the interclass and cross-
gender nature of much of religious life. He points out how people as
diverse as, for example, a widow, a wealthy woman, a slave girl, military personnel and a king each seek out the services of the shaman
(Elisha) for help in time of need (2 Kings 2–5). All, from their very different backgrounds and probably in different ways, hold in common a
belief in the power of the man of God.

b. *Latin American Popular Roman Catholicism as a Test Case*
These insights from an interpretive anthropology approach can be illustrated by means of a brief consideration of Latin American popular
Roman Catholicism.[12] This concrete example can serve to make the
preceding discussion of popular religion more comprehensible.

With the arrival of the Spanish *conquistadores* in the fifteenth and
sixteenth centuries to what is now Latin America came the imposition
of an imperialistic Iberian Christendom (Mires 1986, 1987; Rivera
1992). The cross came with the sword, colonialization with Christian-
ization. Sadly, the invasion was accompanied by a series of devastating
epidemics, as the indigenous peoples suffered for the first time diseases
brought by the Spaniards. The indigenous often were 'converted' with
threats of violence, social destruction and slave labor. Although there
were a few, of whom Bartolomé de las Casas is the stellar example (see
Carroll R. 1995a), who exhibited a genuine concern for indigenous wel-
fare and culture, the process of subduing the continent generally was
quite brutal. There is disagreement over the nature of the hybrid born of
the mixing of the religion of the Catholic clerics and orders and the
religious notions of the Spanish soldiers and settlers with the beliefs of
the conquered peoples. Debate continues over to what degree the resulting syncretism was authentically Christian or 'pagan'.[13]

---

12. A thoroughgoing study of popular religion in Latin America would obviously need to take into account other religious movements and phenomena, such as
the impressive growth of Protestant Pentecostalism. My discussion will be limited
to popular religion within the Roman Catholic tradition.

13. Mention should be made here of the recent movements desiring to reflect
upon the possible relationship between traditional and modern indigenous beliefs
and Christian faith, whether Roman Catholic or Protestant. See Cook 1997.

Since that time the many different countries that make up Latin America have been held together by a common language and a shared set of mores and attitudes, but the Roman Catholic faith also has offered a variously thick culturo-religious umbrella, whose ethos and world view has been nurtured and sustained in part by its rituals, feasts and symbols. The complex popular religion of Latin America incorporates what is presented and taught by the official institutions and personnel of the Roman Catholic Church but celebrates, too, what has been believed and practiced through extra-official traditions over the centuries (cf. Maldonado 1985: 61-179).

Today this popular religion is diagnosed and explained from various points of view (cf. Kselman 1986; Carroll R. 1992: 92-109). To begin with, it is clear from official documents that the Roman Catholic hierarchy acknowledges just how deep are the roots of popular faith in the hearts of Latin Americans. Prayer to saints and Mary, the processions of *Semana Santa* (Holy or Easter Week), the ritual of the mass and rites of passage (such as the baptism of infants, First Communion, weddings, Extreme Unction) are just some of the many pieces of the religious cloth of the continent as a whole. This recognition, however, carries with it an ambiguous evaluation. What are appreciated are the sincerity and spontaneity, as well as the contribution this popular religion can make to propagating at least some level of orthodox belief (e.g. credence in a transcendent deity, the Trinity, sin, the nativity and the crucifixion.). At the same time, the church is wary of the superstition and heterodox syncretism evident in the constellation of phenomena that make up the religion of the people. The hierachy feels that these need purification through catechesis and evangelization (cf. CELAM 1979, par. 444-69, 913-14; 1992, par. 36, 39, 53, 247).

The perspective of liberation theology, in contrast, can be better appreciated by understanding the significance in Spanish of the term *lo popular*. This phrase in common parlance refers to the poor masses and can be applied to any number of spheres.[14] The meaning of *la religión popular* then naturally would denote the beliefs and practices of the disenfranchised, marginalized and subaltern groups in society. The focus, therefore, is not on an extensive, overarching religion but on distinctions dealing with economics, ethnicity and gender.

---

14. E.g., in Spanish, *organizaciones populares* would refer to labor unions and solidarity groups.

Earlier statements by liberationists were critical of the popular religion thus defined. They considered it alienating, because it seemed
characterized by a passive fatalism before the hegemonic claims of the
ruling classes and by a profound superstition unable to challenge the
status quo. In other words, popular religion was devoid of a strong
social consciousness. Significant changes for the benefit of the oppressed could occur only through the efforts of minority, vanguard grass-
roots Christian groups, that would be able to challenge destructive
religious, cultural and socio-political realities (e.g. Segundo 1976: 183-
207; cf. Candelaria 1990: 69-101). This desired sort of religious commitment was supposed to be incarnated in a specific kind of 'popular'
church, the 'base ecclesial communities', which were to live out a new
kind of Christian faith—even if this might mean getting involved in
social protest movements and revolution (Berryman 1984; Dussel 1986;
cf. Carroll R. 1992: 137-39).

More recently liberation theologians have revisited this negative
opinion (e.g. Irarrázaval 1991; cf. Candelaria 1990; Ribeiro de Oliveira
1994; Peterson 1998). Though still feeling that Latin American popular
Roman Catholicism does not seem to perceive properly systemic issues
or offer concrete solutions to social ills, now liberationists commend it
for the spirit of solidarity it sustains, its 'oral' theology of suffering and
survival, the joy of the local festivals, and the involvement of women.
Popular religion is said to be a genuine expression of Christian faith
with a profound potential for liberation and mobilization, if some of the
symbols can be redefined and rituals redirected. This perspective on
popular religion has been championed as well by some social scientists,
who also would like to see the faith of the poor empowered for constructive social change. Parker, for instance, attempts an analysis of
popular religion within the multiple changes wrought by capitalistic
modernization. The 'popular' is contrasted with the religion of the elite
and dominant classes. His is a hope for a liberative 'popular' Christianity to counteract the destructive forces of capitalism and to improve the
life of the poor (1996; cf. Maduro 1982, Levine 1993).

In contrast to this oppositional view, the Roman Catholic Church has
always maintained that the broadly shared popular religion is a crucial
cultural reality that helps hold Latin American societies together:

> This religion of the people is lived preferentially by the 'poor and the
> simple', but it includes every social sector and sometimes is one of the
> few ties that unites people in our nations that are so politically divided.

Yet, it must be recognized that this unity contains multiple diversity according to social, ethnic and even generations (CELAM 1979, par. 447, my translation).

For the purposes of my discussion, it must be noted that liberation theologians, while defending a subaltern perspective on popular religion, at the same time admit that many beliefs and practices do indeed cross class lines in all sorts of ways. Some would even acknowledge that their view of the 'popular' and the 'popular' church never gained many adherents on the ground, that their acute social analysis and idealistic hopes for change have not actually matched the religious perceptions of most Latin Americans. Their rhetoric and ideology were actually quite removed from the majority of Roman Catholics in Latin America, especially the poor (see Berryman 1994). In an important caveat Parker confesses that

it is rather difficult to draw a narrow line between what is popular religion as authentic expression of the subordinate classes and groups, and popular religion as expression of the 'mean' or average manifestations of the gross believing public in mass society ... in Latin American countries, with their Catholic majorities, there are certain religious traits common to the upper and middle classes and the working, subproletarian, peasant, village groups and the mass of unemployed and underemployed. Available data indicate rather the presence of a *continuum* in religious manifestations (1996: 36-37).

He adds

In sum, although the religious element, as part of the cultural field of the classes, does not always maintain a direct correlation with the *objective class situations* of the actors, at least it occurs in correspondence—complex correspondence, and not immediate, via the mediation of the field of practices—with the *class positions* of the actors, and this not in external fashion but on the basis of its role in the constitution and internal configuration of the different class positions (1996: 38).

In other words, differences are visible, but with these there are also commonalities. A helpful example of this cultural religious reality can be found in the veneration of the Virgin Mary. The Virgin became the patroness of New Spain in 1754, and she is believed to have miraculously appeared at different times and circumstances up and down the continent. The shared faith in Mary is evident, for example, in the multiple appeals to her made by Pope John Paul II in his visit to Central America in 1983 (e.g. Pablo II 1983: 117-18, 153-60) and in official

Latin American Church documents (e.g. CELAM 1979, par. 282-303). The most famous of these Virgins is Nuestra Señora de Guadelupe in Mexico City.

This apparition of Mary is said to have occurred in 1531. The impact of the apparition lies in that she appeared to an indigenous convert in native dress and spoke to him in his Nahuatl tongue. Although there is considerable scholarly and ecclesiastical debate about the historicity of the tradition, its ascendance to prominence, and the relationship of the symbolism of the Virgin to the pre-Colombian goddess Tonantzin (contrast Poole 1995 and Elizondo 1997), all agree that ultimately this vision of Mary helped provide access to God for the indigenous. Her utilization of indigenous symbols and language also helped legitimize in part the indigenous culture and allowed for the acceptance, contextualization and propagation of Catholic faith (Gebara and Bingemer 1989: 144-54; Parker 1996: 98-100; Elizondo 1987, 1997; Espín 1997: 73-77; cf. CELAM 1979, par. 282; 1992: par. 229).

Prayers to and worship of the Virgin Mary draw men, women and children from every country and all social classes. This adoration can reflect for some a resignation before the harsh troubles of life; for others she is a compassionate succor in times of trouble; for still others she is a stimulus to charitable deeds. The Virgin can be claimed by Latin American feminist theologians (e.g. Gebara and Bingemer), as well as by pastoral workers among North American Hispanics (Elizondo 1997). In Mexico the Virgin of Guadelupe became the rallying cry for Father Miguel Hidalgo y Costilla's push for national independence from Spain in the early nineteenth century, the revolution of the disenfranchised led by Emiliano Zapata in 1910, and more recently for the Zapatista rebellion in the southern state of Chiapas. Clearly this veneration crisscrosses gender, class and ideological lines and has been maintained over centuries.

To summarize, the data from Latin America demonstrate both profound coherence and many differences within popular religion. Interpretive anthropology views religion within a culture's 'webs of significance', and popular religion therefore as the faith of a people. This concept of popular religion will be the theoretical basis which we will use in our study in the next chapter on popular religion within the book of Amos. There is still one more methodological piece that must be dealt before moving to that biblical text. It is to be remembered that while a fundamental issue in any discussion on popular religion in ancient Israel must be the definition of the term itself, the second is the value of the Bible as a source in that endeavor.

c. *The Bible as a Source for the Study of Popular Religion: A Suggestion*
As was mentioned earlier, it has become a commonplace to minimize the value of the biblical text for the study of ancient Israelite religion on the basis of a claim that its presentation of the religious phenomena is skewed because of its ideology. Of course, not all who investigate Israelite popular religion and who exhibit this 'hermeneutic of suspicion' bent have these same explicit social concerns but are merely interested in recovering what they feel would be a more legitimate picture of religious life in the past.

Nevertheless, it is apparent that in many studies that criticize the text a host of theoretical issues can be either ignored or unsatisfactorily glided over. To begin with, the meaning of the term 'ideology' is sometimes simply assumed without serious reflection. A perusal of social science literature, however, readily reveals that it has been given a wide spectrum of very different definitions (e.g. Giddens 1979: 165-97; Eagleton 1991: 1-31). In addition, more circumspect approaches would acknowledge just how difficult it is to ascertain enough solid information from within and outside a text to identify its possible ideology (the issue of available data) and also would recognize that there is no transparent and neat connection between the ideology of the producers of that text and what is actually 'put down on paper' (the issue of theory: the sociology of literature). One must ask if contemporary attempts to label the ideology of the biblical text have the requisite amount of information concerning the relevant socioeconomic, historical, religious and literary influences and variables that stand behind and within the text to able to speak very confidently of having discovered its ideology (see Jameson 1981; cf. Carroll R. 1992: 31-47, 162-73).

Any attempt to identify the ideology of a text is further complicated if the scholar posits any sort of redactional stages, because then the problems multiply. The challenge now involves not only specifying the discreet ideology of each redactional layer but also comprehending the 're-ideolization' of the earlier levels by the addition of later material. Recent discussions about orality, literacy, and the genesis of the biblical books as written artifacts should exacerbate these issues even further (e.g. Niditch 1996). Lastly, it is important to be cognizant of the history of the ideological interpretations and uses of texts. This information can enlighten the actual and potential utilization of these texts in the present. Is our 'discovery' of a text's ideology simply another self-projection upon that text (Fowl 1995)?

These caveats are not designed to discourage totally the attempts to get at the ideologies of texts, but rather to encourage scholars who study Israelite religion to be more cautious in their pronouncements about ideology. Most who pursue an ideological approach also do so from an oppositional framework. That is, whatever religious ideologies are postulated—and hence the groups that generate (or suffer under) them and the texts and traditions that these groups produce—are situated as polar antagonists. Little room is left for cultural coherence and cohesion, and some level of shared religious experience, belief and practice. In contrast, and not unexpectedly, interpretive anthropology formulates ideology as a realm of culture. Geertz criticizes other principal explanations of ideology and suggests that ideologies should be comprehended within and as systems of meaning (1973: 193-233). This observation, of course, returns to my earlier discussion of popular religion. But at this point of wrestling with the ideology of the biblical text and the question about whether to give it credence, interpretive anthropology can aid the researcher of Israelite religion in yet another way by reorienting the definition of what the biblical text might be taken as.

Instead of reducing the text to little more than a theological piece of a more general hegemonic ideological agenda, I would propose that the biblical text might better be received as *an ethnographic report*—that is, as a description of sociocultural realities from a certain perspective, or, within anthropological parlance, as one native's point of view.[15] Interpretive anthropology has become increasingly self-conscious of how subjective ethnographic accounts are. In a revealing, and often entertaining, 'exposé' of the work of four giants of anthropology (Lévi-Strauss, Evans-Pritchard, Malinowski and Bendict) Geertz demonstrates how factors like personal background, the state of the profession and socio-historical context all contribute to the way anthropological reports are written (1988).[16] His description of tensions in his field today dealing with the acceptability of ethnographic reports sounds much like

15. Whether representative of a particular party or just of one individual is yet another theoretical discussion.

16. In a subsequent book Geertz reflects upon his own field work and writing (Geertz 1995).

what is being heard within biblical scholarship. Objectivity is now suspect, accuracy doubted, written sources maligned:

> What is at hand is a pervasive nervousness about the whole business of claiming to explain enigmatic others on the grounds that you have gone about with them in their native habitat or combed the writings of those who have. This nervousness brings on, in turn, various responses, variously excited: deconstructive attacks on canonical works, and on the very idea of canonicity as such; *Ideologiekritik* unmaskings of anthropological writings as the continuation of imperialism by other means; clarion calls to reflexivity, dialogue, heteroglossia, linguistic play, rhetorical self-consciousness, performative translation, verbatim recording, and first-person narrative as forms of cure (1988: 130-31).

He goes on to add:

> All this is made more dire, leading to distracted cries of plight and crisis, by the fact that at the same time as the moral foundations of ethnography have been shaken by decolonization on the Being There side [i.e. field research], its epistemological foundations have been shaken by a general loss of faith in received stories about the nature of representation, ethnographic or other, on the Being Here side [i.e. the writing of ethnography for an audience]. Confronted in the academy by a sudden explosion of polemical prefixes (neo-, post-, meta-, anti-) and subversive title forms (*After Virtue, Against Method, Beyond Belief*), anthropologists have had added to their 'Is it decent?' worry (Who are *we* to describe *them*?) an 'Is it possible?' one... with which they are even less prepared to deal (1988: 135).

Geertz recognizes that anthropology, and hence ethnographic writing, is profoundly hermeneutical and that questions currently surfacing are very legitimate. But this awareness in no way moves him either to abandon the effort to investigate cultures or to disparage the contributions made by those who strive to write about them. What can be lacking is a clear view of the issues and a balanced approach to the sources.

> The disarray may not be permanent, because the anxieties that provoke it may prove masterable with a clearer recognition of their proper origin. The basic problem is neither the moral uncertainty involved in telling stories about how other people live nor the epistemological one involved in casting those stories in scholarly genres... The problem is that now that such matters are coming to be discussed in the open, rather than covered over with a professional mystique, the burden of authorship seems suddenly heavier. Once ethnographic texts begin to be looked *at* as well as through, once they are seen to be made, and made to persuade, those who make them have rather more to answer for. Such a situation

may initially alarm, producing back-to-the-facts table thumping in the
establishment and will-to-power gauntlet throwing in its adversaries. But
it can, given tenacity enough and courage, be gotten used to (1988: 138).

Much of what Geertz points out can be transferred to research into
ancient Israelite religion. The drive to more adequately comprehend the
religious faith and practices of the ancients (how others lived: the
'Being There') is coupled with modern moral and epistemological mis-
givings, which can lead to the discrediting of the biblical text as a
viable report (the representation of those others to readers of another
place and time: the 'Being Here').

The Bible certainly attempts to persuade its readers of its view of the
nature of the religion of Israel (i.e. its contours and truth value) through
its rhetoric and presentation. Yet, such is what one should expect of any
ethnographic report of a religion and a society. At this point a final constructive notion that can be drawn from interpretive anthropology is the
emic–etic distinction. In simple terms, 'emics' refers to the 'native
point of view', while 'etics' points to the conceptual categories and
analysis of an outside observer. Emic accounts offer descriptions of
cultural phenomena in ways that are understandable and acceptable to
the people in question or which, in fact, actually are given by them. On
the other hand, etic accounts attempt to provide testable and verifiable
procedures to help comparative studies, especially those concerned with
infrastructural causes (Harris 1979: 32-56; Headland, Pike and Harris
1990; Carroll R., 1992: 54-63). The biblical text, therefore, would offer
an emic account, whereas efforts by scholars to ascertain 'objective'
descriptions apart from (or according to critical studies and reconstructions of) that text can be classified as etic studies. Both, of course, are
valuable and necessary; each has its own contribution to make. Accordingly, as an emic account, the biblical text needs to be appreciated and
understood in its own right (cf. Brett 1990). This endeavor requires that
this account be given a careful reading. It is my conviction that an
interpretive anthropological approach to religion can help illuminate the
particulars of this ethnographic report.

Seen in this light, the biblical text can be arrayed alongside of other
ancient written reports and other non-written artifacts as important evidence for the reconstruction of ancient Israelite religion. It will not do
to dismiss this account too summarily. What makes the biblical account
more problematic, to be sure, is its status as Scripture; but it still is *an*
account of the past. Certainly, scholars should continue as well to probe

the possible factions and factors that lie behind the biblical text (while also keeping my aforementioned cautions in mind). Now, however, that text will not be put aside simply because it might have an ideology deemed by some to be unsatisfactory.

4. *Conclusion*

This essay has concentrated on two basic issues within the study of ancient Israelite religion: the definition of popular religion and the use of the Bible in this research. It has been argued that the lens provided by interpretive anthropology allows for a distinct appreciation of religious life and, thus, of the biblical presentation of popular religion in ancient Israel. Popular religion is understood as part of shared cultural realities and not limited to the beliefs and practices of the marginalized. The biblical text can also be read as an ethnographic report and appropriately included with other evidence in the attempt to reconstruct the past.

'FOR SO YOU LOVE TO DO':
PROBING POPULAR RELIGION IN THE BOOK OF AMOS

M. Daniel Carroll R.

1. *Introduction: Religious Polemics in Amos?*

The denunciation of the cult in the Book of Amos has long held the attention of biblical scholars. Convictions concerning the precise nature of the prophetic critique, however, span a wide spectrum of points of view. Scholars differ over whether the book's message targets only some aberrant form of Yahweh worship or if, and to what degree, the text is concerned with adoration of other deities. I offer here a brief summary of various positions with some representative examples. This survey will help set the framework for my own discussion of popular religion in Amos, which will be developed later in this essay.

At one end of the spectrum are those who hold that the text's polemics target the cult per se. Beginning in the last century, a number of Old Testament scholars championed the notion that the prophets (in particular those of the eighth century) sought not to reform Israel's worship but rather that they helped carry Israel's faith in Yahweh to the pinnacle of its ideals by promoting an 'ethical monotheism'—that is, a pure form of that faith grounded in a profound social morality. One of the early proponents of this position, of course, was Julius Wellhausen. According to his reconstruction of the history of religion in Israel, the freedom of religious spirit exemplified by these early prophets was later stymied and eventually killed by the propagation of the Torah following the reforms of Josiah, which were an important first step toward the deadening religiosity that would be put forward as the paradigm in the Exile and afterward (1957: 402-404, 422-25). With his customary eloquence Wellhausen introduces the person of the prophet Amos into his history of Israel. He sets the scene as a cultic celebration at Bethel:

> The multitude were assembled there with gifts and offerings for the observance of a festival, when there stepped forward a man whose grim

seriousness interrupted the joy of the feast. It was a Judean, Amos of Tekoa, a shepherd from the wilderness bordering on the Dead Sea. Into the midst of the joyful tones of the songs which with harp and tabor were being sung at the sacred banquet he brought the discordant note of the mourner's wail (1957: 472).

The ethical message of these prophets, Wellhausen believed, was designed to push Israel beyond nationalism, superstition and ritualism:

> Neither Jehovah nor his prophets recognizes two moral standards; right is everywhere right, wrong always wrong... What Jehovah demands is righteousness—nothing more, nothing less; what he hates is injustice. Sin or offence to the Deity is a thing of purely moral character; with such emphasis this doctrine had never before been heard. Morality is that for the sake of which all things exist; it is the alone essential thing in the world. It is no postulate, no idea, but at once a necessity and a fact, the most intensely living of personal powers—Jehovah the God of Hosts. In wrath, in ruin, this holy reality makes its existence known; it annihilates all that is hollow and false (1957: 472).

In time scholarship reacted against this view,[1] arguing that the prophets were not innovators; instead, it was said, they reworked earlier traditions. What is more, against the Near Eastern background a cultless religion would have made little sense. The 'ethical monotheism' interpretation, therefore, was more of a projection back of modern values onto ancient Israel. Nevertheless, more recently, from a different conceptual framework and with a very distinct motivation, some liberationist biblical scholars have argued for a similar position concerning these prophetic texts. They claim that within the struggles of the oppressed it is now once again recognized that Yahweh can be known only through the practice of inter-human justice. Only this understanding of the prophetic message can properly explain the categorical condemnation of the cult found in passages like Amos 4.4-5; 5.21-25. In other words, there can be no worship without justice and equity (e.g. Miranda 1974: 44-67; Richard *et al.* 1980; Pixley 1988; cf. Carroll R. 1992: 299-306). Other scholars of other persuasions also have expressed an appreciation and sympathy for the understanding of the

---

1.   At a later stage in Amos studies there were those who argued for the opposite of this early view and held that Amos was actually a cultic prophet. Others have been more circumspect and recognize cultic influences (e.g. language, literary forms) but do not see him as a professional prophet serving at the worship centers. For a summary and bibliography, see Carroll R. 1992: 307-309.

nature of eighth-century prophets propounded by Wellhausen (cf. Barton 1986).

A second option accounts for the diatribes against the cult in a political fashion. From this perspective, any possible allusions to other deities are pushed to the background in light of the perceived ideological concerns of the text. For Polley (1989), Amos's attack derives from the prophetic conviction that the only proper place of worship is Jerusalem. Therefore, the prophet criticizes the Northern monarchy and its cult, because it represents a rebellious systemic alternative to the Davidic dynasty—a kingdom approved of by God and sanctioned by the Temple of Zion. Hayes (1988) also interprets the religious polemics politically, but in his particular historical reconstruction the conflict discernible in the book of Amos is between a faction supporting Pekah and his claim to the throne in Samaria and another defending the pro-Assyrian policies of Jeroboam II's regime. Each party would have had rival theological justifications and cults, but both stood under the condemning eye of the prophet.

A third (and the largest) group of scholars contend, as did the first, that the primary focus of the message of Amos lies in a strident demand for social justice. In contrast to that earlier position, however, this ethical call is not presented as the prophetic alternative to the cult. Instead, these interpreters hold that the prophet indicts Israel for religious hypocrisy—that is, for the lack of congruity between the realities of personal and national life and the cultic celebrations. In addition, some of this persuasion would acknowledge that the received text does allude to other deities, although there are those who suggest that these references are later additions and not part of the original message.

Wolff, for instance, opines that the prophet Amos did not direct his diatribe against other gods. Any such material, in his mind, comes from subsequent redactors, beginning with what he calls the 'Amos school' of disciples (1977: 101-103; cf. Coote 1981: 11-45; Albertz 1994: 171-80). Consequently, verses which some cite as possible references to non-Yahwistic worship are either dated after the time of the prophet or interpreted in another fashion: the mention of other deities in 5.26 suggests to Wolff this verse's provenance after the fall of Samaria and the influence brought by Assyrian deportation policies (1977: 112, 265-66; note 2 Kgs 17.29-33); and 8.14 does not point to other gods but rather to local varieties of Yahweh worship (1977: 325-33).

In a similar vein, Jeremias contrasts the clearer reproach of other deities in Hosea with the message of Amos. Thus, 5.26 and 8.14 (the latter of which he does believe speaks of other deities) would be redactional additions (1998: 105, 151-53, respectively). Yet, in his mind, these later lines do not in fact contradict the original preaching of the prophet. Amos's tradents did not simply juxtapose new passages to the foundational words of the prophet in order to meet the theological and pastoral needs of another time and place. They would have sensed a continuity with his criticism of the cult and hence expanded it in a natural and organic way to include the condemnation of other deities.

Other commentators, however, do not date these passages late and propose that almost the entirety of the book of Amos is authentic and can be traced back to the prophet. They, too, would insist that the book of Amos's fundamental emphasis is on social justice and the demand that the cult reflect and encourage proper ethical standards; at the same time, they also hold that the text is concerned with syncretism. Nevertheless, there is disagreement among these scholars about the extent of this concern. For example, Shalom Paul believes that the book does not mention explicitly the worship of idols, with the possible exception of 5.26 (1991: 194-98); 8.14 would speak of different appellations of Yahweh at local shrines (1991: 268-72). On the other hand, Andersen and Freedman do see polemics against other deities at, for instance, 2.7b-8, 5.26, and 8.14 (1989: 318-19, 533-37, 706-711, respectively).

The fourth and final position in this brief overview is that the fundamental aim of the book is to oppose other deities, whom the general populace follow instead of or in addition to Yahweh. The best representative of this position is Barstad. He places the ministry of the prophet Amos within a reconstruction of the rise of monotheistic Yahwism in Israel, a long and complex historico-religious process in which the prophets played a crucial role:

> The fight fought between the Yahwistic prophets was primarily of a religious/polemical, if also of an ethical, character. Their main concern was to convince their fellow countrymen that Yahweh was the only god worth worshipping. He alone could help them in their daily life and with the provision of the fertility so vital to their existence (1984: 10).

According to this Scandinavian scholar, references against Baalism are ubiquitous. Amos's preaching then was a 'missionary activity' to show his people that Yahweh alone could bring prosperity and posterity (4.6-12). Non-Yahwistic elements which had found their way into the cult had to be eliminated (4.4-5, 5.21-24), the syncretistic *marzeaḥ* feast avoided (2.7b-8, 4.1, 6.4-7), and other deities shunned (5.26, 8.14).

It is evident that there is a wide range of opinions concerning the meaning of the religious polemics in the book of Amos. The challenge for this essay will be to try to offer a reading of this prophetic text which can make sense of its critique of religious life in Israel.

2. *Methodological Considerations*

The theoretical underpinning for this discussion comes from the perspective on religion offered by interpretive anthropology in the previous essay. By way of a brief summary, it will be remembered, to begin with, that for interpretive anthropology religion, through its belief system, set of symbols and activities, helps give a particular culture or society a measure of coherence, meaning and transcendent legitimation. This cohesiveness, however, does not imply absolute homogeneity. Individuals, groups and social classes can celebrate some different religious ceremonies, have different understandings of the religion's symbols and cult, and even seek out other deities or divine beings; there also might very well be some measure of conflict over religious meanings. Still, some interconnectedness exists that transcends social particulars because of what is shared by all. This shared religious canopy, the 'popular religion', can include elements of both official and extra-official religion.

In addition, I also proposed that the biblical text be considered an ethnographic report—that is, a perspective from one 'native's point of view'—of life in ancient Israel. An important task then, whatever one's stance vis-à-vis the historical reliability of the Bible, is to try to read carefully that report as part of the gathering of evidence on ancient Israelite religion. My purpose here is to attempt such a reading of the book of Amos.

Two other preliminary issues need to be articulated before proceeding to my study of this prophetic text. First, I recognize that there are a plethora of theories concerning the composition of Amos.[2] Nevertheless, for this essay, I will present just two understandings of the textual data. One will work with the premise that all of the book can be considered as reflective of the general cultural context of the eighth-century

---

2. Helpful surveys of these theories can be found in the commentaries and in introductions to the book (e.g. Martin-Achard 1984: 52-74; Auld 1986: 50-59; Hasel 1991: 91-99).

prophet or his immediate circle. The other will reflect the fact that for many critical scholars two key passages for my discussion are later redactional expansions (5.26, 8.14). I will have to consider if and in what way their addition might alter the picture of what was actually the state of religious life in the days of Amos. This decision to limit the readings to two for some might appear to oversimplify the interpretive options, but it will make the material in Amos more manageable for an essay such as this. In addition, it also reflects the notion that cultural backdrops can cover broad sweeps of time (Overholt 1996a: 1-23), so the credibility of the readings is therefore not necessarily compromised.

Finally, there are several verses which will not be included in the following discussion. On the one hand, some will not be considered, because their possible contribution is dependent on a hypothetical emendation and/or the proposals of some scholars have not met with widespread acceptance. Such is the case for suggestions that references to Molech/Milchom appear at 1.15 and 2.1 (e.g. Puech 1977; Albright 1968: 209; yet see Heider 1985: 301-10; Day 1989: 72-81) and that Baal worship is alluded to at 4.1 (e.g. Watts 1972; Williams 1979; Neher 1981: 82-85; Barstad 1984: 37-47; Jacobs 1985). On the other hand, other verses that could be veiled allusions and indirect polemics against other deities also will not be scrutinized. Such is the case, for instance, of the so-called doxologies of Amos, where Yahweh is presented as the one who strides over the 'high places' (4.13) and is the creator of the stars (5.8; e.g. Wolff 1977: 217-18, 224; Watts 1997: 9-27). Even though a fully comprehensive survey of the book's material would incorporate and evaluate all of this information, the limitations of this essay require that I concentrate on those passages that speak more explicitly of religious activities, centers and attitudes.

3. *'Popular Religion' in Amos: A Prophetic Ethnography*

a. *The 'What' and the 'Who' of Israel's Worship*
The religious scene within the book of Amos is complex. I begin my study of the material by identifying the activities and the participants in Israel's religious life. After a survey of the religious activities, the next major section of this essay will attempt to articulate the purpose and essence of the prophetic critique of Israel's popular religion.

Some passages seem to describe the religious activities of those who in some way are in positions of authority and influence, while others

Rethinking Contexts, Rereading Texts

record the worship of the nation in general. What can make the effort to correlate activities with specific segments of the population difficult is that a close reading of the text reveals a constant movement back and forth within the same literary units between phrases and passages that include both the broader populace as well as more particular groups within Israel.

Four passages dealing with dominant groups or personalities stand out. The first is 2.8, which occurs in the initial pericope denouncing the social sins of Israel (2.6-8).[3] Interpreters disagree over the referents for 'every altar' and בית אלהיהם. Is the text speaking of things that are occurring at various yahwistic cultic centers, such as that which might occur at the holy places explicitly named later in the book?[4] Or, is it pointing to shrines that might be found in the private residencies of those, such as the merchants, who are better off than most (cf. 8.4-6)? Another option is that the target is the worship places of other deities (see below at 5.26, 8.14).[5] Could 'every altar' be linked in any way to the enigmatic high places of 7.9? Whatever the precise nature and location of worship in view here, these sacrilegious excesses are possible only because the powerless have been taken advantage of. Nevertheless, at the same time, the wider context of the oracle (2.6-16) incorporates the people as a whole into the prophetic condemnation. The introductory formula is directed at the nation (2.6a), as is the recounting of Yahweh's gracious acts on behalf of Israel early in her history (2.9-11) and the sweeping list of casualties that closes this section (2.14-16). More pertinent to our concern is the mention of the rejection by the 'sons of Israel' of the nazarites and prophets raised up by God (2.11-12). In this oracle, in other words, the unacceptable worship practices of a

---

3. Some would include v. 7 within the religious critique, because of the clause at the end of the verse (למען חלל את־שם קדשי; cf. Ezek. 20.30; 36.20-22; Lev. 20.3; 22.2, 32). Barstad holds that 2.7-8 refers to a *marzeaḥ* feast, for which the maiden in v. 7 would be the hostess (1984: 33-36). Hammershaimb believes that what is alluded to is cultic prostitution or some sort of immoral sexual practices (1970: 48-49). Andersen and Freedman connect the girl to 8.14, suggesting that this is a reference to a female deity (1989: 318).

4. That is, Bethel, Gilgal, Dan and Beersheba. Note especially the reappearance of 'altar' in relationship to Bethel at 3.14 and 9.1.

5. In that interpretation, אלהיהם could be translated as a plural ('gods'). The translation would reflect the interpreter's understanding of to whom the household shrines are dedicated.

few is part of a wider refusal to respond properly to the voice and will of Yahweh.

The second passage is 6.4-7. Evidence from across the Ancient Near East has helped clarify this celebration as a *marzeaḥ* feast. These banquets, which apparently could go on for several days, were sponsored by wealthy fraternal associations which provided drink and a sumptuous meal. These verses in Amos actually use the term (מִרְזַח, v. 7) and mention several other elements—such as lounging in luxury, fine meats, revelry, and abundant wine and oil—that are readily associated with such a scene. Scholars are not in agreement, however, over the religious significance of the practice. Many relate the *marzeaḥ* to some kind of funerary rites or cult, where mourners could be comforted and the dead (and/or ancestors) or other patron deities honored (see Pope 1972, 1981; Barstad 1984: 127-42; King 1988: 137-61; Smith 1990: 126-32; Bloch-Smith 1992: 125-32; Toorn 1996: 206-35; cf. Jer. 16.7-8). In contrast, Schmidt minimizes the religious component of the *marzeaḥ* in general and in Amos 6.4-7 in particular (1996: 22-23, 62-66, 144-47; cf. Wolff 1977: 277-78; Lewis 1989: 80-94, esp. 88). This text, he says, does not explicitly affirm an interest in the dead, let alone detail any cultic activities. The passage is simply another instance of the book's diatribe against the opulence of the uncaring upper classes.

In my view, although caution is advisable, it seems that the evidence on occasion perhaps does favor the idea of a religious component. It is significant, therefore, that the following verses in fact are concerned with death and mention calling on Yahweh (6.8-10).[6] In addition, unacceptable worship practices are intertwined with injustice elsewhere in the text (2.6-8; 5.4-7, 21-25; 8.4-6), so to say that the pericope is highlighting oppression in no way precludes the possibility of a religious context.[7] It is not clear whether Yahweh or some other deity or spirit is the 'divine' consoler at the banquet. What is unambiguous is that one

6.   This calling on Yahweh in 6.10 is a notoriously difficult line to interpret. On the one hand, although it is not very clear what relatives are trying to do with the dead (see the commentaries and, e.g., Bloch-Smith 1992: 119), the point at issue here is the reality of pervasive loss of life. Schmidt acknowledges this important juxtaposition, but takes the verse as unrelated to 6.7 (1996: 146). On the other hand, there are a wide range of views concerning the meaning of the refusal to call on the name of Yahweh. Note my interpretation below, n. 19.

7.   It is true that in 2.8 and 5.21-25 the text lists specific religious activities. My view is based on a cluster of textual clues in Amos 6 (cf. 2.6-8, 8.4-6), coupled with background of the Ancient Near East.

acquires yet another glimpse of religious activity of a well-to-do sector of society, an activity from the text's point of view which is once more exposed as callous to the realities of those who suffer (v. 6b).

A literary approach can place this pericope about the *marzeaḥ* in 6.4-7 within a coherent structure for the entire chapter, a fact that again suggests that what is performed by smaller groups is in some fashion linked to the attitudes and/or actions of the larger population (cf. Carroll R. 1992: 254-73). To begin with, death comes to all, but yet none desire to call on Yahweh (vv. 9-10). Both the great *and* the small houses will be destroyed in the coming judgment (v. 11). The masses will not wail the loss of life and property within the context of a lavish feast, but they too shall weep all the same in their own way in every place (cf. 5.16-17, 8.10). In other words, no social class will escape the mourning, and no group responds to death and Yahweh in ways the text would consider appropriate.

The third passage relates the confrontation between the prophet and Amaziah the priest at Bethel (7.10-17). Scholars, even those who argue for a redactional history behind the received text, have increasingly come to recognize the multiple interconnections between these verses and the two visions that surround them (i.e. 7.7-9, 8.1-3; see, e.g., the recent discussions in Andersen and Freedman 1989: 751-99; Williamson 1990: 101-105; Clements 1996; Jeremias 1998: 135-42; Noble 1998). This literary fact can help the reader appreciate its present role within the broader religious indictment of chs. 7 and 8.

Amos 7.9 announces the destruction of the 'high places of Isaac' and 'the sanctuaries of Israel'. As with 2.8, the allusion to places of worship is a bit vague: are these sanctuaries and high places for the veneration of Yahweh or of other deities (cf. Catron 1995; Emerton 1997)? Nevertheless, מקדשי ישראל is picked up in 7.10-17, as one particular sanctuary is singled out. There Bethel is called the 'sanctuary of the king (מקדש מלך) and the house (i.e. temple) of the kingdom' (7.13). That is, 7.10-17 present the specification and illustration of judgment of the third vision. Amaziah is concerned about the religious and socio-political issues that the prophetic message might raise for the crowds who come to the temple and alerts the king. In his mind, the reason for the existence of the temple and the kind of worship permitted there are tied up with the fortunes of the kingdom. The priest decries Amos's words as treasonous to the crown (7.10-13).

The prophet's words of doom in 7.17 are followed by the fourth vision (8.1-3). This pericope describes the weeping in the היכל (v. 2), a fitting word choice in light of the preceding prophetic pronouncement of exile and death. The term can mean either 'palace' or 'temple'.[8] The first option could hark back to, for instance, 7.9, 11, 17, while the latter serves as a reminder of 3.14 and could anticipate 9.1. In the case of the former, the scene could be the response to death among the royal family, entourage, and officials (7.9, 11); if the referent is the temple, then the circle of death broadens to include all the worshippers.

In the following verses, the fourth and last passage of this set, unjust merchants surface again in the context of religious activities (8.4-6; cf. 2.6-8). The text reveals that they are participating in the New Moon and Sabbath, while plans of machiavellian greed occupy their thoughts. In contrast to the two more ambiguous passages dealt with earlier (2.8, 6.4-7), there is no doubt that these two celebrations deal with involvement in Yahweh worship by those in positions of privilege and this at yahwistic sanctuaries such as Bethel.[9]

Once more, in accordance with the established pattern, the literary contexts of 7.10-17 and 8.4-6 juxtapose the religious activities and attitudes of the privileged with the people as a whole, who never totally fade from view.[10] The mention of high places and sanctuaries in 7.9 demonstrates an awareness and concern beyond the central sanctuary and cult at Bethel (and also, most assuredly, beyond the other cited worship centers). The prophetic call is to speak against 'my people Israel' (7.15), and Israel will go into exile from its land even as Amaziah will lose his land (7.17). The wailing in the temple will be for the nation Israel, which has become like a basket of over-ripe summer fruit and whose dead lie everywhere (8.1-3, 10). The people, who had rejected the word of God, will suffer a famine for his word throughout the

---

8.   Noble tries to defend the idea that the reference is to the private homes of the wealthy (1998: 432-35).

9.   There has been debate, of course, concerning the possible non-yahwistic background to the New Moon festival (cf. Hallo 1977; Keel and Uehlinger 1998: 298-323; Keel 1998: 102-109). This passage, however, envisions only a context of Yahweh worship.

10.   The juxtaposition of worship and power at Bethel with words against the nation also appears at 3.13-15. There the chastisement decreed for the nation ('house of Jacob' and 'Israel') involves the tearing down of the Bethel altar, as well as of the seasonal homes of the monarchy and the luxurious houses of the wealthy. This passage, however, does not describe any religious activity per se (cf. Carroll R. 1992: 198-201).

land (8.11-13; cf. 2.11-12). In other words, from the perspective of the text, both those privileged by social or economic station as well as the masses go to the same holy places and join together in the same cult. Even if agendas and motivations differ, all are part of a shared religious life and rhythm that Yahweh abhors and will judge at a terrible cost.

Four other passages that bear consideration are 4.4-5, 5.4-6, 5.21-27, and 8.14.[11] None of these, in contrast to the previous four, can be limited to any specific groups within the nation. All underscore the divine rejection of the entire nation's religion. The first is an oracle directed at the 'sons of Israel' (4.5), the second and the third at the 'house of Israel' (5.5, 25), and the context of the last clearly envisions the people as a whole (8.8, 10-12). Each has in view regular cultic activities, and three of the four mention traditional Yahwistic shrines: Bethel (4.4, 5.5), Gilgal (4.4, 5.5), Beersheba (5.6, 8.14), and Dan (8.14). Each passage, as well, has its own particular way of describing Israel's popular religion. 4.4-5 list 'sacrifices', 'tithes', 'thank offerings', and 'free will offerings'; 5.21-23 give another catalogue of rituals: 'festivals', 'solemn assemblies', burnt offerings', 'grain offerings', offerings of 'fatlings', and music. These lists of rites and ceremonies read like a register of familiar items now codified in the Law. Amos 5.4-6 and 8.14, on the other hand, allude to pilgrimages to sacred sites. Interestingly, in 8.14 some of those who swear do so by Beersheba, a site beyond the boundaries of Israel and in the south of Judah (cf. 5.5). Lastly, 5.25 contrasts the unacceptable worship of the present with Israel's relationship with the deity in the desert.[12] In other words, Israel, on the face of things, has a substantially yahwistic tone to its worship.

Two verses, however—5.26 and 8.14—could affect this initial impression of a primary allegiance to Yahweh and have been, in fact, the foci of extensive scholarly debate. The primary interpretive problems of 5.26, which are important for our discussion, can be categorized as lexical (to what do the phrases סכות מלככם and כיון צלמיכם refer?) and historical (can the passage be dated to the eighth century?).[13] In regards

---

11. For detailed readings of 4.4-13, 5.1-17 and 5.21-27 see Carroll R. 1992: 206-18, 221-41 and 245-50, respectively.

12. Some scholars have tried to interpret this verse as a definitive statement of prophetic attitudes to the cult. For a reading of this line within the context of the book of Amos, see Carroll R. 1992: 249-50.

13. The other issues are syntactical: the tense of the verbal form ונשאתם and word order.

to the lexical issue, scholars have generally seen these phrases as some sort of references to other deities, although to exactly whom has proven to be a point of disagreement. Some suggest that סכות and כיון should be repointed[14] and translated in such a way as to mean 'booth' or 'pedestal', with the construct nouns 'your king' and 'your images' as being allusions to other gods or spirits (in addition to the commentaries, see e.g. Weinfeld 1972: 149-50; Gevirtz 1987; Smith 1990: 129, 137; Albertz 1994: 193, 342-43; de Moor 1997: 348-52; DDD 478, 722-23).[15] Many, on the other hand, take סכות to be the transliteration of the name of a Mesopotamian astral deity ([d]SAG.KUD) and כיון to indicate Saturn. Whoever the deity might be, it does not appear to be Yahweh.[16]

The other item of contention in 5.26 concerns the possible dating of the line. There are those who associate the introduction of astral deities into the area with the Assyrian foreign policy of mixing populations, which of course would have occurred after the fall of Samaria (2 Kgs 17.19-31). Amos 5.26 then would be a later Deuteronomistic redaction reflecting the religious realities of the seventh century and could not have played a part in the religious accusations of the historical prophet (e.g. Wolff 1977: 265-66; Loretz 1989; Albertz 1994: 330-31, 342-43; Jeremias 1998: 105; cf. Keel and Uehlinger 1998: 283-372). Other scholars disagree and claim that the worship of astral bodies could have come into Israel earlier via Aramaean influence and contact (McKay 1973: 45-59, 67-73; Cogan 1974: 103-104; cf. Barstad 1984: 118-26; Andersen and Freedman 1989: 533-37; Paul 1991: 194-98). All agree, therefore, that there is some allusion here to the worship of other gods. What is disputed are their identity and the dating of the text.

Amos 8.14 presents a similar array of problems. Once more, the most serious are lexical: what are the meanings of the phrases אשמת שמרון and דרך באר־שבע? The basic interpretive options are that these terms signify other deities or that they are regional appellations of Yahweh. In

14. It is commonly assumed that the present vocalization of סכות and כיון derives from שׁקוץ ('detestable things'; cf. 1 Kgs 11.5; 2 Kgs 23.13).

15. The authors cited do not agree in all the particulars of their interpretation. For example, Weinfeld (followed by Albertz) posits that the line is speaking of Adad and Ishtar; Smith suggests that *mlk* refers to the leader of the dead; de Moor takes סכות as 'stele' (cf. DDD 478, 723). Another pertinent phrase, of course, is כוכב אלהיכם, which has also generated much debate.

16. One who would claim that 5.26 does refer to Yahweh is Hayes, who interprets the verse as describing a procession celebrating Yahweh's re-enthronement at the fall festival (1988: 178-79).

regards to the first phrase, among those who believe another deity is in view, there are some who see here a reference to the goddess (or cult object) A/asherah on the basis of an emendation or by identifying the phrase (translated as 'the guilt of Samaria') with her (or 'it'. See Tigay 1986: 26 n. 31; Andersen and Freedman 1989: 828-29)—a possibility now more intriguing after the finds at Kuntillet 'Ajrud and Khirbet el-Qom (for a recent discussion and bibliography see Keel and Uehlinger 1998: 210-48). Others suggest that a slight revocalization of אשמת yields the goddess Ashima (e.g. Barstad 1984: 157-81; Toorn 1992: 91; Jeremias 1998: 151-52; cf. 2 Kgs 17.30; yet note DDD: 106). If one does not take the phrase to refer to another deity, but instead under-stands it to be a barb directed at a local Yahweh cult, then 'the guilt of Samaria' could be a reference to the calf/bull cult at the state sanctuary at Bethel (e.g. Paul 1990: 269-70; cf. 1 Kgs 12.28-30). The book, how-ever, in contrast to another eighth-century prophetic text (Hos. 8.5-6; 10.5, 8), never explicitly mentions that particular cult object. Still another related possibility would be that this is simply a derogatory description of and a reference back to the nationalistic cult overseen by Amaziah at Bethel, which had been denounced in the preceding chapter (7.10-17) and whose destruction is announced by the prophet (3.14, 9.1).

Another disputed phrase in 8.14 is דרך באר־שבע. Some of the more common of the interpretive options are that the word be taken simply as 'the way of Beersheba'—that is, the pilgrimage route to that city (e.g. Wolff 1977: 323-24; Paul 1990: 271-72); that it be connected with Ugaritic *drkt* ('power'; e.g. Amsler 1965: 237; Barstad 1984: 191-98; Jeremias 1998: 152-53); and that דרך be emended to *dod^{e}ka*, 'your kinsman' (cf. 6.10) which is then taken as meaning the patron deity in parallel with the preceding phrase אלהיך דן (note most recently Olyan 1991). These words, 'your god(s), O Dan', do not prove to be a lexical challenge as do the other two phrases. Their significance depends in part on the determinations made for אשמת שמרון and דרך באר־שבע and the interpretive choice concerning the nature of popular religion in Israel in general. The literary interweaving of 7.7-17 and 8.1-14 men-tioned earlier, the thematic link between 8.11-13 and 2.11-12 and 4.4-8, and the juxtaposition with 9.1 (which appears to refer to Bethel) could strengthen the possibility that each of the three phrases in the verse could best be interpreted as alluding to different local epithets of Yah-weh instead of to other deities or non-yahwistic cult objects.

Two further observations on 8.14 are pertinent at this point. First, some commentators, who do believe other deities are meant, date this verse later than the time of the prophet (Wolff 1977: 332; Jeremias 1998: 152-53). As a result, as with 5.26, an allusion to other deities is removed from consideration in the discussion of popular religion in the days of Amos. Second, whatever the identity of the god(s) in 8.14 might be, the religiosity of the nation is highlighted in yet another manner: the taking of oaths and the making of pilgrimages to different points of the compass and even across national boundaries attest to its deep-rootedness in the life of the people.

In sum, if one were to try summarize the picture of popular religious activity painted by the text, several observations could be made. First, on the whole, Israel as a people is very active at the sanctuaries and willing to travel to express their devotion at various cult centers. At the same time, the text also points out on a number of occasions the separate religious activities and attitudes of those who are somehow privileged (2.8, 6.4-7, 7.10-13, 8.5). What is not totally clear in 2.8 and 6.4-7 is whether non-yahwistic ceremonies are also being alluded to. The same could be said for the general population at 5.26, 7.9, and 8.14. The additional issue for 5.26 and 8.14 is whether they should be included in the portrait of popular religion of the eighth-century prophet. If not, how might their exclusion affect the portrait of religion in Amos? The next section will attempt to present the text's analysis and evaluation of the content of Israel's religious activity and thought.

b. *The 'Why' of the Announced Destruction of Israel's Worship*
From a cultural anthropology perspective, religious life is complex and is a component of a broader multidimensional tapestry. Many religious convictions and rituals are a part of and also are the supernatural legitimation of what for the nation would be the 'natural order of things'. There are, therefore, several general aspects of Israel's religious life—her popular religion—which interconnect with national existence, that the ethnography of Amos targets with biting sarcasm and harsh denunciation. I will begin by looking at that faith and religion centered on Yahweh before moving on to the possible allusions to other deities.

First, the nation's religiosity seems to be characterized by celebration: Yahweh is a god of blessing. 4.4-5 mention the traditional cult centers at Bethel and Gilgal and then enumerate several rituals performed at those sanctuaries. It is noteworthy that none are for transgression against the deity. All, in one way or another, are grounded in thanksgiving to and fellowship with Yahweh. 'For so you love to do', decries Yahweh. From the divine–prophetic point of view, in other words, the ceremonies have as one of their primary goals to satisfy the religious impulses of the people. Religious commitments are fulfilled and are to be broadcast for all to see. For Yahweh, though, it is so much sin.

What makes the religious life of the nation so incomprehensible— and self-destructive—is that it stands as a striking contradiction to the harsh experiences of hunger, thirst, plague and death in warfare (4.6-11). Worship, it seems, has little to do with actual life on the ground. The refusal to see these tragedies as movements of Yahweh's hand of discipline to bring them to a proper view of reality and of himself is a testimony to just how far Israel truly is from the one whom the nation claims to worship. The climax at 4.12-13 calls Israel to face the god who can utterly destroy cities and has the incomparable power to control nature itself: 'Yahweh, god of hosts, is his name!' (for details see Carroll R. 1992: 206-21).

Not surprisingly, such a religion is lacking in ethical demands. This second attribute is the item which most commentators on the book have observed and highlighted. The multitude of rituals and the pilgrimages are divorced from concern for the powerless. The merchants are singled out at 8.4-6, a scene that in many ways echoes 2.6-8 and reminds the reader of 6.4-7 (if these last two passages indeed can be considered as well as referring to the yahwistic religious practices of the well-to-do). These three pericopes express that the perversion of the moral demands of faith in Yahweh is present in both the minds and activities of these privileged sectors, at the national sanctuaries and within the confines of private homes and fraternal meeting houses. Their actions 'profane the holy name' of Yahweh (2.7b). But, as mentioned earlier, the entire nation—not just the privileged—falls under the same condemnation (5.4-5, 21-25). Is it then the case that the prophetic ethico-religious critique is to be limited strictly to certain groups of people, who consciously manipulate religious life for their own ends and lusts and who make no connection between their adoration and social ills? Or, is the text communicating that the popular religion of Israel itself generates an ambiance and ethos that allows and never questions such attitudes and actions?

In my opinion, cultural anthropology and the textual data support the latter option. Such an interpretation obviously also would lend credence

to those who envision that the socio-economic abuse described by the
text to be more complicated than simply a rich class–poor class dichotomy (cf. Sicre 1984: 89-168; Carroll R. 1992: 22-47; 1993). The lack
of a social conscience and the divorce between morality and faith in
Yahweh would appear to be endemic to society in general. Some sectors, of course, precisely because of their greater resources and higher
social position, would benefit from this socio-religious reality in more
visible ways that would have a profound social impact. If this tension is
in fact a broad phenomenon, this state of affairs is all the more tragic,
because the nation as a whole never questions this religion. Those in
power revel in their detestable religious practices, even as the poor are
trampled under foot and march into debt slavery (2.6-8, 8.4-6). Ironically, the unfortunate look to those over them, these very ones who
have no feeling for the 'ruin of Joseph' (6.2, 6). The masses continue to
congregate, along with their leaders, at the traditional cult centers and
praise Yahweh as a god of abundance and prosperity. Life goes on with
all of its inconsistencies, and the harps still play (5.23). One might say
that the Marxist claim that religion is the opiate of the people holds true
(cf. Kee 1990: 1-127; Dussel 1993), even in ancient Israel.

The text rhetorically conveys its critique in multiple, powerful ways.
As has long been recognized, 5.1-17 exhibits a chiastic structure whose
center is at 5.8 (cf. Carroll R. 1992: 221-41). Woven into the hymn of
5.8-9 that describes the power of god is the proclamation: 'Yahweh is
his name'. This emphasis on Yahweh's sovereign strength and name,
recalls the climax at 4.13. Here Yahweh warns that the sanctuaries will
be brought down, and he will reject this popular religion with an
almighty power. These verses contain a call to choose Yahweh, life and
justice over empty ritual (5.4-6, 14-15). What awaits religious hypocrisy and blindness are death and mourning in a true encounter with the
almighty god (5.16-17).

A case can be made for a chiastic structure, too, for 5.18-27 (Carroll
R. 1992: 240-54). The center lies at 5.24, with its well-known line 'let
justice roll down like waters, and righteousness like an ever-flowing
stream'. The rituals of 5.21-23 are thus undermined by the clarion call
for a different kind of society where justice would never be lacking.
Disaster is again in the offing for those with a false sense of hope and
security in Yahweh (5.18-20, 26-27). The close of this passage returns
to the 'name' (5.27).

The text in a variety of manners is communicating what we might call a 'name' theology. In the book of Amos ten different names are used of the god of Israel a total of 86 times (Dempsey 1991).[17] What is at stake, in other words, in the view of this prophetic book is the person of Yahweh himself. The deity being worshipped by Israel has that same name but is a mere creation and reflection of the popular religion. The nation as a society and culture claims to be his and to be blessed by him, but Yahweh can only announce its irrevocable demise.

This point leads to a third area of concern. The condemning eye of the prophet also falls on what we might label the official religious ideology of the state. The prevailing attitude of those in power and of the populace as a whole appears to be confidence in the country's military strength and success (e.g. 6.1-2, 13). From this perspective Yahweh is the national deity, who protects and grants success to the armies of Israel. To question victory and stability amounts to treason against the monarchy; it is to bring into disrepute the very significance and centrality of Bethel, Israel's principal sanctuary (7.9-13).[18] To announce defeat and exile, in the opinion of the chief priest, is more than the nation should bear. At this sanctuary any word from a prophet of God should be in support of the regime; the messenger of any other kind of revelation would not be tolerated. At the same time, it is important to note that the nationalistic religion, which all seem to support, is not limited by an absolute boundary. That is, official religion is more restricted than the parameters of popular belief. Pilgrimages are still made to Beersheba in southern Judah (5.5, 8.14). The people's Yahweh is not limited to a neatly defined theology. There is still an irresistible draw to venture south to that venerable holy place. In other words, Yahweh is a complex figure—at once transcendent and local, shared and socially

17. This figure disagrees with the number of occurrences in LXX. Note the comments in Auld 1986: 57-58 with a response in Carroll R. 1992: 263-64 n. 1.

18. Hayes, Polley and Rosenbaum also see the book's message as an attack against the reigning socio-political and religious ideology. Each, however, understands what this means differently according to his particular historical reconstruction. Rosenbaum believes that Amos was a native of the North and a 'civil servant' of the state of Israel, who rose up to denounce its unjust system (1990). As mentioned in the first section of this essay, Hayes envisions a rivalry between Jeroboam II and Pekah. Amos would have spoken against the religious support of both (1988). Polley argues that Amos's religious polemics have as their aim to denounce any alternative to the monarchy and state religion of Judah (1989: esp. 28-54, 83-111).

defined—and each conceptualization of his person contributes to the complexity of the popular religion.

It is possible to read the entire book of Amos as a sustained attack upon the military pretense and this political pride of Israel (cf. Carroll R. 1995, 1996a, 1996b). For example, the nation is included among the nations in the first two chapters who are to experience destruction and exile; 2.14-16 announce total military defeat (the flight and retreat of seven different kinds of troops); an enemy will surround the land and bring its fortresses, altars, fine homes, and walls crashing down (3.11–4.1; 5.9; 6.11,14); and the trek into exile awaits the survivors of the imminent invasion (4.2-3; 5.5, 27; 6.7; 7.17).[19]

Several of the visions can also be explained along these same lines. Because of its juxtaposition with the closing lines of ch. 6 (6.11-14) and the announcement of death and exile in 7.9-17, could not the twice-repeated phrase 'he is so small' in the first two visions (7.2, 4) be a reference to Israel's defenselessness and military helplessness before the threat of war? I would offer another, corresponding, interpretation of the enigmatic third vision that would underscore the military delusions of Israel. The particular difficulty in this vision lies in ascertaining the meaning of אֲנָךְ (7.7-8; cf. Williamson 1990; Weigl 1995). Traditionally this term has been taken to refer to an iron plumb-line, which was then understood to be a metaphor for placing the divine standard (such as the prophet, his message, or the Law) against the present condition of Israel; found wanting, the nation was to be judged. More recently, scholars have come to recognize that this word is a cognate of an Akkadian term for tin. This find has baffled scholars, because tin is a soft metal, and this meaning would appear to them to be irrelevant in this context. Therefore, some appeal to the practice of mixing tin with copper to produce bronze, a stronger alloy used to manufacture weapons. The imagery of bronze would communicate in a general sense the military power that God is bringing against Israel, or could point more specifically to the weapons (note the mention of 'sword' in 7.9) yielded by the coming enemy or metaphorically by Yahweh. This

---

19. I would suggest that the refusal to call on the name of Yahweh in 6.10 is not based on any superstition that the deity might return again in judgment, but rather that people are not going to utter his name because what he has done/allowed (i.e. invasion, exile) is a betrayal of their national god ideology. Instead of a fear of Yahweh, this line could reflect profound disappointment and ultimately the rejection of the god who has failed them.

meaning then is extended to incorporate the notion that the tin/bronze (and, hence, the military threat) would be placed in Israel's midst. This confusion has led some scholars to return to the interpretation of the plumb-line (e.g. Williamson 1990: 110-19; Hoffmeier 1998). In con-tradistinction to these suggestions, and in accordance with the overall tone of the book, however, I would argue that the best interpretive option is still 'tin', precisely because of its connotation of frailty and weakness. The resulting picture would have Yahweh standing upon a wall of tin—that is, the self-deluding defenses of Israel. Though indeed a 'metallic wall', the fortresses are easily scaled and torn apart (cf. 3.9-11; 4.3; 5.9). Yahweh in disgust hurls a piece of this flimsy military illusion at the feet of his people. Defeat is certain; humiliation inevitable.

What the reader witnesses in the message of Amos is the forceful declaration of the end of a culture and society that claims to be Yah-weh's nation. The popular religion celebrates his benevolent and sup-portive hand in Israel's life. Yet the deity will have none of this. He will not permit his name to be associated with this cultural construction of reality, which he through the prophet sees as blind in its celebrations, perverse and callous in its immorality, and deceived by its military hubris. Yahweh through the prophet announces the end of this socio-religious world, in which all participate both collectively and in more individual ways. Their position as the heirs of the traditions of Yah-weh's deliverance cannot be any guarantee of safety; rather, those actions on their behalf in the past are an important foundation for the prophetic indictment in the present (2.9-10; 3.2; 4.10; 9.7; cf. 1 Kgs 12.28).[20] Their trust in a 'day of the Lord' will be exposed as a false hope, as it will bring darkness instead of light (5.18-20); the 'day(s)' that is coming will bring sorrow and pain (2.16; 3.14; 4.2; 8.9-11, 13). The most prominent representatives of this religious construct are named and given a specific sentence: the dynasty of Jeroboam the king will come to an end (7.9); Amaziah the high priest will see his family violated, and he will go into exile (7.17). What is more, the central

20. Toorn labels the Exodus the 'charter myth' of the Northern monarchy (1996: 287-315). Of course, there are critics who would understand the use and dat-ing of this historical tradition in a very different way. Note Lemche's argument within another context that Pentateuchal traditions did not play a significant role within the eighth century. In his reconstruction passages alluding to the Exodus are for the most part dated late (1985: 308-12).

sanctuary of this popular religion will be torn down by Yahweh himself (9.1; cf. 3.14).

What remains to be discussed are 5.26 and 8.14. The first question that must be raised is, are these verses polemics against other deities? It appears that of the two 5.26 is the clearest allusion to other deities, even though debate continues over the precise identity of those mentioned. On the other hand, I have suggested that 8.14 perhaps should be taken as referring to regional or local Yahweh cults, each of which could have its own particular characteristics.

The second issue concerns the dating of these two passages. If both are dated late, then one might say that Amos's religious message considers *only* what was considered unacceptable Yahwism. Any references to other deities, therefore, are expansions that would have been added by the tradents of Amos, meaning that the present text's message has been updated to meet the religious challenges of a later time. Of course, other vague verses (such as 2.8, 7.9) or religious activities (like 6.4-7) also would have to be brought into line with this interpretation. They have to be understood as pointing to some sort of Yahweh worship or, if not, should be dated late as well to fit within the chosen religious reconstruction. In light of the archaeological evidence, from this perspective there is no doubting the existence of syncretism in the time of the prophet. Questions revolve instead around whether the original prophetic message dealt with it.

On the other hand, if one believes that 5.26 can be considered as describing syncretistic belief and practice within the time frame of Amos, the religious picture changes accordingly. To opt for this interpretation, of course, brings yet more complexity to the nature of this biblical representation of popular religion. The challenge of deciding how best to handle 2.8, 7.9 and 6.4-7 still remains. If these verses refer to non-yahwistic practices, then a stronger case for this book's concern about other deities could be made; if not, then these passages would be further instances of a misguided faith in Yahweh.

Whatever kinds of non-yahwistic rituals and beliefs might have been prevalent in the first half of the eighth century—whether items mentioned in the text of Amos or not—one must ask, why are these elements either ignored, downplayed, or expressed in such veiled language? Some scholars, for instance, have attempted to bring attention and clarification to these enigmatic data in the text by discovering the 'true meaning' of these allusions...some to the extent of saying that syncretism was actually the prophet's principal concern (witness Barstad)! Others might suggest that certain issues were not thought actually to be a problem at that time; the religion of Israel, in other words, was at a stage within its process of development in which certain practices and beliefs, which later would be rejected, were acceptable (cf. Olyan 1988: 8-9, 17, 38). This latter explanation, although it might be historically correct, does not wrestle adequately, I believe, with the text's presentation.

An anthropological perspective would argue that this prophetic book has taken concentrated aim at a particular construction of reality. This text is an ethnography dedicated to presenting a Yahweh who demands an alternative life for Israel, because that people and state do not deserve to carry his name. The Yahweh of Israel is a sinful and selfish creation, and is nothing more than a projection of popular desires and the national ideology. This conceptualization of the message relativizes the impact of the historical decision concerning 5.26 (and 8.14). Whatever interpreters at some point finally decide, ultimately the text's primary message is only nuanced by that choice; the thrust of that message in the main is not significantly changed.

The end of the book can be interpreted as the hope for national reconstruction after the obliteration of this socio-religious world called Israel.[21] In this dream of a new Israel, interestingly, there are no altars, temples or palaces, yet there will be political and material blessings and a closer relationship with the deity. 'Yahweh of hosts', who soon will be sending armies of destruction, one day will be 'Yahweh your God', who will restore them to a bountiful and peaceful land (9.11-15).

4. Conclusion

This essay has been an initial attempt to consider the book of Amos as an ethnography of popular religion in eighth-century Israel. As such, this prophetic text offers a certain perspective on national religious life. The text does have, so to speak, an agenda: it presents very compellingly its own interpretation of the people's religious attitudes, values and practices. This text, therefore, is only one 'native's point of

---

21. Issues of dating 9.11-15 would surface at this point. On the other hand, no matter one's option on that point, literarily these verses clearly now serve the function of negating the realities of the present as well as the effects of the imminent invasion described in the rest of the book.

view', but as such it is one more piece of evidence within a much broader and ongoing interdisciplinary study. A comprehensive understanding of the religion of that time necessarily will require continued study of this text and corrections to our reading. Much work remains to be done, too, in coordinating archaeological findings with this and other biblical material. It is hoped that our effort can serve as a contribution to that fascinating and important task of trying to understand more accurately the faith of ancient Israel.

DIALECT AND REGISTER IN THE GREEK
OF THE NEW TESTAMENT: THEORY

Stanley E. Porter

1. *Introduction*

Catford makes a useful distinction between varieties of language. He distinguishes two types—those that are permanent and those that are transient. The permanent kinds of varieties include idiolect, which is the particular variety of an individual, and dialect, which is determined along geographical, temporal and social lines. The transient types of varieties include what Catford calls register, style and mode (Catford 1965: 84-85). These two categories (though problematic to distinguish and maintain) well encapsulate the difference in perspective of traditional discussion of the language of the New Testament (e.g. the study of dialects) and a sociolinguistic perspective (of which register is a part). Sociolinguistics as a sub-discipline of the field of modern linguistics dates to around 1960, as several areas of study began to be integrated, in particular, but not exclusively, sociology and linguistics (see Giglioli 1972 for early studies). Linguists such as Ferguson (1959) and Fishman (1967) were some of the first to appreciate that various social factors have an influence on linguistic usage of individuals, especially in their varying definitions and applications of the term 'diglossia'. Their observations were complemented by anthropological insights promoted by such instrumental figures as Gumperz and Hymes (1972), especially as the role of speech communities came to be more fully realized. As the discipline developed, an increasing emphasis was placed upon issues of change and variation, that is, the attempt to measure how it is that people speak and write (Labov 1972). Along with this emphasis came an attempt to quantify results in what was perceived to be a scientific way, rather than being content with taxonomic descriptive labels, such as functional linguistics was seen to provide (see Newmeyer 1988 for recent developments). The entire field of sociolinguistics, but especially many of the early practitioners who set the agenda for study, has recently left itself open for criticism that the discipline has failed to analyze its critical assumptions. These include, in particular, the social models first developed in the nineteenth century with regard to social evolution, and continued in the twentieth century with regard to social norms. This was especially reflected in discussion of diglossia, which worked according to linguistic typologies, a continuing emphasis of much sociolinguistic research (see Williams 1992 for a strong and useful critique).[1] The goal of this paper, and the following paper with analysis of an extended example, is not to chronicle this debate, or to arbitrate the disputants, since that is not appropriate or necessary here. Instead, I wish to show how advances in Hallidayan functional sociolinguistics, which has in several ways avoided many of the pitfalls noted above, can offer new insights to the study of the Greek of the New Testament in its several varieties (see de Beaugrande 1991: 223-64; Sampson 1980: 212-35).

2. *Dialects and Varieties of Greek*

The usual discussion of the varieties of Greek found in the Hellenistic world, including the Greek of the New Testament, traditionally devotes attention to Catford's permanent kinds of varieties.[2] Thus, in a useful discussion of the language of the New Testament, Hemer (1987) distinguishes eight categories for brief consideration: dialect, the diverse influences of substratal languages, social and stylistic variations, borrowings, semantic interference, varieties of formulation, choice of synonyms, and technical terms. What Catford characterizes as transient types of varieties have been virtually neglected in recent discussion of New Testament Greek, including Hemer's treatment (see also, for example, Black 1988; Cotterell and Turner 1989; Turner 1995; Egger 1996; but cf. Horrocks 1997: 32-127; Brixhe 1996). I will use Hemer's article as a point of entry into discussion of various sociolinguistic issues, moving from matters of dialect towards those of register.

In discussing dialect, for example, Hemer repeats Thumb's conclu-

---

1.   The issue of diglossia has been a matter of discussion in Hellenistic Greek and New Testament studies recently, and will probably continue to be so in the future. See Niehoff-Panagiotidis 1994; Watt 1997.

2.   This is, of course, a relevant and important part of sociolinguistics, just not the only one. See Chambers and Trudgill 1980.

sion that Koine Greek was essentially a dialectless language, without major phonetic, structural and syntactical distinctions, as opposed to the differences among Ionic/Attic, Doric and Aeolic, the major dialects during the 'dialect' age (Thumb 1901: 162-201; cf. Thumb 1909).[3] Nevertheless, Hemer still also claims that it is possible to show that there were 'locally-based variations within the "common" Greek' (1987: 68), some of which he attempts to illustrate in his discussion. Several sociolinguistic concepts have been inadvertently introduced by Hemer here. These include 'standard language', prestige language, variety, dialect, regional dialect and accent. What Hemer appears to be saying is that he accepts that Koine Greek had the status of a 'standard language' or 'standard variety' (for recent discussion, see Joseph 1987). A standard language is described by Hudson as the language that results from 'direct and deliberate intervention by society. This intervention, called "standardisation", produces a standard language where before there were just "dialects" (i.e. non-standard varieties)' (1980: 32).[4]

Alexander the Great's initial conquest of Greece and subsequent conquest of the Mediterranean world in the fourth century BC directly intervened into the use of not only varieties based on geography (regional dialects) in mainland Greece, but the broader varieties of language[5] of Asia Minor, Palestine, Egypt and elsewhere. The use of a regularized variety of Attic Greek as the 'standard language' would have been a virtually conscious choice by Alexander due to his own education and inclinations, and his utilization of Greek mercenaries as the basis of his army, reinforced in its regularity by those who attached themselves to him and his troops, including those conquered and various hangers-on,

---

3.   For a discussion of the matter of dialect in Hellenistic Greek, see Porter 1989: 141-56. This paper attempts to refine comments made there with particular use of the concept of register.

4.   In the only extensive sociolinguistic analysis of Hellenistic Greek known to me (Frösén 1974), it is concluded that the language is a creole. But Hudson (1980: 61-71) points out (1) that a creole is just another variety and therefore not of particular linguistic interest, and (2) that its distinguishing feature is its origins in the pidgin, a variety that is not the result of borrowing from another variety since it has no pre-existing variety, no morphology and no native speakers. Cf. Holm 1988, for a survey of the subject.

5.   There is some dispute over how the terms 'language' and 'dialect' should be used. I distinguish between broad and narrow varieties in much the same way as Hudson does (1980: 23-25); Wardaugh 1992: 22-54. Cf. Haugen 1972: 97-111, esp. 99.

such as merchants and traders, who were compelled to learn this variety of Greek.[6] The function of this 'standard Greek', although not formally codified, was elaborated in all walks of life, including government, bureaucracy, education, science and business throughout the Hellenistic and then Greco-Roman worlds, even to the point of being used by artisans and local businessmen in Palestine (see Palmer 1980: 174-96; Horrocks 1997: 17-127 *passim*; Teodorsson 1977: 25-35; Porter 1994; 1997a). This 'standard Greek' had a very strong unifying force upon the Hellenistic world.

Even though Greek was the 'standard language' or 'standard variety' of the Hellenistic world, this does not mean that there were not still variations in pronunciation (i.e. accent or 'dialect') of this language, differing according to region, social level, sex, education and age, nor does it mean that the standard language was the only variety in use. To the contrary, the concept of a 'standard language' implies, or even requires, other varieties of language (see Brixhe 1987; Brixhe [ed.] 1993; 1996, for examples and discussion). Greek as the standard language constituted the prestige language throughout at least the eastern Roman Empire, apart from when Latin was used for official documents and the military (see Haugen 1950 on prestige language; Fitzmyer 1991: 129-33 on Latin in Palestine). Other varieties continued to be used in definable contexts, such as other varieties of Greek in Greece and elsewhere (Asia Minor, Egypt), and broad varieties such as Aramaic in Palestine and possibly Hebrew in certain Jewish religious contexts (the linguistic situation in Palestine was clearly multilingual, not merely diglossic in Ferguson's original sense; Hudson 1980: 55; Ferguson 1959; Porter 1994: 123-29).

There are at least two other significant kinds of differences in varieties worth noting. For example, in Greece and elsewhere, certain persistent differences that Hemer notes are typical of various geographical regions and are hence best called regional dialects (Hemer's locally based variations). In the light of increased mobility in the Hellenistic world, one must also consider social dialects, which category takes into consideration such significant factors as social status, sex and age. Hemer recognizes the question of differences between men's and women's language in his section on social and stylistic variations, noting that little has been done with Greek, although he claims there is

---

6. On Alexander and his conquests, see Lane Fox 1973; Wilcken 1967.

'scant evidence' of lexical divergence (1987: 71). These various dialectical factors are not consistently distributed across a population, but are
to be distinguished from simple differences of pronunciation (i.e.
accent). Many of the kinds of variation that Hemer cites seem to be
matters of accent reflected in orthography, rather than differences of
variety. Thus, in Hemer's simple paragraph on dialect, a number of
issues regarding the users of varieties of language are raised, although
not in a precise sociolinguistic way.[7]

In his discussion of social and stylistic variations, Hemer focuses on
the Atticistic movement, citing a number of words frowned upon by
Phrynichus but used in the New Testament. Hemer characterizes the
Atticistic ideal as artificial and contrary to the prevailing changes in the
Greek of the time, in which there are 'differing levels of style even
within the New Testament' (1987: 71). Hemer, like many classical
philologists, seems to equate style with the characteristics of the language user (such as Luke or Paul), and hence treats style as a matter of
'social distinction in linguistic usage' (1987: 71), even though social
factors are only one category of influences upon language use. More
important in discussing the Atticistic movement, however, is the issue
of a 'standard language' and varieties. This movement provides an
important contrast to the linguistic standardization brought about by
Alexander. A number of Atticists attempted to intervene in the development of Greek, but this effort at standardization ultimately failed.
This movement may well have had an influence upon which works the
Alexandrian librarians decided to have copied and may have thus
resulted in the relative paucity of first-century Greek writing apart from
scientific and Christian literature, but Atticists were never able to
impose this variety as the 'standard language' of the Hellenistic world.
It proved impossible to impose a variety confined to artificial literary
creations and word-books. This is seen in the fact that even noted
Atticistic writers did not maintain the standards codified in Phrynichus
(see Horrocks 1997: 79-83, with examples). Although influential in certain literary and educational circles (including some of the Church
Fathers in their attempts to win acceptance in the ancient world), this
literary variety was not used in government, business or commerce, and
certainly not in scientific and much popular writing of the time. Consequently, it was not a unifying linguistic force in the Hellenistic world.

---

7.   One of few scholars to study dialects of the New Testament writers was
Wifstrand 1947. There is no systematic study of the entire corpus known to me.

In his discussion of the influence of what he calls substratal languages, Hemer invokes Gignac, who has noted the frequency in Egyptian papyri of the voiceless bilabial stop [p] (Greek π) for the voiced [b] (Greek β) and voiceless alveolar stop [t] (Greek τ) for voiced [d] (Greek δ) as possible evidence for a 'distinctively Egyptian substratum' (Hemer 1987: 69; Gignac 1970). Furthermore, the Greek inscriptions of Phrygia, according to Hemer, reveal 'a strangely illiterate patois with recurring eccentricities' (Hemer 1987: 69).[8] Hemer seems here to be discussing multilingualism and, in particular, the issue of interference, which can occur in relation to lexicon, morphology, syntax and phonology, as well as involving code switching (see Baetens Beardsmore 1986: 43-84; cf. Klein 1986: 1-14; Watt 1997: 41-51). While some of the differences noted may simply be orthographic reflections of differences in pronunciation (i.e. accent), others may reveal non-standard use of Greek. The Phrygian instances may reveal a number of characteristics typical of multilingual contexts, in which attempts are made due to various social, economic and political reasons to acquire and use the prestige variety by those who know a non-prestige variety of language. These can and do include spelling changes, misuse of words and constructions, and calques (loan translations) taken over where a specific word is needed. Hemer, like many who discuss Semitic influence on the Greek of the New Testament, seems to treat these as if the non-prestige language is having an effect upon the prestige language. What he is describing is worth noting, but it is only evidence of the non-prestige language user's 'imperfect grasp of the receptor language' (Hemer 1987: 73). Multilingual speakers (in fact, any speakers) often use varieties with varying degrees of precision, and often switch codes in a way that reveals not their linguistic limitations, but their co-ordinated or compounded multilingualism. The local non-prestige variety, especially as a first language, may well have had an influence upon the idiolect of a user of Greek, but that is not the same as saying that the local variety has influenced the 'standard language'. It provides very little evidence,

8.   He is perhaps referring to the findings of Gibson (1978: 96), but who seems to conclude oppositely: 'The same evolution was taking place all over Asia Minor, as inscriptions show, and these features of pronunciation and syntax foreshadow those of modern Greek, facts which are ignored by those (even Petrie! [and Hemer apparently]) who consider the existence of this non-Classical Greek to be evidence that the spoken language of Phrygia was Phrygian. Many of the elements of modern Greek are here already' (Gibson 1978: 97). See also Ramsay 1915: 65-78.

therefore, for the larger linguistic profile of the Hellenistic world.

In his sections on borrowings, semantic interference and technical terms,[9] Hemer discusses how the Greek of the Hellenistic period was supposedly influenced by other varieties of language in the Hellenistic world. In the first category, a Greek user incorporates into his lexical stock a word for an institution for which there is no Greek word. In the second, the writer's semantic categories are influenced by those of another variety. In the third, the use of words either uniquely in the New Testament or discontinuously with extra-biblical usage is treated. The significance of these categories in discussion of the Greek of the New Testament is revealed in the fact that Hemer devotes three of his eight sections to them. These categories are appropriate in a discussion of sociolinguistics and the Greek of the New Testament, although the results will probably disappoint many biblical scholars. New Testament scholars often place a great deal of emphasis upon Semitic or other words that make their way into New Testament usage (as calques or other forms of borrowing), possibly by way of the Septuagint, but it is widely recognized that langauge varieties in geographical or cultural contact often transfer words to and from each other, since words tend to move across various dialectical boundaries along with the items that they denote (Hudson 1980: 44-48). The result may be a certain amount of recognizable similarity or resemblance among varieties that have borrowed from each other or other varieties that they have come into contact with, even if these languages are quite distinct varieties. Theological and other culturally specific terminology is particularly subject to borrowing, but virtually any set of words is subject to such replacement. This proves very little about the influence of one variety upon another. It is syntax that is a better indicator of such influence, and it is surprisingly resistant to such interference (Weinreich 1953: 29; Hudson 1980: 46-48).

Although Hemer has marshalled significant instances and examples for examination, his treatment is ultimately unsatisfactory. He is unable—even with the amount of evidence available—to offer the kind of linguistic profile of Hellenistic Greek that he desires, that is, one that addresses the question of dialect in a systematic way.

---

9.   Hemer (1987: 77-79) also discusses synonymy, but this is beyond the scope of this paper, sociolinguistics and most discussions of synonymy as well.

3. *Register in a Hallidayan Sociolinguistic Context*

One of the reasons for Hemer's apparent analytical shortcomings appears to be the failure to utilize a model that has a clear conception of what dialect is or how it relates to other categories of linguistic usage, especially sociolinguistic ones. This is not to say that this work is not important, or that it should not continue, or to say that the categories introduced above could not be used further to re-analyze the data into important and helpful categories (as I have begun to do). Nevertheless, this kind of approach still neglects a number of very important linguistic questions. For example, rather than allowing a single user to speak for an entire dialect, what of linguistic contexts where 'the same person may use very different linguistic items to express more or less the same meaning on different occasions'? (Hudson 1980: 48). This has been defined as a 'variety according to use' or register, as opposed to a 'variety according to the user' or dialect (Halliday in Halliday and Hasan 1985: 41; first found in Halliday, McIntosh and Strevens 1964: 88-89; cf. Ure and Ellis 1977). Very little work has been done from this perspective with the language of the New Testament, although it addresses many of the same kinds of questions suggested by the above analysis. One of the few treatments that introduces the concept of register to the study of the Greek New Testament is Reed (1997a: 34-122; cf. Reed 1995), with a few other references occasionally made to the importance of a Hallidayan approach to sociolinguistics (e.g. Malina 1991: 8; 1996: 80). This perspective merits further development in the light of the kind of textual evidence that is available (as noted above).

The concept of register has been developed by Hallidayan linguistics to provide a framework for approaching varieties of language from the perspective of their use in context (there is no systematic and comprehensive discussion of register in Halliday, but see Halliday in Halliday and Hasan 1985; Halliday 1973a; 1973b: 98-100; 1975: 125-33; 1978: 31-35, 60-64, 110-11, 130-45, 186-89, 221-27; Hudson 1980: 48-55; Gregory and Carroll 1978: chapter 6).[10] Register, as the term is employed by Halliday and others in systemic-functional linguistics,

10. For a useful summary and critique, see Butler 1985: 62-68, 92. For the best critical analysis to date of Hallidayan register, see de Beaugrande 1993: 7-25. De Beaugrande (1993: 14) notes that Halliday backs away from the concept of register in Halliday 1985, who claims that 'we are only beginning to be able to characterize' register structure (p. xxxv).

seems to include all that Catford mentions under his category of transient characteristics of varieties, such as register, style and mode, as well as overlapping significantly with the concept of dialect (see Halliday in Halliday and Hasan 1985: 43; Hasan 1973; Berry 1975: 2). It is difficult to distinguish between what one language user typically says (i.e. dialect) and what another language user may say on an occasion (i.e. register) (see Hudson 1980: 51).[11] Whenever a communicative act occurs, speakers or writers position themselves in relation to a grid with two major axes, that of other kinds of linguistic behaviour and that of their sociolinguistic context (i.e. the location of their linguistic actions). To use Halliday's formulation: 'It is *which* kinds of situational factor determine *which* kinds of selection in the linguistic system' (1978: 32). This is what Halliday calls the context of situation, and it is this context that register attempts to define.

Context of situation is to be distinguished from two other related concepts fundamental to the Hallidayan framework. One is the context of culture and the other is the co-text. Context in its inclusive sense is concerned with 'extra-linguistic factors that influence discourse production and processing', and consists of the context of situation, defined as 'the immediate historical situation in which a discourse occurs' (Reed 1997a: 42), and the context of culture, which includes such extra-linguistic factors as setting, behavioural environment, language itself, including the category of genre (see Butler 1989: 13-19, for discussion), and extra-situational factors, often referred to as frames or scenarios (see Duranti and Goodwin 1992). Co-text refers to levels of linguistic units specific to a particular linguistic environment (such as words, groups, and clauses). A basic and useful definition of register is provided by Halliday himself:

> the notion of register is at once very simple and very powerful. It refers to the fact that the language we speak or write varies according to the type of situation...What the theory of register does is to attempt to uncover the general principles which govern this variation, so that we can begin to understand *what* situational factors determine *what* linguistic features (1978: 31-32).[12]

11. As most linguists recognize, everyone is involved in code or dialect switching. See Halliday 1978: 34.

12. Halliday goes on to admit that 'little is yet known about the nature of the variation involved, largely because of the difficulty of identifying the controlling factors' (1978: 32).

Although many recognize the clear usefulness of the category of register, a major complaint is a failure on Halliday's part to define terminology precisely and consistently (see de Beaugrande 1993: 9-17). This is not the place to engage in a full-scale assessment of Hallidayan linguistics, although a close analysis of his categories of thought, especially as applied to New Testament studies, may be in order in the future. Nevertheless, certain terms require comment. The labels 'tenor' and 'mode' are particularly difficult. Whereas 'field' accurately conveys what Halliday means by a 'field of discourse', 'tenor' is opaque. It seems to be related to the concept of direction (as in 'the tenor of his remarks'), but the term is a much more specific and focused concept in Hallidayan linguistics related to participant structure. Whereas 'tenor' is simply unclear, 'mode' is potentially misleading, since it is so closely related to such terms as mood and modality. As will be seen below, these concepts are used by Halliday, but in terms of interpersonal semantics and hence under tenor of discourse, where they rightly belong, even if defined differently in terms of the Greek verbal network. In Halliday's thinking, register has developed from a set of constraints on language into a semantic category (contrast Halliday 1978: 32 with Halliday in Halliday and Hasan 1985: 38). A clearer formulation of the relation of register to semantics and formal structures of language would be greatly welcome, since it would enable more precise lines of influence to be established between extra-linguistic factors and the particulars of the lexico-grammatical system. Likewise, other linguists have proposed a number of different components of register (Fawcett 1980: 84-85), and have arranged the components differently (Gregory 1987: 97-104). Nevertheless, Halliday's model of register does not seem to be seriously improved or compromised (only slightly confused) by such efforts.

In order to determine which linguistic features of a discourse result from which situational factors, Halliday proposes three conceptual categories of analysis of the situation: field of discourse, tenor of discourse and mode of discourse. These categories are somewhat impressionistically based on what he sees as informational, interpersonal and, less precisely defined, aesthetic and related functions of language, as described by linguists across a range of theoretical orientations (see Bühler 1990; Malinowski 1923; Halliday in Halliday and Hasan 1985: 15-23; cf. Gregory 1987: 94-97). Register does not directly determine the specific lexico-grammatical realizations that may be used in a given

utterance, but it constrains a number of semantic or functional components. These constraints do not constitute the text, but they determine
the linguistic parameters in which it is realized. Thus the situational
factors correlate with the semantic component, which governs formal
realization. For Halliday, the semantic component of language is divided into a triadic structure as well: ideational meanings, interpersonal
meanings and textual meanings. There is thus seen to be a direct
realizable correlation between the situational determinants and semantic
components, such that each of the situational dimensions activates a different semantic component, and these semantic components are realized
in lexico-grammatical structures. A spoken text is then expressed
phonologically, and a written text graphemically (Matthiessen 1993:
227). Assumed here is that there is a language system that unites
situation, semantic components, lexico-grammatical realizations and
either phonological or graphical substance.[13] The definition, unification
and full exemplification of all of these units has so far eluded even
Halliday,[14] although each merits further significant attention. This essay
will focus upon register, semantic structures, and some of their realizations (see de Beaugrande 1993: 17), in order to explore in the subsequent essay what the exegetical usefulness might be for analysis of
the New Testament.

a. *Mode of Discourse Realized by Textual Semantic Component*
Mode or medium of discourse

> refers to what part the language is playing, what it is that the participants
> are expecting the language to do for them in that situation: the symbolic
> organisation of the text, the status that it has, and its function in the con-
> text, including the channel (is it spoken or written or some combination
> of the two?) (Halliday in Halliday and Hasan 1985: 12).

The mode of discourse activates the textual component in terms of
several structuring factors (see Halliday in Halliday and Hasan 1985:

---

13. In other words, this is very similar to what has come to be called a model for
discourse analysis. See Ventola 1988: 58, who defines language in terms of discourse, lexicogrammar and phonology; Reed 1997a.

14. For example, in an essay of 1975 he saw the semantic components as realized in the grammar (reprinted in Halliday 1978: 108-26) but in a 1977 essay and
then in 1980, the semantic components are seen to constitute the semantic level
(reprinted in Halliday 1978: 128-51; Halliday in Halliday and Hasan 1985: 15-28).
See Butler 1985: 63.

35). These include theme, cohesion and information structure—all features of the textual semantics, in that they are part of the texture of the discourse. Theme is indicated in Greek by grammatically explicit subjects, which establish those persons and items that create the primary information flow. Theme, which marks the point of departure for conveyance of information, is established in contrast to rheme, which develops thematic material (Halliday 1985: 38). In contrast to languages such as English (and hence to Halliday's thought at this point), theme is not always in prime position (the first syntactical unit), but may be in subsequent position. Not every sentence has a theme, since in Greek the subject of a clause may not be grammaticalized. Cohesion is concerned with such nonstructural semantic features as reference, substitution and ellipsis, conjunction and lexical cohesion such as reiteration and collocation. Hence, it is established through a variety of means, including reference to the larger context of situation or even culture (exophoric reference), or to elements within the text (endophoric reference). These items may be fully expressed (e.g. nouns) or partially reduced to pronouns or fully reduced through ellipsis. Cohesion is also established through various conjunctions, or words used to link larger units within a discourse. Lexical patterning, through repetition of various lexical items that fall within similar or related semantic domains, or which collocate in identifiable patterns, may also establish cohesion. Information flow is concerned with how these elements are distributed within a discourse, usually in terms of sub-units. Since the textual semantic structure is concerned with thematic and informational structure, including focus (Halliday 1985: 38-67), how the information is focused (i.e. prominence, or salience) is also important. This often is realized in terms of voice—that is, for example, whether the agent is the explicit subject—and various deictic indicators of time, place, and so on. This is not part of the linguistic structure itself, but is a part of the textual semantic feature by which information is distributed and structured so that there is focus. Textual structure is determined by appropriate thematic patterning of this information. These elements of the textual component will be more fully exemplified in my subsequent essay on the Gospel of Mark.

Concern for the means or medium of communication, most notably though not exclusively by speech or writing, that is, how the communication actually took place, would appear to render this dimension of analysis very straightforward, since all of the New Testament is in written form, as is all of the evidence for Greek that we have from the Hellenistic period. Nevertheless, at least two potentially insightful questions are raised by this analysis. The first concerns the relationship of mode of discourse to the traditional categories of historical-literary analysis, such as form criticism. The second concerns spoken language in the New Testament, such as in the words of Jesus in the Gospels, as well as other instances, and the degree of its recovery through the mode of written discourse, the only mode of discourse available for study.

The mode of discourse constrains the textual semantic component, including its discourse type (but not generic structure, since conventional literary patterns such as these are part of the context of culture), textual structure and cohesion. These are what distinguishes a text from randomness or what is not a text. These are not a part of the linguistic structure defined in terms of the clause as the largest unit of structure, but are part of the semantic system, yet they are realized through formal features of text. Thus discourse type is not a property of linguistic structure (confined to the level of the clause) but of the textual semantic structure, constrained by the mode of discourse. Every text has, or rather is, a discourse type, regardless of whether it directly correlates with formal literary genres. Most other models of register equate context of situation with register (see Reed 1997a: 53; following Hasan in Halliday and Hasan 1985: 68-69), but in many of these schemes there seems to be ambiguity regarding levels, with the result that my analysis has led me to place genre within the context of culture, distinct from register (see Ventola 1988: 57-58; cf. Halliday 1978: 134). The concepts of genre and discourse types (or forms, in form-critical terminology) have always been difficult ones in biblical studies, as well as literary studies. The tendency has been to give genres a kind of independent status apart from the texts that are described by the generic label and certainly apart from the social-semiotic context out of which they arise. Seeing genre as part of the context of culture allows its formal features to be maintained, while recognizing and not hindering the constitutive nature of the context of situation for communication (see Pearson and Porter 1997). Similarly, one of the apparent difficulties in discussion of discourse types in New Testament studies is the failure to appreciate at least the following factors: the context of situation as predictor of language usage, the aggregate (and dependent) nature of discourse structure, the differentiation of discourse structure from formal literary genre, and the multi-dimensional—including structural and nonstructural—properties of textual semantic structure. This illustrates that the traditional generic categories used in New Testament studies are in need of serious re-thinking from a sociolinguistic standpoint. For example, a typical division is between Gospel and epistle, but this kind of generic division is a blunt tool for distinguishing the Synoptic Gospels from John, as well as distinguishing important features of the Synoptics themselves. The difficulty with traditional categories is seen further in the dispute over the book of Acts, not only in relation to Luke's Gospel (if these are two different genres, how can they be linked as they are?), but in terms of whether Acts is a historical or fictional narrative. There is the further category of apocalypse often invoked, not only for Revelation but for portions of the New Testament, such as Mark 13 and 1 Thessalonians. Definition of apocalyptic litera-ture is probably the closest that current discussion of genre in New Testament studies comes to a socio-semiotic treatment of genre or dis-course types, since the matrix view of apocalyptic considers social context in its analysis (see Collins 1979). The debate over the unique-ness of the Gospels, and whether they are forms of Greco-Roman bio-graphy, also appeals to a sociological dimension, but not in a principled linguistic way. Distinction from *Hoch-* and *Kleinliteratur*, and the dis-cussion of supposed uniqueness, alongside the category of biography, apparently mixes categories. Clarification of these categories in terms of context of situation and textual semantic structure would seem to promise a productive development of discussion of discourse in New Testament studies, by integrating it into linguistic discussion.

At several places Halliday suggests that rhetorical structure is part of textual structure (Halliday 1978: 223; Halliday in Halliday and Hasan 1985: 12).[15] By this he means that the rhetorical use of a text to per-suade, teach, describe, etc., is part of the textual structure. If this is provable, it would appear to call for a complete reorientation of rhetori-cal study of the New Testament. Rather than working from the assump-tion that all language is rhetorical and hence rhetoric is the governing framework for all textual analysis, rhetorical analysis will need to be seen within a larger sociolinguistic framework. Halliday does not develop this notion of rhetorical structure, but I am not convinced that it belongs in the textual semantic component. Since rhetoric seems to deal

---

15. Cf. Matthiessen 1992: 61-62, 71-72, who attempts to justify the rhetorical element in the textual metafunction using rhetorical structure theory, but which is pretty far away from what most would think of as rhetorical theory.

with participant relations, for example, the relation of teacher–pupil, politician–polis, lawyer–jury, and since persuasion, teaching, and description seem to be functions of mood, I think that rhetoric is perhaps better considered a part of the interpersonal semantic component. Nevertheless, wherever it may be placed, it is clearly a part of the semantic component of language-use, and must be considered within this larger sociolinguistic framework, not as a separate or independent category that governs all other interpretation.

The analysis of supposed spoken language recorded within written language presents a different set of (perhaps insurmountable) problems. Most work on textual structure of *written* texts with dialogue does not differentiate between dialogue as written text and dialogue that may record oral text. This is not to say that it could not be done, however, but one would have to rely upon criteria found in the analysis of contemporary spoken discourse. This provides a further problem for discussion of ancient Greek, however, since the assumption that spoken language now reflects similar features as ancient Greek is one that must be proved and cannot be assumed (but see Biber 1988).

Another course would be to undertake investigation of a wide range of language that purports to record spoken texts, but this has not proved successful to date. For example, the undue regard for the language of Plato and other ancient writers as representative of the language of Attica has only recently given way to the recognition that these dialogues, like the speeches of Lysias, Isocrates and Demosthenes, are not transcripts of normal conversational discourse, as the Gospels purport to record, but a highly artificial literary variety of purported speech, or written texts meant for public reading (Dover 1981; Teodorsson 1979). Because the textual component of these discourses is analyzably different, their contexts of situation are different. The non-documentary papyri, although they reflect many features of a non-standard variety of Greek, reflect a different context of situation altogether, being ephemeral written texts from the start (see on Paul's letters below).

b. *Tenor of Discourse Realized by Interpersonal Semantic Component*
Tenor of discourse is concerned with participant structure, that is, who is taking part in the discourse, and the relationships that exist between the participants, including their status, permanence and role relationships. Two kinds of social relationships enter into discourse considerations: extra-linguistic and intra-linguistic (Halliday 1978: 144). Extra-

linguistic relations are those defined apart from language, although they will often be defined in and by language, and the intra-linguistic relations are those defined by the linguistic system. The former are called first-order social roles and the latter second-order social roles. For example, the relationship of Jesus to his disciples and Paul to his churches are extra-linguistic social relations. The discourse functions of questioner, informer, responder, are intra-linguistically formulated. There are, however, noteworthy correlations between these social relations. For example, Jesus often plays the role of questioner or informer to his disciples and others who act as responders.

The tenor of discourse constrains the selection of interpersonal semantic options in the language system (this is where rhetorical structure should probably be located). Whereas the textual semantic component has nonstructural features (features larger than the sentence), all of the interpersonal semantic features are structural (features realized at the sentence or below) (Halliday 1978: 133, 144). That is, they are realized by features of the language, in particular at the clause level. For example, at the clause level, the system of mood is realized, in the statement, declaration, demand and interrogation. At the group level, both verbal and nominal, there is realization of person (first, second and third) and polarity (positive or negative), that is, whether the discourse is in first, second or third person and what role these persons play in the discourse, and whether positive or negative formulations are realized.

Several significant questions for New Testament language use emerge from this analysis as well. The first is with regard to the amount of information needed to be known of a context of situation in order to assess accurately the constraints on the tenor of discourse. There is an abundance of linguistic data, but there is a clear lack of contextual indicators. As Collinge says, 'it is still too rarely seen that in the interpretative process of relating text to context it is usually hard, and often impossible to know the situation in which the text was uttered' (1960: 82). In other words, since so little is known of the social relations implied by the Gospels, what effect does this have on the use of this category for informing our analysis? Can one extrapolate from the text back to re-creation of the context of situation, as Halliday seems to want us to be able to do (see the next chapter for an attempt at this)? The second is the related problem of the Pauline opponents, another problem in determining the context of situation. The sociolinguistic categories would appear to have potential for analysis of the Pauline situation, but there are several mitigating circumstances related to the texts themselves. One is the artificial and one-sided discourse of the epistles, such that all of the information is filtered through the Pauline text. Another is the random and haphazard focus upon these topics, seen for example in a book such as Philippians, where there are hints at inter-personal relations with opponents in 1.15-18, 3.2 and 3.19, but not much more. Within the confines of these limitations, what is needed is a more highly refined set of categories and more attention given to a par-ticular letter to arrive at a more plausible reconstruction. The potential benefit of a sociolinguistic analysis such as Halliday's is that at least the rudiments exist of a framework of criteria to evaluate the reconstruction of the context of situation.

c. *Field of Discourse Realized by Ideational Semantic Component*
Field of discourse is concerned with the purpose and the subject-matter of the communicative act. The field of discourse may be concerned with extra-linguistic or intra-linguistic items, and the reasons for their being selected for linguistic action. For Halliday, extra-linguistic fields of dis-course include a range of subjects in which language may play no role or may only play a subordinate role. Intra-linguistic fields of discourse depend upon language for their very existence (Halliday 1978: 143-44). The field of discourse may include any item that falls within the larger ideational sphere of human existence, although to define field beyond the scope of language events may be too broad to be useful. It is of course in the second of the two categories—intra-linguistic fields of discourse—that the writings of the New Testament, as well as other religious discourse, fit.

The field of discourse constrains the ways in which the ideational semantic component is realized. Halliday treats the ideational semantic component in terms of two distinct sub-components, the experiential and the logical. The logical has never been as well defined as the expe-riential, partly because it appears that the logical was originally con-ceived of in terms of pure logic, as something outside of language itself. More recently Halliday has apparently rethought the concept of the logical semantic component in terms of natural language. The result is that at least parts of the logical semantic component can be located in and realized by structures of language (the shift can be observed in Halliday 1978: *passim*; see Ellis 1987: 107-114), making it question-able whether the sub-components are necessary to be distinguished. For example, according to such a distinction, the verbal group realizes the aspect system as part of the logical semantic component (but it is also part of the transitivity network), and the relations between clauses (e.g. hypotaxis and parataxis) are part of the logical component as well. The experiential component is realized in terms of grammar and lexicon, a major part of which is the transitivity network.

The transitivity network is realized at the clause level (see Halliday 1985: 144-57; cf. Davidse 1992). For Halliday, transitivity is much more than whether a verb is transitive or intransitive. It includes the verb and everything that depends upon it. At the level of group, the verbal group specifies the types of processes, the nominal group the kinds and types of participants, and their class, quality and quantity, and the adverbial group (prepositional groups) the types of circumstances. One of the major innovations of Halliday's concept of transitivity is the relation between a process, voice and agency, including ergativity, where the subject of a verb is the internal cause of the action, as opposed to a clause where the subject is not the cause, or, as with a passive voice verb, the cause is external.

The lexicon is part of the experiential semantic component as well. There is a complex relation between lexicon and grammar, in which, for Hallidayan grammar, the lexicon is the most delicate level of structure (Hasan 1987). For example, a nominal group, when specifying participants, draws upon the lexicon, and must use specific words to do so. Thus, the individual word (from a class of words) constitutes a paradigmatic choice of element of structure in the nominal group (headterm, modifier).

3. *Conclusion*

In conclusion, I wish to make several observations about a socio-linguistic or functional approach to the language of the New Testament, and offer several areas of potential future exploration. It is to be noted that the terms of discussion have been changed. The shift that I have suggested is away from an almost arbitrary accumulation of random examples from the ancient world that point to the idiosyncrasies of individual users, categorized and analysed in terms of pre-linguistic categories, to an attention to texts that illustrate functional usage, ana-lysed in terms of a sociolinguistic framework. As a result, the conclu-sions will be quite different, but I would argue that, whereas sociolinguistic analyses should not eliminate the kinds of investigations previously conducted, sociolinguistic studies should be encouraged for several reasons.

First, they are able to appreciate and utilize the limitations of the evidence, by focusing upon instances of language use. The predictive capacity of the model, in the sense that the context of situation constrains the field, tenor and mode, has, by implication (so far undeveloped), potential for reconstruction of the original context of situation on the basis of the evidence of field, tenor and mode at hand (this is explored further in the subsequent essay). Perhaps this can provide, at least from a linguistic standpoint, some controls on the kinds of reconstructions that biblical scholars are usually accustomed to offering. Secondly, the model is integrative and enables the kinds of evidence that figure into traditional discussions of dialect to be included in a much larger framework. One of the limitations of contemporary New Testament studies is its fragmentation due to the development of various sub-disciplines. A functional linguistic perspective is not to be seen as the great unifying force of biblical studies, but it does provide one model that allows for possible integration of historical, literary, sociological and, above all, various linguistic features into one conceptual framework (see Hudson 1980: 51, on the necessary multi-dimensional analysis of register).

REGISTER IN THE GREEK OF THE NEW TESTAMENT:
APPLICATION WITH REFERENCE TO MARK'S GOSPEL

Stanley E. Porter

1. *Introduction*

In my previous chapter in this volume, I have offered a definition of register in distinction to other related linguistic categories, especially that of dialect, and in terms of the three meta-functions within the context of situation. As I said above, in order to determine which linguistic features of a discourse result from which situational factors, Halliday proposes three conceptual categories of analysis of the situation: field of discourse, tenor of discourse and mode of discourse. These categories constitute register (on register, see Halliday in Halliday and Hasan 1985; Halliday 1973a; Halliday 1973b: 98-100; Halliday 1978: 31-35, 60-64, 110-11, 130-45, 186-89, 221-27; Halliday 1975: 125-33; Hudson 1980: 48-55; Gregory and Carroll 1978: chapter 6). Register does not directly determine the specific lexico-grammatical realizations that may be used in a given utterance, but it constrains a number of semantic or functional components. These constraints do not constitute the text, but they determine it. Thus the situational factors correlate with the semantic component, which governs formal realization. For Halliday, the semantic component of language is divided into a triadic structure as well: ideational meanings, interpersonal meanings and textual meanings or meta-functions. There is thus seen to be a direct, realizable correlation between the situational determinants and semantic components, such that each of the situational dimensions activates a different semantic component, and these semantic components are realized in lexico-grammatical structures. To understand only one of the components of register, according to this Hallidayan functional model, is to have an inadequate picture of the context of situation. All three must be analysed to appreciate the predictive force of register in terms of activating the semantic component of a text.

To this point, the Hallidayan concept of register has been used as a means of accounting for what is in a discourse on the basis of the constraints of the various meta-functions. For contemporary texts, this is probably its most useful purpose. When studying ancient texts, however, there is much of the context of situation that is unknown to the interpreter, with the interpreter being left simply with the evidence within the discourse, and perhaps a vague notion of the 'context' out of which the text arose. To date, to my knowledge, there have been no fully-developed linguistic models proposed that have serious potential for reversing the interpretative process, so that, on the basis of the textual evidence, one can attempt a reconstruction of the original context of situation—even though this process is one that is engaged in incessantly in the study of ancient texts by means of forms of historical criticism.[1] The Hallidayan concept of register might be able to reverse this interpretative flow in New Testament studies, however, since this sociolinguistic system has a reciprocal character that may prove useful. As Halliday says, 'If the observer can predict the text from the situation, then it is not surprising if the participant, or "interacting", who has the same information available to him, can derive the situation from the text; in other words, he can supply the relevant information that is lacking' (1978: 62). As noted in the first essay above, however, the linguistic variables involved are highly complex, so much so that Halliday's paraphrase of the reciprocal process of possible reconstruction appears to be almost reductionistic (Halliday has been accused of being overly programmatic in his approach: see Butler 1985).

This linguistic model, nevertheless, provides potential for uniting traditional historical criticism, with its concerns for reconstructing the original context in which a text was created and out of which it emerged, and a modern linguistic methodology, with its (at least in this framework) concern for describing this historical environment in terms of a linguistic context of situation that constrains textual choice. In terms of the New Testament, one has a choice of working within the broad categories of the expositions or the narratives, that is, the letters attributed to Paul and the so-called general epistles, or the Gospels and Acts. To a considerable degree, this method of Hallidayan linguistics, especially as a form of discourse analysis, has already been applied by Reed (1997a; cf. Reed 1997b) to analysis of the Pauline book of Philip-

---

1. Many of these forms of criticism are presented and exemplified in Porter (ed.) 1997.

pians.[2] After defining in some detail a Hallidayan framework regarding context of situation, Reed applies his findings, as well as his method, to the question of literary integrity in Philippians. The question of literary integrity in Philippians is one that has bedeviled recent discussion, since many scholars are undecided whether the canonical letter is a single letter, originally penned in its entirety by Paul, or a composite of any number of other letters (two, three and five letters being the most frequent—but by no means the only—proposals). Reed generally concludes for the literary integrity of the letter, but with the major caveat that the method of discourse analysis that he employs is not necessarily well-suited to resolving such questions as this. Despite Reed's recognition of the limitations of his method of analysis, in particular because of assumptions regarding the nature of discourse analysis, most New Testament scholars would probably believe that deriving the context of situation of a text is a task more easily accomplished in terms of a letter—especially an authentic letter, where such basic issues as authorship are already decided—than with regard to a text such as a Gospel or Acts, since questions of chronology, dating and authorship are, almost by definition, the major points of debate regarding these books. Thus, partly as a complement to Reed's work, and partly as an attempt to see if linguistic insights can be gained from a Hallidayan approach to register in the New Testament, I have selected the book of Mark as a suitable text for analysis.

2. *Previous Applications*

Before taking a closer look at Mark through the Hallidayan concept of register (defined in my previous article), I would like to note previous research into Mark's Gospel that may have a bearing on this study. A quick survey of several of the major commentaries and monographs on the Gospel is not encouraging with regards to a linguistic analysis, especially one of anything more involved than the study of basic syntax and semantics. Like most commentaries, most monographs are no better than Hengel's (1985) excellent historically-based study of Mark's Gospel. In a chapter on the 'Time of Origin and Situation', a title that is in itself quite promising, Hengel discusses the tradition of the early Church, a few indications in the Gospel itself (e.g. Mk 9.1; mention of

---

2.   Halliday 1985 is an explicit attempt to relate his categories of grammar to text analysis (1985: x).

Peter) and Mark 13. The only sustained discussion of a linguistic problem is that of the time-frame in which translation of Jesus' words from
Aramaic into Greek took place (Hengel 1985: 12), a discussion not
informed by modern linguistic issues.[3] In one chapter, Kee (1977) discusses the social and cultural setting of the Markan community, drawing upon various social-scientific models regarding prophetic and
sectarian movements. After much discussion, he attempts to draw historical links between these movements and the Markan community, and
then posit a historical and geographical setting of the Gospel. Kee's linguistic discussion seems to be confined to noting that Mark's linguistic
character indicates a predominantly Greek-speaking environment,
although with traces of Semitic influence (Kee 1977: 101). One notes
with some wonder how it is that a recent book on new approaches to
Mark (Anderson and Moore [eds.] 1992) has no chapter on any form of
linguistic criticism or analysis, although it has plenty on other forms of
criticism, such as reader-response and deconstruction.

Most commentaries on Mark's Gospel have little to offer besides the
standard discussions of authorship, date and provenance. A few of the
older commentaries have comments on the Greek used in the book of
Mark. For example, Swete has an insightful section on the 'Vocabulary,
Grammar, and Style' (Swete 1909: xliv-l) and V. Taylor has a similar
one on 'The Vocabulary, Syntax, and Style' (Taylor 1952: 44-52).
Whereas Taylor's discussion amounts to little more than a list of particular syntactical constructions, Swete includes this as well as lists of
vocabulary items. Mann (1986: 165-72) has an even shorter and briefer
discussion of the same. A discussion of interchange in the verb tenses
by Swete (1913: xlix-l) is as close as any of these commentaries comes
to a linguistic discussion. Not even this is to be found in a commentary
such as Guelich's (1989). Hurtado (1989: 4-8) and Lane (1974: 12-17)
both have sections that use the words 'circumstances' or 'situation' to
describe discussion of the environment that gave rise to Mark's Gospel,
but these are not more linguistically informed than traditional discussions of authorship, date and provenance. Arguably, the low-point in
discussion of such issues was reached by the commentary of D. Taylor,
who seems to take pride in noting that he has arrived at a number of
what he characterizes as literary conclusions regarding Mark's Gospel

---

3.   E.g. Hurst (1986) is not part of the discussion. This is perhaps the best-
informed article about this issue.

without finding anything more substantial than vague conceptual support for them (1992: vi-ix).

This situation regarding secondary scholarly research on Mark's Gospel is both discouraging, for those who look to these traditional resources for serious textual analysis, and encouraging, for those who are looking for areas of possible application of recently developed linguistic methodologies. More potentially promising are two attempts to utilize linguistic models to analyze texts of the New Testament. One is a detailed and insightful study of Mark's Gospel, and the other is an avowed attempt to utilize the categories of Hallidayan register in the study of Galatians.

The first is the monograph-length study by Paul Danove on Mark (1993a). This detailed work merits fuller comments than can be devoted to it here, as does his entire approach—construction grammar—developed by the linguist Charles Fillmore (Danove 1993b: 120-27; Danove 1993a: esp. 30-36; Danove relies upon mostly unpublished work by Fillmore). What I am interested in here is Danove's methodological perspective. Construction grammar is a descriptive, non-transformational grammar that depends upon two major concepts: semantic frames and valency. The descriptive characteristic distances it from a variety of formal grammars (see, for example, Palmer 1995), that is, those predicated upon a formal semantic calculus that exists apart from or prior to observation of actual locutions. In this respect, construction grammar has a presupposition in common with a Hallidayan functional grammar: both are concerned with the functions of the structural units of a language, although construction grammar, as will be noted below, tends to work on the basis of language universals in a way that Hallidayan functional grammar does not. The description of construction grammar as non-transformational follows on from its descriptive character, in that it attempts to describe the particular syntactical patterns that are associated with a given semantic structure, rather than these structures depending upon transformational rules acting upon underlying structures.

When the notions of semantic frames and valence are introduced, however, construction grammar must part company with systemic linguistics. Fillmore, according to Danove, begins from the standpoint of belief in a deep structure consisting of semantic cases, which, though supposedly empirically discoverable, constitute a finite set of universal, semantic relations. This is an obvious development from Fillmore's earlier work on universal case theory, taken up and extended in New Testament studies by the work on Paul's letters by Wong (1994; 1997).[4] Thus, Fillmore attempts to devise a relationship between semantics and syntax predicated upon what is called a 'case frame'. The case frame appeals to semantic notions that are part of the cognitive processes activated and drawn upon by utterances (on semantic frames, see Brown and Yule 1983: 236-56). The representation at the syntactical level that leads to invoking a particular semantic frame is the Valence Description of a predicator, by which are determined the functions of the complements of the predicator, their semantic functions and their lexical realizations.

There are several major points of criticism regarding this scheme as presented by Danove. One is that the relationship among Valence Descriptions, their semantic functions and their cognitive semantic frames is an imprecise one in English, to say nothing regarding ancient Greek and its context of culture or any possible context of situation. Access to the context of situation, as noted in the previous essay, is through linguistic usage, not the reverse as is necessary in semantic-frame theory, and construction grammar fails to address this major shortcoming by failing to deal with constructions larger than the clause (for example, how would such a basic notion as conjunction between clauses be analysed?). In this sense, construction grammar can never proceed beyond any clause-limited grammar, and does not have within its definitional capabilities larger structures such as sub-discourse (paragraph) or discourse structures. An attempt to extend its analysis beyond the clause invokes the concept of semantic frames, which are not grammatically of the same type of description. Another serious deficiency is that several of the major concepts, such as semantic frames and semantic cases, are subject to much criticism. For example, frames seem to be best examined in terms of higher discourse levels, such as the context of culture, rather than lower levels of context of situation. Semantic cases found in the deep structure are an attempt to deal with language universals, an effort that many linguists have lately abandoned in favour of analysis of finding language typologies. In other words, instead of positing notional roles, which may or may not have a determinable relationship to any given language, cases are better seen in terms of grammatical roles, for which there are realizations specific to

---

4.   Wong's proposal has already been criticized in Porter (1994) and (1997: 120-22). See Porter (1997: 122-24) for a proposal on defining case.

the analysed language (see Palmer 1994: 1; Blake 1994: 5-11 *passim*). Thus, although Danove's attempt to bring a linguistic methodology to his analysis of Mark is highly commendable, it comes as little surprise that his method must invoke other approaches, such as rhetorical theory, in order to provide an analysis of the whole of Mark, since rhetorical categories must be used to extend his analysis beyond the clause without jumping to the highly abstract level of semantic frames.

Whereas Danove is rigorous in his application of construction grammar to Mark, despite its obvious methodological limitations, the same cannot be said of Boers's use of Halliday's concept of register in his analysis of Galatians (1994: 65). His discussion is only tangential to the major thrust of his analysis of Galatians, but his treatment is so potentially misleading that it merits comment here. In analysing Gal. 3.1–5.12, Boers divides the section into five sub-sections. In these five sections, he sees an alternation between sections that function 'as interactions with the readers and those which function to provide information'. He sees in this a correlation with Halliday's 'interpersonal' and 'ideational' components of a discourse: 3.1-5 is interpersonal; 3.5-22 ideational = exposition; 3.23–4.20 interpersonal; 4.21-31 ideational = exposition but with an interpersonal conclusion in v. 31; 5.1-12 interpersonal. In a footnote (p. 65 n. 53) Boers also notes that Halliday distinguishes the 'textual' component, citing Halliday at some length on the three meta-functions (1973a: 99).

That Boers has misunderstood Halliday is clear. He has mistaken the Hallidayan concept of grammar and treated the individual meta-functions of register as if they can exist in compartmentalized and isolated units. What Halliday says, even in the quotation given by Boers, is that these various meta-functions are 'part of the grammar', not that (as Boers seems to take it) each constitutes a different part of the text. All components of the grammar—textual, interpersonal and ideational—are always functioning, by definition, even if one of the components is brought to the fore, since discourse is always conveyed by a textual medium, specifies participants, and has an ideational component. To analyse it otherwise appears too much like taking a theory and making it work in support of a previously determined hypothesis. It also runs the risk of making the analytical linguistic task appear to be different, and perhaps easier, than it really is or can be.

3. *A Hallidayan View of the Register of Mark's Gospel*

In the light of what has been said above, I wish here to make some preliminary and initial observations regarding Markan register from a Hallidayan functional–grammatical perspective. Without a substantial previous tradition of commenting from this perspective, these comments
are meant to be instigatory rather than definitive. Nevertheless, I think
that they can help us to realize a way forward for subsequent, insightful
work from this methodological perspective.

The usual (although simplified) view of Mark's Gospel, the earliest
of the four Gospels, is that it is a simple narrative, reflecting either the
thought-patterns of the writer, whose native competence was in Aramaic, or a type of language that most approximates spoken language
(see, for example, Maloney 1980: 2 and chapter 1; cf. Horrocks 1996:
92-95 for a contrasting linguistic approach). A conclusion such as this
is usually—at least, in its best form—dependent upon analysis of individual examples of linguistic usage, gathered and assessed in the way
noted in the previous essay regarding Hemer's article, and found in
many of the standard commentaries, such as Swete (1909) and V. Taylor
(1952). An analysis of the register of Mark's Gospel, however, looks
quite different.

a. *Mode of Discourse Realized by Textual Semantic Component*
The mode of Mark's discourse is that it was created and preserved as a
written text, although probably originally meant to be read aloud (see
Achtemeier 1990; Gilliard 1993), with some sections created around
quotations of Old Testament texts (see Fairclough 1992: 101-36, for
comparisons in other types of literature). The language is supportively
descriptive, especially of the character of Jesus, with various connected
discourse sub-units (pericopes) illustrating his actions and utterances.
The patterned alternation between sub-units including actions and utterances belies any notion of casual or haphazard composition.

The form of the discourse is that of narrative, with connected
descriptive sub-units, involving both actions and dialogue. The question
of genre is a question that is best discussed in terms of the context of
culture, since it concerns formalized literary patterning particular and
peculiar to a specific linguistic community. Therefore, the question of
Markan genre is one that falls outside the discussion of register, but
would be important in terms of a full discourse analysis of the book

also considering its context of culture. It is at this highest and most abstract level that various social and cultural conventions, often invoked through scenarios, play their most decisive role. The question of historicity of the Gospel accounts would here find its most suitable place for discussion, since this question draws upon the question of exophoric reference, that is, how and whether the discourse invokes events or people outside of the discourse itself. In the light of the referentiality of Jesus, one can plausibly posit that there is at least an appearance of attempting to write a historically-based narrative, in so far as the context of culture is concerned, and in terms of literary genres available in the Greco-Roman world should probably be classified as biography (see Burridge 1992, who invokes linguistic criteria in trying to establish a family resemblance between the Gospels, including Mark, and other Greco-Roman biographies).

I am here concerned, however, with the context of situation, which extends only so far as the discourse in its textual component is concerned. Questions of historical referentiality, made through various forms of deixis, are beyond the scope of such analysis. The textual structure of Mark's Gospel follows a very straightforward, apparently roughly chronological, thematic structure (see below on the use of 'and' and 'immediately/then', and how they serve in creating this textual structure; but cf. Mk 4.1, where the scene is not necessarily consecutive), beginning with John the Baptist and ending with the empty tomb. Thus the text moves on two levels from given to new information for the reader or hearer (see Halliday 1985: 278-79). The first level is that of the discourse itself, where the given situations and characters proceed to the new situations and characters. The discourse begins with identification of the major character, Jesus Christ, by quotations from the Old Testament, which is treated here as known and recognizable sacred text, and ends with resurrection. At the end of the Gospel, if resurrection was not an unexpected concept in the ancient world (see Porter 1999), it certainly was not part of ordinary experience, and leaves the women at the tomb fearful.[5] A similar pattern is to be found at the level of sub-units such as paragraphs or pericopes within the discourse. Within individual sub-units, the apparently normal narrative pattern of Mark's Gospel is to establish the location, time and characters in the first one or two verses of the episode, before elaborat-

---

5.   I take it that the Gospel of Mark ended at 16.8.

ing the episode. For example, in Mk 10.1-2, we have an indication of movement to a specified place (Judea beyond the Jordan), those who accompanied Jesus (crowds), those who opposed him (Pharisees), and Jesus' beginning his teaching. In terms of clause structure (anticipating what is perhaps more properly discussed under the field of discourse), the book of Mark appears to follow the general Hallidayan patterns for marked and unmarked thematization (Halliday 1985: 44-45). Here is a point where Greek linguistic structure must be appreciated, since included in analysis of thematization is the fundamental consideration that Greek syntax of the verb does not require an expressed or grammaticalized subject (i.e. finite verbs are monolectic). For an assertive clause, the assumed subject is the unmarked thematic element, a pattern found not only throughout Mark but in much of the Greek of the New Testament and elsewhere (see Porter 1993). In narrative, it appears likely that there will often be more thematized subjects than there are in exposition, as new characters are introduced to the scene. Nevertheless, a sub-unit, for example one such as Mk 10.1, can begin with a verb with an assumed subject, in this instance, Jesus. It is unnecessary to mark the theme in this kind of structure, since it continues the pattern of Jesus being the one who performs the action. Specification of the subject marks the thematic structure, and placement of the subject in relation to the verb seems to indicate degrees of markedness. The use of voice is part of this thematic (as well as informational) structure, with the passive voice used to thematize the medium, rather than the agent, of the process as the subject. For example, in Mk 11.2, the colt is described as bound (with the marked perfect tense-form, grammaticalizing stative verbal aspect), using the passive form of the verb, in distinction to the use of active voice verbs (realized by active forms) used in the vast majority of instances, especially at the beginning of sub-units. It is the colt that is the bound element, with the agent not grammaticalized, and hence not significant for the situation. The rheme is realized by the verb and its complements and adjuncts. Theme and rheme are not iconistic with 'given' and 'new', since theme and rheme are concerned with the language user's structuring of what is known (given) and unknown (new) for perception by the language receiver (Halliday 1985: 278). With regard to the Markan narrative, it appears that such characters as Jesus Christ (Mk 1.1 and *passim*) and John the Baptist (1.4), and the authoritative status of the Old Testament (1.2-3), are part of the 'given' context of situation of the Markan audience.

Since all three are invoked at the outset without description or identification,[6] this indicates a Christian audience, with re-enforcing, possibly even informational, rather than evangelistic, purposes for the Gospel. Peter/Simon is also possibly a part of this 'given' information, since his introduction in 1.16 is simply by name, in contrast to Andrew, who is specified as Peter's brother (1.16). The sons of Zebedee are introduced and then described as leaving their father, who was a fisherman (1.19-20). It is against the backdrop of these known characters, implying a Christian audience for whom Jesus Christ, John the Baptist and Peter were known characters, that the episodes unfold and are thematized. The thematized material reflects the author's bringing to the fore incidents and events for particular appreciation. The context of situation may well indicate that the Gospel has links between a Petrine origin and Palestinian reception, linking communities that might know both Peter and John the Baptist.

The cohesiveness of the text of Mark is established through the use of several different kinds of linguistic items (see Halliday and Hasan 1976, for the most thorough discussion of the following categories). The forms of cohesiveness are what gives a text its texture, and ultimately what make it possible for a text to cohere, as well. One of the elements of cohesiveness is the frequent repetition of various lexical items, for example, in Mark's Gospel the adverb[7] often translated 'immediately/then' (εὐθύς). Often in conjunction with 'and', this adverb can indicate immediate succession within a discourse sub-unit. It is used in such a way in Mk 1.10, when Jesus comes up out of the water after his baptism; in 1.18 and 20 when Jesus calls his disciples; and in 1.23 when Jesus confronts the man with the unclean spirit; this pattern appears consistently throughout the Gospel. This adverb is also used occasionally at crucial junctures to link discourse sub-units, indicating 'temporal succession between prior and upcoming' discourse sub-units (Schiffrin 1987: 246). It is used in such a way in Mk 1.12 to mark the end of the announcement of Jesus' ministry by John and Jesus' being tempted, the formal beginning of his own ministry; 1.21 and 1.29 to indicate the first healings by Jesus, the first of an individual and the second of many others; in 6.45 to link Jesus' walking on the

---

6. The presupposition pool of the Markan audience must be determined on the basis of a complex of linguistic, cultural and historical factors, all of which are part of the context of culture. See Cotterell and Turner 1989: 257-59.

7. The word is formally an adjective, but is used adverbially as a fixed form.

water with his feeding of the five thousand, two contrastive yet revela-
tory miracles (see 6.52, where the discourse indicates the connection);
14.43 to join Jesus' being in the garden with his disciples and the
coming of Judas to betray him; 15.1 to contrast Peter's denial of Jesus
with his appearance before Pilate. A second category is the use of the
conjunction 'and' (καί), not only to connect individual clauses but to
begin new sub-units (see Schiffrin 1987: 128-52), a very frequent
Markan characteristic. The two primary functions of coordination and
continuation tend to be demonstrated by these two uses. This is an
example of cohesion created through grammar and lexis, since both
elements—the function of the syntax and the meaning of the lexical
item—are operative.

The relatively non-periodic syntax of Mark has given rise to much
speculation among scholars, especially about its possible origins in
Semitic or oral contexts. There are similarities in the use of 'and' with
Semitic paratactic style, but the same patterns can be found in pre-Hel-
lenistic and Hellenistic Greek especially of a non-artificially literary
type (see Reiser 1984: 99-137; cf. Porter 1989: 140-41), as a means of
joining together elements of the discourse in a serial and often chronological fashion. Origin in an oral context is not necessarily the case
either, however, as recent studies in differences between spoken and
written language indicate. These features of Mark's Gospel, instead of
necessarily indicating origins in Semitic or oral discourse, point rather
to the Gospel as discourse always being a written text, regardless of
whether individual episodes may have originated in the spoken words
of Jesus.[8] Recent study has shown that facile distinctions, on the basis
of typifications of spoken and written language, simply do not hold
(Biber 1988; cf. also Brown and Yule 1983: 14-19; Fleischmann 1990:
187-88, 191-92). Nevertheless, typical of spoken language in the
extreme is a surprisingly complex syntax, often so complex that it cannot be deciphered when transferred to written form (Halliday 1978:
224). By comparison, it appears that, at least in places, the Pauline
epistles reflect spoken language written down for subsequent reading
(dictation?) rather than the Gospel of Mark, or even some of the other
letters, such as Hebrews and 1 Peter, where the syntax is more regular

---

8.   Again, the question of whether the words of Jesus in Mark's Gospel reflect
the actual words of Jesus (whether in translation from Aramaic or originally uttered
in Greek) must begin with the context of culture, and not with the context of situation, with which register is concerned.

and less orally complex. This would seem to be a conclusion that moves in the opposite direction from most regarding the linguistic relationships among these bodies of writing, as well as confirming theories regarding some Pauline syntax (such as the complexity of Eph. 1.3-14, arguably the longest single—yet perhaps overly convoluted—'sentence' in the New Testament).

Another explanation of the Markan syntax is perhaps necessary. The context of situation implied is one in which there is a sense of irresistible logic or succession seen behind the events conveyed. In the same way that, for example, other non-literary Hellenistic texts present their material as simply unfolding for the reader, Mark's Gospel appears to have originated in a context of few literary pretensions, but where the events were seen to unfold in a logical and connected succession. The initial endorsement of Jesus Christ by means of sacred tradition does not use connective 'and', but rather asyndeton, the use of parataxis not appearing until 1.5. Similarly, asyndeton is used in high concentration in Mark at three other places: 8.35-38, 10.27-30 and 13.33-36. The first is where Jesus calls for his disciples to follow after him, a way that leads to death and resurrection; the second, where Jesus discusses further with his disciples the importance of commitment to his cause; and the third, where Jesus says that the day and hour of the coming of the son of man is unknown. The final endorsement of Jesus is made through his resurrection. One can perhaps see that the connective pattern of alternation between 'and' and asyndeton reflects belief in a divine supervision of successive events, framed by and interspersed with important scenes that comment on the importance of following Jesus to his death and resurrection. This perhaps indicates a context of situation in which instruction and edification of Jesus' followers is paramount.

A third means of establishing cohesion is through the person of the verb. The use of third person singular verbs, often with an unstated subject such as Jesus, serves to create cohesion through co-referentiality between individual sub-units. The theme of a given sub-unit may well be a continuation in terms of participant structure of the previous unit, such as Jesus and his disciples. For example, in Mk 10.32, the group of Jesus' followers is the assumed subject, but then Jesus is specified to distinguish him from the group. A fourth category of cohesive devices involves reference, substitution and ellipsis. These categories are invoked when grammatical means such as pronouns are used. Once reference is established through an explicit reference, such as using the name of the person, there are other means of utilizing the information without repeating the same term, such as substitution with a pronoun or utilization of a verb in the third person (singular or plural, depending upon the actor or actors involved), in order to bring cohesion to the discourse. A common pattern in Mark, as well as other Greek narrative, is the initial identification of a participant, and then subsequent reference by means of a pronoun, especially use of the genitive singular intensive pronoun (αὐτοῦ) to indicate 'possession'—that something is 'his'. For example, in Mk 14.10, Judas Iscariot is introduced and defined, since he is new to the narrative in an active capacity, but then referred to with a pronoun (v. 11). However, Jesus is referred to with the pronoun 'him' (αὐτόν), even though he is not explicitly mentioned, because he is the major actor in the narrative.

Since Mark's is a written text (though perhaps initially and in subsequent contexts used orally), it does not have textual informational structure indicated by intonation, as would a spoken discourse. Consequently, paragraphs or pericopes (or other sub-units), as well as clauses, provide the framework for creating informational structure. In Mark, sub-units are fairly clearly marked, especially with the use of 'and' (see above). Like many written texts, this one seems to follow the 'good reason' principle (see Halliday 1978: 133). This principle states that when one information structure is mirrored upon another, the unmarked form is used except where there is a good reason for a marked form to be used. This might involve, for example, use of an explicit subject or use of a complex nominal group to indicate new material, as in Mk 10.35, where James and John, specified as the sons of Zebedee, come to Jesus. This is a marked thematic structure indicated by a complex nominal group, even though in secondary position syntactically following the main verb.

b. *Tenor of Discourse Realized by Interpersonal Semantic Component*
The tenor of Mark's text is monolingual, in that the narrator is the one who presents all of the speakers and actors. Many literary studies of Mark debate the so-called omniscience of the narrator,[9] but perhaps a different approach through tenor of discourse, and drawing upon the interpersonal semantic component, can prove equally enlightening to

9.   See, for example, Petersen 1980.

the interactive dimension of the Gospel discourse. Second order—linguistically- or discourse-based—interpersonal roles (Halliday 1978: 144) in the text consist of an overwhelmingly predominant use of third person (mostly singular, but also plural) in the narrative frame itself, with first and second person virtually confined to the interspersed dialogue sections and not found with great frequency. First person is used mostly by Jesus and appears in the singular, although he also uses second person when speaking to individuals (singular) or groups (plural, for disciples, etc.) and third person (e.g. Mk 13 in the so-called apocalyptic discourse); those who speak to Jesus use second person singular. There is relatively little use of the third person to speak about Jesus. The role relationships depicted in the Gospel are highly involved, with an intensive introduction and reintroduction of characters throughout. The relationship of first and second person is semantically more closely related than that of third person, since first and second persons include either speaker or addressee [+ participants], but third person includes neither [- participants] (see Levinson 1983: 69). Therefore, third person is a way of linguistically creating distance in the discourse between speaker–addressee and others–events, since there is a grammaticalized differentiation and distancing of any specific participant-role in the text. The use of the locution 'son of man' poses difficulties, mostly because of this semantic function of person. The question for interpretation is whether the speaker, Jesus, is using this third-person locution to be self-referential (as most scholars think today, for at least some of the 'son of man' statements) or whether he is using it with reference to someone else (as scholars such as Bultmann have thought in the past). Even by using it of himself, the third-person structure distances the speaker from himself, so that explanations that use of 'son of man' is the same as using 'I' may be accurate in so far as reference goes but are inaccurate so far as other semantic features are concerned, taking the referent and distancing it from the speaker, even if the two are the same. Furthermore, the narrative itself, by using the third person, does not specify any particular participant structure, whereas episodes in which Jesus speaks with people define participant roles. For example, in Mk 10.13 the sub-unit opens with a description of children coming to Jesus and the disciples rebuking them, with both the children and the disciples grammatically specified. Jesus is then thematized so that he can speak. He addresses the disciples to permit the children to come to him, and then offers a statement on harming them. The context of situation implied by this participant structure is one typically found in narrative, in which the focus is upon Jesus and those to whom he speaks and about whom he speaks. Even though, as noted above, this is a discourse that is addressed to a Christian community, the use of the third-person narrative style indicates an attempt at an objective depiction of the major participants. The occasional use of first and second person maintains Jesus as the centre of attention, with very little use of third person by others to speak about Jesus.

The tenor of the discourse makes definition of the interpersonal role relationships relatively easy to determine concerning Jesus and those who approach him for help or instruction. This is also the case in adversarial scenes when Jesus deals with the Jewish leaders and the Romans. The possible relationships between Jesus' compatriots and adversaries are more difficult to establish, due to the limited number of scenes in the discourse when they come into contact with each other. However, establishing a relationship between the narrator and the original audience is very complex, since this requires extra-linguistic analysis. The Jewish religious leaders are viewed as adversaries and the others, especially Jesus' closest followers, the disciples, are seen in a sympathetic light, despite their often failing to understand his actions (Mk 8, 9). The relations between Jesus' followers and adversaries, however, are left undefined in the discourse. Although one cannot specify the original context of situation in terms of place and date using register analysis (that is not its purpose or aim), the evidence indicates one in which close interpersonal relationships of the characters are not the primary emphasis of the discourse. The lack of a sense of needing to defend the participants, along with the objective third-person characterization, may seem surprising in a Christian document, unless one concludes that the context of situation was a non-apologetic one, in which the events and characters are unfolded by means of the interconnected narrative.

In terms of the mood and modality networks, the Greek language organizes its interpersonal semantic component differently than does English (for Greek see Porter 1989: 109, 163-78; cf. Halliday 1985: 71-75). The attitudinal system at the level of clause, realized by the mood forms at the level of the verbal group, is concerned with expression of degrees of probability (Halliday's modality system), as well as ways of expression such as assertion, command, etc. (Halliday's mood system), within the constraints of discourse structure (Halliday 1978: 223). Questions (simple, or with implied positive or negative answers, that is, polarity) are a matter of clause and discourse structure. In Mark, as in most Greek narrative, assertion (realized by the indicative) is the basis of the narrative, with commanding (realized by the imperative, etc.), projection (realized by the subjunctive), etc., reserved mostly (though not exclusively, to be sure) for dialogue, including Jesus' healing and teaching. Assertion is used in didactic portions as well (e.g. a parable). For example, when the leper comes to Jesus (Mk 1.40, 41), he phrases his request for healing in terms of a third class conditional structure, utilizing the subjunctive verb form in the protasis. Jesus' response of healing consists of two clauses, one with an indicative verb and the other with an imperative. One makes an assertion, that is, that Jesus desires to heal the leper, and the other directs a course of action, that is, Jesus tells the man to be healed.[10]

c. *Field of Discourse Realized by Ideational Semantic Component*
The field of discourse indicates the subject matter and the purpose of the discourse. It draws upon the ideational semantic component, including both the experiential and the logical sub-components. The subject of the Gospel of Mark is 'the gospel of Jesus Christ [son of God]' (Mk 1.1).[11] This is stated at the outset, and developed throughout the Gospel, including, for example, the baptism where God endorses his beloved son in the opening scene of the text (1.15) and the acclamation of the centurion that this man was the son of God at the end (15.39; note that this serves as a cohesive lexical tie as well). It is also clear that son of God language is prominent here, whether it be defended from a Semitic or a Hellenistic background (see Porter forthcoming). The Semitic background is to be found in a variety of sources, including recently published Dead Sea texts and others (e.g. 4Q246), and the Hellenistic background is attested in Greco-Roman inscriptional evidence (the most famous being, perhaps, the Priene inscription of 9 BCE which celebrates the 'birthday' 'of the God', referring to Augustus [OGIS 458]).

With regard to the logical semantic component, the Markan discourse is arranged paratactically, with an abundant use of 'and' sometimes accompanied by a word translated 'immediately' or 'then' (εὐθύς), as noted above regarding cohesion. 'And' is used at the beginning of sub-

10. Note that the passive voice verb is used, thus making the leper, the medium, the subject of the clause, rather than the agent, who remains unspecified.
11. The variant 'son of God' is most likely original to the Gospel—at least it has the strongest textual support.

units, as well as to conjoin clauses. Representative would be the parable of the sower in Mk 4.1-9, where roughly 20 of 26 clauses begin with 'and'. Halliday (1985: 75) attaches time to the verb (probably because his analysis is based upon English), and considers this a part of the logical semantic component; however, in Greek, temporal relations are, in Hallidayan terms, better considered nonstructural, since they are not part of clause structure, but are part of the logical semantic component. Establishment of temporal relations is part of the discourse, but not realized structurally, the way verbal aspect is. The Markan discourse begins with the verbless clause regarding the good news of Jesus Christ, son of God, and then recounts this good news by means of events and dialogue. The semantic domain of words of communication is drawn upon heavily throughout the discourse; it is the most frequent semantic domain, apart from those of function words (e.g. indicating relations). On a macro-level, the discourse puts forward Jesus as the good news (Mk 1.1), but on the micro-level, Jesus is the one who is the speaker of the good news, whether that consists of words of healing (e.g. Mk 3.5, where Jesus speaks to heal), instruction (e.g. Mk 4.11, where Jesus comments on his purpose for giving parables, most of which begin with Jesus 'saying' something, e.g., 4.1, 13, 21, 26, 30; 12.1), or information about future times (Mk 13.2, 4). A second semantic domain to note is that of linear motion. Words of motion are frequent in the Gospel, especially to indicate where Jesus is going. These words of motion often are used to introduce a sub-unit. For example, the Markan discourse says in 1.16 that Jesus went along the sea of Galilee, in 1.21 that he entered Capernaum, in 1.29 that he left the synagogue, in 1.35 that he departed and went away to a desert place, 1.40 that he came to a leper, 2.1 that he entered Capernaum, etc. (see also 2.13; 3.1, 13, 20, 31; 5.1, 21; 6.1, 6, 53; 7.24, 31; 8.11, 22, 27; 9.14, 30, 33; 10.1, 17, 32, 46; 11.1, 12, 15, 27; 13.1; 14.32, with decreasing frequency after his entry into Jerusalem). These two ideational domains indicate two of the major functions of Jesus, his speaking including teaching, and his moving toward his destiny in Jerusalem. Consistent with what was said above regarding the context of situation, the discourse indicates that it may well have originated in a community interested in what Jesus said and did, within the framework of his ordained and vindicated life and ministry.

The transitivity network for Hallidayan linguistics is fundamental to the ideational component, especially its experiential sub-component, and encompasses all of the relations between verbs and their phrases, in terms of the kind of process expressed in the clause. One of the dimensions of process is verbal aspect. In terms of verb structure in Greek, the aspectual and attitudinal (mood) systems are a coordinated network, grammaticalized by selection of single forms (on aspectual and attitudinal systems in Greek, see Porter 1989: 109), but in a Hallidayan framework of sociolinguistic analysis, they draw upon two different semantic components. Whereas the mood system draws upon the interpersonal system (as noted above), the aspectual system draws upon the ideational system, and more particularly the experiential system, that is, how the process is seen or thought to be experienced by the language user. In Mark, narrative transitivity expressed by verbal aspect relies heavily upon the perfective and imperfective aspects. The perfective aspect, realized by the default form, the aorist, creates the framework of the narrative, with the marked imperfective aspect, realized by the present tense form as well as the imperfect form, selected as a choice in semantic contrast, to in some way mark a particular verbal process. In the Markan discourse, sometimes the imperfective aspect marks a process within a sub-unit (e.g. the use of the imperfect form used of a verb of communication, e.g., Mk 11.28). However, a more noteworthy use of the imperfective aspect in Mark is to introduce a sub-unit or new participants in the narrative, as well as to close a sub-unit (see Porter 1989: 192-98, where numerous examples are cited).

Participant identification as indicated by verb choice is also part of the ideational semantic component. A good example is found in Mk 3.31, where Jesus' mother and brothers are introduced with the present tense verb-form (imperfective aspect), but in the following sub-unit, where Jesus, who has already been introduced and is the focus of the narrative, is already known, his activity is described using the aorist tense-form (Mk 4.1). The participant structure in the nominal groups reflects this same ideational structure. New participants are often introduced with complex nominal groups (e.g. Mk 1.5 with 'all the country of Judea and all the Jerusalemites'), whereas known participants are often reintroduced by implicit participant reference or simple nominal groups.

4. *Conclusion*

To return to the initial question regarding register and the Gospel of Mark, the question must be asked whether knowledge of the textual, interpersonal and ideational semantic components allows for a recon-

struction of the context of situation of the discourse. Several conclusions are worth drawing. First, one must face the possibility that the
conclusions drawn using register analysis may not readily supplant
those of traditional historical criticism. One obvious reason for this is
that the kind of evidence drawn into that discussion—while being
highly instructive and forming part of what is meant by the context of
culture—is often not clearly correlated with the semantic structure of
the discourse itself. As was noted above, there is a clear lack of
significant analysis of the linguistic structure of Mark's Gospel, and a
similar situation is found in relation to other New Testament texts.
Thus, the kinds of conclusions reached regarding context of situation
might be quite different from those of historical criticism. Secondly,
with regard to the Gospel of Mark, a number of further conclusions can
be drawn regarding the context of situation. While many of these correlate with traditional conclusions, a small but significant number are
new, or at least newly reformulated—and all supported by quantifiable
linguistic evidence. For instance, the text was written in a literate culture, designed for conveying information regarding the figure of Jesus
Christ. The material is presented in a narrative that displays who he is
through what he does and says, including a series of meetings and relationships with a variety of people. One of the major semantic domains
throughout the discourse, not so much because of frequency of these
words as their discourse placement, is wording regarding 'good news'
and its proclamation. The context of situation of the original reading of
the Gospel appears to be one in which the recipient community already
was convinced of who Jesus was. Although some traditional Markan
scholars have viewed Mark's Gospel in this way, we can now see linguistic reasons for this conclusion. Jesus' identity is announced at the
beginning of the Gospel, and the episodes are presented in a consistently given–new fashion through the events of his life. There is no
necessary implication that Jesus' interpersonal relations with the Jewish
leaders is reflective of that of the audience of the work, since the relationship between Jesus' followers and the authorities is not developed,
an observation that merits further analysis. Nor is there a use of language reflecting a situation in which Jesus' followers are under perceived threat from without, since there is little interpersonal relation
between Jesus' followers and the authorities. Instead, the discourse is
concerned to represent in an orderly and progressive written/read fashion the actions, expositions and conversations of this figure, Jesus, who

dominates the Gospel in terms of specified grammatical reference. Thirdly, one can utilize these findings, in so far as they are linguistically well-founded in the points raised above, to say something about the larger context of culture and what we know of the formation of early Christianity. This discourse was probably written before there was serious tension between the Church and the Roman world. There may have been some tension with Judaism, although this is probably minimal, due to the way in which the Jewish leaders are presented in terms of Jesus, not his followers. If correlation can be found on other grounds between the events purported to have happened, and even the words purported to have been spoken, then one would be on good ground for seeing this discourse as a historical narrative, and hence a biography of its dominant character, Jesus.

BIBLIOGRAPHY

Abercrombie, N., S. Hill, and B.S. Turner
    1980   *The Dominant Ideology Thesis* (London: George Allen & Unwin).
Achtemeier, P.J.
    1990   '*Omne verbum sonat*: The New Testament and the Oral Environment of Late Western Antiquity', *JBL* 109.1: 1-12.
Ackerman, S.
    1992   *Under Every Green Tree: Popular Religion in Sixth-Century Judah* (HSM, 46; Atlanta: Scholars Press).
Adorno, T.W.
    1951   *Minima Moralia: Reflexionen aus dem beschädigten Leben* (Suhrkamp Verlag). ET E.G.N. Jephcott, *Minima Moralia: Reflections from a Damaged Life* (London: Verso, 1974).
    1967   *Negative Dialektik* (Frankfurt am Main: Suhrkamp Verlag, 2nd edn).
    1969   *Dialektik der Auflärung* (Frankfurt am Main: Fischer Verlag).
    1970–86 *Gessamelte Schriften* (ed. R. Tiedemann; Frankfurt am Main: Suhrkamp Verlag).
    1972   *Ästhetische Theorie* (Berlin: Suhrkamp Verlag, 2nd edn). ET C. Lenhardt, *Aesthetic Theory* (London: Routledge & Kegan Paul, 1984); Re-translation by R. Hullot-Kentor (Minneapolis: Minnesota University Press, 1996).
    1998   'Geschichtsphilosophischer Exkurs zur Odyssee', in Tiedemann (ed.) 1988: 37-88.
Adorno, T.W. *et al.*
    1950   *The Authoritarian Personality* (Studies in Prejudice, 1; New York: Harper).
Albertz, R.
    1994   *A History of Israelite Religion in the Old Testament Period*. I. *From the Beginnings to the End of the Monarchy* (trans. J. Bowden; London: SCM Press).
Albright, W.F.
    1968   *Yahweh and the Gods of Canaan: A Historical Analysis of Two Contrasting Faiths* (Winona Lake, IN: Eisenbrauns).
Alt, A.
    1953   *Kleine Schriften zur Geschichte des Volkes Israel*, II (Munich: C.H. Beck).
Alter, R.
    1981   *The Art of Biblical Narrative* (New York: Basic Books).
    1990   *The Pleasures of Reading in an Ideological Age* (Berkeley: University of California Press).
    1992   *The World of Biblical Literature* (London: SPCK).

Alter, R., and F. Kermode (eds.)
1987 *The Literary Guide to the Bible* (London: Fontana).
Althusser, L.
1977 *Lenin and Philosophy and Other Essays* (trans. B. Brewster; London: New Left Books).
1985 *For Marx* (trans. B. Brewster; London: Routledge, Chapman & Hall).
1994 'Selected Texts', in Eagleton (ed.) 1994: 87-111.
Amsler, S.
1965 *Amos* (Commentaire de l'Ancien Testament, 11a; Neuchâtel: Delachaux & Niestlé).
Andersen, F.I., and D.N. Freedman
1989 *Amos* (AB, 24; Garden City, NY: Doubleday).
Anderson, J.A., and S.D. Moore (eds.)
1992 *Mark and Method: New Approaches in Biblical Studies* (Minneapolis: Fortress Press).
Anonymous
1980 'Kracauer, S.', *Neue Deutsche Biographie*, XII (Berlin: Dunckler & Humblot).
Ardener, E.
1972 'Belief and the Problem of Women', in J.S. LaFontaine (ed.), *The Interpretation of Ritual* (London: Tavistock): 135-58.
Asad, T.
1983 'Anthropological Conceptions of Religion: Reflections on Geertz', *Man* NS 18: 237-59.
Ashton, E.B.
1973 *Negative Dialectics* (London: Routledge).
Auer, D., T. Bonacker and S. Müler-Doohm (eds.)
1998 *Die Gesellschaftstheorie Adornos: Themen und Grundbegriffe* (Darmstadt: Wissenschaftliche Buchgesellschaft).
Auld, A.G.
1986 *Amos* (OTG; Sheffield: JSOT Press).
Baetens Beardsmore, H.
1986 *Bilingualism: Basic Principles* (Clevedon: Multilingual Matters, 2nd edn).
Bakhtin, M.
1981 *The Dialogic Imagination: Four Essays* (trans. C. Emerson and M. Holquist; Austin, TX: University of Texas Press).
Barfield, T. (ed.)
1997 *The Dictionary of Anthropology* (Oxford: Basil Blackwell).
Barrett, M.
1991 *The Politics of Truth: From Marx to Foucault* (Stanford, CA: Stanford University Press).
Barstad, H.M.
1984 *The Religious Polemics of Amos: Studies in the Preaching of Am. 2, 7B-8; 4, 1-13; 5, 1-27; 6, 4-7; 8, 14* (VTSup, 34; Leiden: E.J. Brill).
1993 'No Prophets? Recent Developments in Biblical Prophetic Research and Ancient Near Eastern Prophecy', *JSOT* 57: 39-60.

Barthes, R,
    1977   'The Struggle with the Angel', in R. Barthes, *Image, Music, Text* (trans.
                S. Heath; London: Fontana Collins): 125-41.
Barton, J.
    1986   *Oracles of God: Perceptions of Ancient Israelite Prophecy in Israel after
                the Exile* (London: Darton, Longman & Todd).
Batstone, D. *et al.* (eds.)
    1997   *Liberation Theologies, Postmodernity, and the Americas* (London: Rout-
                ledge).
Batton, L.W.
    1913   *Ezra and Nehemiah* (ICC; Edinburgh: T. & T. Clark).
Beaugrande, R. de
    1991   *Linguistic Theory: The Discourse of Fundamental Works* (Longman Lin-
                guistics Library; London: Longmans).
    1993   ' "Register" in Discourse Studies: A Concept in Search of a Theory', in
                Ghadessy (ed.) 1993: 7-25.
Benhabib, S.
    1986   *Critique, Norm, and Utopia: A Study of the Foundations of Critical The-
                ory* (New York: University of Columbia Press).
Berger, P.L., and T. Luckman
    1967   *The Social Construction of Reality: A Treatise in the Sociology of Knowl-
                edge* (Harmondsworth: Penguin Books).
Berlinerblau, J.
    1993   'The "Popular Religion" Paradigm in Old Testament Research: A Socio-
                logical Critique', *JSOT* 60: 3-26.
    1995   'Some Sociological Observations on Moshe Greenberg's *Biblical Prose
                Prayer as a Window to the Popular Religion of Israel*', *JNSL* 21.1: 1-14.
    1996   *The Vow and the 'Popular Religious Groups' of Ancient Israel: A Philo-
                logical and Sociological Inquiry* (JSOTSup, 210; Sheffield: Sheffield
                Academic Press).
Bernstein, B. (ed.)
    1973   *Classes, Codes and Control.* II. *Applied Studies towards a Sociology of
                Language* (London: Routledge & Kegan Paul).
Berry, M.
    1975   *Introduction to Systemic Linguistics.* I. *Structures and Systems* (London:
                Batsford).
Berryman, P.
    1984   *The Religious Roots of Rebellion: Christians in Central American Revo-
                lutions* (Maryknoll, NY: Orbis Books).
    1994   *Stubborn Hope: Religion, Politics, and Revolution in Central America*
                (Maryknoll, NY: Orbis Books).
Bhabha, H.
    1985   'Signs Taken for Wonders', *CritInq* 12: 144-65.
    1994   *The Location of Culture* (London: Routledge).
Biber, D.
    1988   *Variation across Speech and Writing* (Cambridge: Cambridge University
                Press).

Bible and Culture Collective
    1995   *The Postmodern Bible* (New Haven, CT: Yale University Press).
Bird, P.A.
    1997   *Missing Persons and Mistaken Identities: Women and Gender in Ancient Israel* (OBT; Minneapolis: Fortress Press).
Black, D.A.
    1988   *Linguistics for Students of New Testament Greek: A Survey of Basic Concepts and Applications* (Grand Rapids, MI: Baker Book House).
Blake, B.J.
    1994   *Case* (CTL; Cambridge: Cambridge University Press).
Blenkinsopp, J.
    1988   *Ezra–Nehemiah* (OTL; Philadelphia: Westminster Press).
Bloch-Smith, E.
    1992   *Judahite Burial Practices and Beliefs about the Dead* (JSOTSup, 123; JSOT/ASOR Monograph Series, 7; Sheffield: Sheffield Academic Press).
Blum, E.
    1990   *Studien zur Komposition des Pentateuch* (Berlin: W. de Gruyter).
Boers, H.
    1994   *The Justification of the Gentiles: Paul's Letters to the Galatians and Romans* (Peabody, MA: Hendrickson).
Bolte, G.
    1989   *Unkritische Theorie: Gegen Habermas* (Lüneburg: Dietrich zu Klampen Verlag).
Brenner, A. (ed.)
    1993   *A Feminist Companion to Genesis* (The Feminist Companion to the Bible, 2; Sheffield: Sheffield Academic Press).
Brett, M.G.
    1990   'Four or Five Things to do with Texts: A Taxonomy of Interpretative Interests', in Clines, Fowl and Porter (eds.) 1990: 357-77.
    1991a   *Biblical Criticism in Crisis? The Impact of the Canonical Approach on Old Testament Studies* (Cambridge: Cambridge University Press).
    1991b   'Motives and Intentions in Genesis 1', *JTS* 42.1: 1-16.
    1993   'The Future of Reader Criticisms?', in F. Watson (ed.), *The Open Text* (London: SCM Press).
    1995a   'Nationalism and the Hebrew Bible', in Rogerson, Davies and Carroll R. (eds.) 1995: 136-63.
    1995b   'The Political Ethics of Postmodern Allegory', in M.D. Carroll R., D.J.A. Clines, P.R. Davies (eds.), *The Bible in Human Society: Essays in Honor of John Rogerson* (JSOTSup, 200; Sheffield: Sheffield Academic Press, 1995): 67-86.
    1996a   'Interpreting Ethnicity: Method, Hermeneutics, Ethics', in Brett (ed.) 1996: 3-22.
    1996b   'The Implied Ethics of Postcolonialism', *Semeia* 75: 219-28.
    2000   *Genesis: Procreation and the Politics of Identity* (London: Routledge).
Brett, M.G. (ed.)
    1996   *Ethnicity and the Bible* (BIS, 19; Leiden: E.J. Brill).

Briggs, S.
    1992   'The Deceit of the Sublime: An Investigation into the Origins of Ideolog-
            ical Criticism of the Bible in Early Nineteenth-Century German Biblical
            Studies', in Jobling and Pippin (eds.) 1992: 1-23.

Brixhe, C.
    1987   *Essai sur le Grec Anatolien au début de notre ère* (Travaux et memoires:
            Etudes anciennes, 1; Nancy: Presses universitiares de Nancy).
    1996   *Phonétique et phonologie du grec ancien.* I. *Quelques grandes questions*
            (Bibliothèque des cahiers de l'institut de linguistique de Louvain, 82;
            Louvain-la-Neuve: Peeters).

Brixhe, C. (ed.),
    1993   *La koiné grecque antique.* I. *Une langue introuvable?* (Travaux et mém-
            oires: Etudes anciennes, 10; Nancy: Presses universitaires de Nancy).
    1996   *La koiné grecque antique.* II. *La concurrence* (Travaux et mémoires:
            Etudes anciennes, 14; Nancy: Presses universitaires de Nancy).

Brown, G., and G. Yule
    1983   *Discourse Analysis* (CTL; Cambridge: Cambridge University Press).

Brueggemann, W.
    1988   *Israel's Praise: Doxology against Idolatry and Ideology* (Philadelphia:
            Fortress Press).
    1993   'Trajectories in Old Testament Literature and the Sociology of Ancient
            Israel', in Gottwald and Horsley (eds.) 1993: 161-85.
    1997   *Theology of the Old Testament: Testimony, Dispute, Advocacy* (Min-
            neapolis: Fortress Press).

Bühler, K.
    1990   *Theory of Language: The Representational Function of Language* (trans.
            D.F. Goodwin; Amsterdam: John Benjamins [1938]).

Burridge, R.
    1992   *What are the Gospels? A Comparison with Graeco-Roman Biography*
            (SNTSMS, 70; Cambridge: Cambridge University Press).

Butler, C.
    1985   *Systemic Linguistics: Theory and Applications* (London: Batsford).
    1989   'Systemic Models: Unity, Diversity, and Change', *Word* 40: 1-35.

Cahill, L.S.
    1995   'Sex and Gender Ethics as New Testament Ethics', in Rogerson, Davies
            and Carroll R. (eds.) 1995: 272-95.

Candelaria, M.R.
    1990   *Popular Religion and Liberation: The Dilemma of Liberation Theology*
            (Albany: State University of New York Press).

Carr, D.
    1996   *Reading the Fractures in Genesis* (Louisville, KY: Westminster/John
            Knox Press).

Carroll R., M.D.
    1992   *Contexts for Amos: Prophetic Poetics in Latin American Perspective*
            (JSOTSup, 132; Sheffield: Sheffield Academic Press).
    1993   'Los profetas del octavo siglo y su crítica de la economía: Un diálogo con
            Marvin Chaney', *Kairós* 13: 7-24.

1995a   'The Bible and the Religious Identity of the Maya of Guatemala at the Conquest and Today: Considerations and Challenges for the Nonindigenous', in Rogerson, Davies and Carroll R. (eds.) 1995: 193-212.

1995b   'Reflecting on War and Utopia in the Book of Amos: The Relevance of a Literary Reading of the Prophetic Text from Central America', in M.D. Carroll R., D.J.A. Clines, and P.R. Davies (eds.), *The Bible in Human Society: Essays in Honour of John Rogerson* (JSOTSup, 200; Sheffield: Sheffield Academic Press): 105-21.

1996a   'God and his People in the Nations' History: A Contextualized Reading of Amos 1 & 2', *TynBul* 47.1: 39-70.

1996b   'The Prophetic Text and the Literature of Dissent in Latin America: Amos, García Márquez, and Cabrera Infante Dismantle Militarism', *BibInt* 4.1: 76-100.

forthcoming   'Latin American Liberation Theology Hermeneutics', in J. Rogerson (ed.), *The Oxford Illustrated History of the Bible* (Oxford: Oxford University Press).

Carroll, R.P.

1990   'Whose Prophet? Whose Social Reality? Troubling the Interpretative Community Again: Notes Toward a Response to T.W. Overholt's Critique', *JSOT* 48: 33-49.

1995   'An Infinity of Traces: On Making an Inventory of our Ideological Holdings. An Introduction to *Ideologiekritik* in Biblical Studies', *JNSL* 21.2: 25-43.

Carter, C.E., and C.L. Meyers (eds.)

1996   *Community, Identity, and Ideology: Social Science Approaches to the Hebrew Bible* (SBTS, 6; Winona Lake, IN: Eisenbrauns).

Catford, J.

1965   *A Linguistic Theory of Translation* (London: Oxford University Press).

1967   'Translation and Language Teaching', in *idem, Linguistic Theories and their Application* (n.p.: AIDELA): 125-46.

Catron, J.E.

1995   'Temple and *bamah*: Some Considerations', in S.W. Holloway and L.K. Handy (eds.), *The Pitcher Is Broken: Memorial Essays for Gösta W. Ahlström* (JSOTSup, 190; Sheffield: Sheffield Academic Press): 150-65.

CELAM

1979   *Puebla: La evangelización en el presente y en el futuro de América Latina* (III Conferencia General del Episcopado Latinoamericano, Puebla, México; Bogotá, Colombia: Editora L. Canal y Asociados, 3rd edn.).

1992   *Nueva evangelización, promoción humana, cultura cristiana* (IV Conferencia General del Episcopado Latinoamericano, Santo Domingo, República Dominicana, 12–28 de octubre, 1992; Antigua, Guatemala: CELAM).

Certeau, M. de

1985   *The Practice of Everyday Life* (Berkeley, CA: University of California Press).

Chambers, J.K., and P. Trudgill

1980   *Dialectology* (CTL; Cambridge: Cambridge University Press).

Clements, R.E.
1996 'Amos and the Politics of Israel', in R.E. Clements (ed.), *Old Testament Prophecy: From Oracles to Canon* (Louisville, KY: Westminster/John Knox Press): 23-34.

Clements, R.E. (ed.)
1989 *The World of Ancient Israel: Sociological, Anthropological and Political Perspectives* (Cambridge: Cambridge University Press).

Clines, D.J.A.
1984 *Ezra, Nehemiah, Esther* (NCB; London: Marshall, Morgan & Scott).
1993 'Metacommentating Amos', in H.A. McKay and D.J.A. Clines (eds.), *Of Prophets' Visions and the Wisdom of Sages. Essays in Honour of R. Norman Whybray on his Seventieth Birthday* (JSOTSup, 162; Sheffield: Sheffield Academic Press).
1995 *Interested Parties: The Ideology of Writers and Readers of the Hebrew Bible* (Sheffield: Sheffield Academic Press).

Clines, D.J.A, S.E. Fowl and S.E. Porter (eds.),
1990 *The Bible in Three Dimensions: Essays in Celebration of Forty Years of Biblical Studies in the University of Sheffield* (JSOTSup, 87; Sheffield: Sheffield Academic Press).

Cogan, M.
1974 *Imperialism and Religion: Assyria, Judah and Israel in the Eighth and Seventh Centuries BCE* (Missoula, MT: Scholars Press).

Collinge, N.E.
1960 'Some Reflexions on Comparative Historical Syntax', *Archivum Linguisticum* 12: 79-101.

Collins, J.J. (ed.)
1979 *Apocalypse: The Morphology of a Genre* (Semeia, 14; Chico, CA: Scholars Press).

Comaroff, J.
1985 *Body of Power, Spirit of Resistance: The Culture and History of a South African People* (Chicago: University of Chicago Press).

Comaroff, J., and J. Comaroff
1991 *Of Revelation and Revolution: Christianity, Colonialism and Consciousness in South Africa* (Chicago: University of Chicago Press).

Cook, G. (ed.)
1997 *Crosscurrents in Indigenous Spirituality: Interface of Maya, Catholic and Protestant Worldviews* (Studies in Christian Mission, 18; Leiden: E.J. Brill).

Coote, R.B.
1981 *Amos among the Prophets: Composition and Theology* (Philadelphia: Fortress Press).

Coote, R.B., and M.P. Coote
1990 *Power, Politics, and the Making of the Bible: An Introduction* (Minneapolis: Fortress Press).

Cotterell, P., and M. Turner
1989 *Linguistics and Biblical Interpretation* (London: SPCK).

Crüsemann, F.
    1996   'Human Solidarity and Ethnic Identity: Israel's Self-Definition in the
                Genealogical System of Genesis', in Brett (ed.) 1996: 57-76.
Danove, P.L.
    1993a   *The End of Mark's Story: A Methodological Study* (BIS, 3; Leiden: E.J.
                Brill).
    1993b   'The Theory of Construction Grammar and its Application to New Tes-
                tament Greek', in S.E. Porter and D.A. Carson (eds.), *Biblical Greek
                Language and Linguistics: Open Questions in Current Research*
                (JSNTSup, 80; Sheffield: JSOT Press): 119-51.
Davidse, K.
    1992   'Transitivity/Ergativity: The Janus-Headed Grammar of Actions and
                Events', in Davies and Ravelli (eds.) 1992: 105-35.
Davies, M., and L. Ravelli (eds.)
    1992   *Advances in Systemic Linguistics: Recent Theory and Practice* (London:
                Pinter).
Davies, N.
    1996   *History of Europe* (Oxford: Oxford University Press).
Davies, P.R.
    1992   *In Search of 'Ancient Israel'* (JSOTSup, 148; Sheffield: Sheffield Aca-
                demic Press).
Day, J.
    1989   *Molech: A God of Human Sacrifice in the Old Testament* (University of
                Cambridge Oriental Publications, 41; Cambridge: Cambridge University
                Press).
Dempsey, S.
    1991   'The Lord Is his Name: A Study of the Distribution of the Names and
                Titles of God in the Book of Amos', *RB* 98.2: 170-89.
Dever, W.G.
    1987   'The Contribution of Archaeology to the Study of Canaanite and Early
                Israelite Religion', in Miller *et al.* (eds.) 1987: 209-47.
    1994   'The Silence of the Text: An Archaeological Commentary on 2 Kings
                23', in M.D. Coogan, J.C. Exum and L.E. Stager (eds.), *Scripture and
                Other Artifacts* (Festschrift P.J. King; Louisville, KY: Westminster/John
                Knox Press): 143-68.
    1995   ' "Will the Real Israel Please Stand Up?" Part II: Archaeology and the
                Religions of Ancient Israel', *BASOR* 298: 37-58.
    1997   'Folk Religion in Early Israel: Did Yahweh Have a Consort?', in Shanks
                and Meinhart (eds.) 1997: 27-56.
Donaldson, M.
    1981   'Kinship Theory in the Pentateuchal Narratives', *JAAR* 49: 77-87.
Douglas, M.
    1993   *In the Wilderness: The Doctrine of Defilement in the Book of Numbers*
                (JSOTSup, 158; Sheffield: Sheffield Academic Press).
Dover, K.J.
    1981   'The Colloquial Stratum in Classical Attic Prose', in G.S. Shrimpton and
                D.J. McCargar (eds.), *Classical Contributions: Studies in Honour of M.F.
                McGregor* (Locus Valley, NY: Augustin): 15-25.

Duranti, A., and C. Goodwin (eds.)
    1992   *Rethinking Context: Language as an Interactive Phenomenon* (Studies in
                the Social and Cultural Foundations of Language; Cambridge: Cambridge
                University Press).
Dussel, E.
    1985   'El concepto de fetechismo en el pensamiento de Marx: Elementos para
                una teoría general marxista de la religión', *CrSoc* 87: 67-91.
    1986   'Religiosidad popular latinoamericana, hipótesis fundamentales', *CrSoc*
                88: 103-12.
    1988   *Ethics and Community* (trans. R.R. Barr; Liberation and Theology Series,
                3; Tunbridge Wells: Burns & Oates).
    1993   *Las metáforas teológicas de Marx* (Navarra, Spain: Verbo Divino).
Dutcher-Walls, P.
    1996   *Narrative Art and Political Rhetoric: The Case of Athaliah and Joash*
                (JSOTSup, 209; Sheffield: Sheffield Academic Press).
Eagleton, T.
    1976   *Marxism and Literary Criticism* (London: Methuen).
    1978   *Criticism and Ideology: A Study in Marxist Literary Theory* (London:
                Verso).
    1991   *Ideology: An Introduction* (London: Verso).
Eagleton, T. (ed.)
    1994   *Ideology* (London: Verso).
Egger, W.
    1996   *How to Read the New Testament: An Introduction to Linguistic and His-
                torical-Critical Methodology* (trans. P. Heinegg; Peabody, MA: Hen-
                drickson [1987]).
Eissfeldt, O.
    1965   *The Old Testament: An Introduction* (Oxford: Basil Blackwell).
Elizondo, V.
    1987   'La Virgen de Guadelupe como símbolo cultural', in P. Richard (ed.),
                *Raíces de la teología latinoamericana: Nuevos materiales para la histo-
                ria de la teología* (San José, Costa Rica: DEI, 3rd edn): 393-401.
    1997   *Guadelupe: Mother of the New Creation* (Maryknoll, NY: Orbis Books).
Elliott, J.H.
    1993   *What Is Social Science Criticism?* (Guides to Biblical Scholarship, New
                Testament Series; Minneapolis: Fortress Press).
Ellis, J.
    1987   'The Logical and Textual Functions', in Halliday and Fawcett (eds.)
                1987: 107-29.
Emerton, J.
    1988   'The Priestly Writer in Genesis', *JTS* 39.2: 381-400.
    1997   'The Biblical High Place in the Light of Recent Study', *PEQ* 129.2: 116-
                32.
Eskenazi, T.C.
    1992   'Out from the Shadows: Biblical Women in the Postexilic Era', *JSOT* 54:
                25-43.

Eskenazi, T.C., and K.H. Richards (eds.)
    1994   *Second Temple Studies*. II. *Temple Community in the Persian Period* (JSOTSup, 175; Sheffield: Sheffield Academic Press).

Esler, P.F.
    1994   *The First Christians in their Social Worlds: Socio-Scientific Approaches to New Testament Interpretation* (London: Routledge).

Espín, O.O.
    1997   *The Faith of the People: Theological Reflections on Popular Catholicism* (Maryknoll, NY: Orbis Books).

Exum, J.C.
    1995   'The Ethics of Biblical Violence against Women', in Rogerson, Davies, and Carroll R. (eds.) 1995: 248-71.

Fairclough, N.
    1992   *Discourse and Social Change* (Cambridge: Polity).

Fawcett, R.
    1980   *Cognitive Linguistics and Social Interaction: Towards an Integrated Model of a Systemic Functional Grammar and the Other Components of a Communicating Mind* (Heidelberg: Groos).

Fawcett, R.P., and D.J. Young (eds.)
    1988   *New Developments in Systemic Linguistics*. II. *Theory and Application* (London: Pinter).

Ferguson, C.A.
    1959   'Diglossia', *Word* 15: 325-40.

Fewell, D., and D. Gunn
    1991   'Tipping the Balance: Sternberg's Reader and the Rape of Dinah', *JBL* 110.2: 193-212.

Finnegan, R.
    1988   *Literacy and Orality: Studies in the Technology of Communication* (Oxford: Basil Blackwell).

Firth, R.
    1964   *Essays in Social Organization and Values* (London: Athlone Press).

Fish, S.
    1980   *Is There a Text in this Class?* (Cambridge, MA: Harvard University Press).
    1989   *Doing What Comes Naturally* (Oxford: Clarendon Press).

Fischer, A.
    1997   *Skepsis oder Furcht Gottes?* (BZAW, 247; Berlin: W. de Gruyter).

Fishman, J.A.
    1967   'Bilingualism with and without Diglossia; Diglossia with and without Bilingualism', *Journal of Social Issues* 23: 29-38.

Fitzmyer, J.A.
    1991   'The Languages of Palestine in the First Century AD', in S.E. Porter (ed.), *The Language of the New Testament: Classic Essays* (JSNTSup, 60; Sheffield: JSOT Press): 126-62.

Fleischmann, S.
    1990   *Tense and Narrativity: From Medieval Performance to Modern Fiction* (London: Routledge).

Foley, J.M.
1995 *The Singer of Tales in Performance* (Bloomington, IN: University of Indiana Press).
Foucault, M.
1972 *The Archaeology of Knowledge and the Discourse of Language* (New York: Harper & Row).
Fowl, S.
1990 'The Ethics of Interpretation; or, What's left over after the Elimination of Meaning', in Clines, Fowl and Porter (eds.) 1990: 379-98.
1995 'Texts Don't Have Ideologies', *BibInt* 3.1: 15-34.
Friedeburg, L. von, and J. Habermas (eds.)
1983 *Adorno-Konferenz 1983* (Frankfurt am Main: Suhrkamp Verlag).
Frösén, J.
1974 *Prolegomena to a Study of the Greek Language in the First Centuries AD: The Problem of Koiné and Atticism* (Helsinki: University of Helsinki).
Frostin, P.
1988 *Liberation Theology in Tanzania and South Africa: A First World Interpretation* (Lund: Lund University Press).
Fulton, J.
1987 'Religion and Politics in Gramsci: An Introduction', *Sociological Analysis* 48.3: 197-216.
Galling, K.
1964 *Studien zur Geschichte Israels im persischen Zeitalter* (Tübingen: J.C.B. Mohr).
Gates, H.L.
1988 *The Signifying Monkey: A Theory of African American Literary Criticism* (New York: Oxford University Press).
Gebara, I., and M.C. Bingemer
1989 *Mary: Mother of God, Mother of the Poor* (trans. P. Berryman; Theology and Liberation Series; Maryknoll, NY: Orbis Books).
Gee, J.P.
1994 'Orality and Literacy: From the Savage Mind to Ways with Words', in J. Maybin (ed.), *Language and Literacy in Social Practice* (Clevendon: Multilingual Matters): 168-92.
Geertz, C.
1960 *The Religion of Java* (London: Glencoe).
1973 *The Interpretation of Cultures: Selected Essays* (New York: Basic Books).
1983 *Local Knowledge: Further Essays in Interpretative Anthropology* (New York: Basic Books).
1988 *Works and Lives: The Anthropologist as Author* (Stanford, CA: Stanford University Press).
1995 *After the Fact: Two Countries, Four Decades, One Anthropologist* (Cambridge, MA: Harvard University Press).
Geuss, R.
1981 *The Idea of a Critical Theory: Habermas and the Frankfurt School* (Cambridge: Cambridge University Press).

Gevirtz, S.
1987   'A New Look at an Old Crux', *JBL* 87.3: 267-76.
Ghadessy, M. (ed.)
1993   *Register Analysis: Theory and Practice* (London: Pinter).
Gibson, E.
1978   *The 'Christians for Christians' Inscriptions of Phrygia* (HTS, 32; Missoula, MT: Scholars Press).
Giddens, A.
1979   *Central Problems in Social Theory: Action, Structure and Contradiction in Social Analysis* (Berkeley: University of California Press).
1984   *The Constitution of Society* (Oxford: Polity).
1987   *Social Theory and Modern Sociology* (Oxford: Polity).
1992   *The Transformation of Intimacy: Sexuality, Love and Eroticism in Modern Societies* (Cambridge: Polity Press).
Giglioli, P.P. (ed.)
1972   *Language and Social Context: Selected Readings* (Harmondsworth: Penguin Books).
Gignac, F.T.
1970   'The Pronunciation of Greek Stops in the Papyri', *TAPA* 101: 185-202.
Gilliard, F.D.
1993   'More Silent Reading in Antiquity: *Non omne verbum sonabat*', *JBL* 112.4: 689-96.
Girardi, G.
1986   *Sandinismo, marxismo, cristianismo: La confluencia* (Managua, Nicaragua: Centro Ecuménico Antonio Valdivieso).
Giroux, H.A.
1985   'Introduction', in P. Freire (ed.), *The Politics of Education* (London: Macmillan): xi-xxv.
Gnuse, R.K.
1997   *No Other Gods: Emergent Monotheism in Israel* (JSOTSup, 241; Sheffield: Sheffield Academic Press).
Goldberg, D.T.
1994   *Multiculturalism: A Critical Reader* (Oxford: Basil Blackwell).
Gotay, S.
1985   'Las condiciones históricas y teóricas que hicieron posible la incorporación del materialismo histórico en el pensamiento cristiano en América Latina', *CrSoc* 84: 25-48.
Gottwald, N.K.
1979   *The Tribes of Yahweh: A Sociology of the Religion of Liberated Israel 1250–150 BCE* (Maryknoll, NY: Orbis Books).
1985   *The Hebrew Bible: A Socio-Literary Introduction* (Philadelphia: Fortress Press).
1993a   *The Hebrew Bible in its Social World and Ours* (SBLSS; Atlanta, CA: Scholars Press).
1993b   'Sociological Method in the Study of Ancient Israel', in Gottwald and Horsley (eds.) 1993: 142-53.

1995   'Theological Education as a Theory-Praxis Loop: Situating the Book of
                Joshua in a Cultural, Social Ethical, and Theological Matrix', in Roger-
                son, Davies and Carroll R. (eds.) 1995: 107-18.

Gottwald, N.K., and R.A. Horsley (eds.)
1993   *The Bible and Liberation: Political and Social Hermeneutics* (Maryknoll,
                NY: Orbis Books).

Gowan, D.E.
1986   *Eschatology in the Old Testament* (Edinburgh: T. & T. Clark).

Gramsci, A.
1971   *Selections from Prison Notebooks* (trans. Q. Hoare and G.N. Smith; Lon-
                don: Lawrence & Wisehart).
1985   *Selections from Cultural Writings* (eds. D. Forgacs and G.N. Smith; trans.
                W. Boelhower; London: Lawrence & Wisehart).

Greenblatt, S., and G. Gunn (eds.)
1992   *Redrawing the Boundaries: The Transformation of English and American
                Literary Studies* (New York: Modern Language Association).

Gregory, M.
1987   'Meta-Functions: Aspects of their Development, Status and Use in Sys-
                temic Linguistics', in Halliday and Fawcett (eds.) 1987: 94-106.

Gregory, M., and S. Carroll
1978   *Language and Situation: Language Varieties and their Social Contexts*
                (London: Routledge & Kegan Paul).

Grünwaldt, K.
1992   *Exil und Identität: Beschneidung, Passa und Shabbat in der Priester-
                schrift* (Frankfurt: Anton Hain).

Guelich, R.A.
1989   *Mark 1–8:26* (WBC, 34A; Dallas, TX: Word Books).

Guha, R.
1983   'The Prose of Counter-Insurgency', in R. Guha (ed.), *Subaltern Studies*
                (New Delhi: Oxford University Press): 1-42.

Gumperz, J.J.
1977   'Sociocultural Knowledge in Conversational Inference', in M. Saville-
                Troike (ed.), *Linguistics and Anthropology* (Washington, DC: George-
                town University Press): 191-211.

Gumperz, J.J., and D. Hymes (eds.)
1972   *Directions in Sociolinguistics: The Ethnography of Communication* (New
                York: Holt, Rinehart & Winston).

Gunkel, H.
1910   *Genesis* (Göttingen: Vandenhoeck & Ruprecht).

Habel, N.C.
1995   *The Land Is Mine: Six Biblical Land Ideologies* (Minneapolis: Fortress
                Press).

Habermas, J.
1972   *Knowledge and Human Interests* (trans. J.J. Shapiro; London: Heine-
                mann).
1984   *The Theory of Communicative Action.* I. *Reason and the Rationalization*
                of Society (trans. T. McCarthy; London: Polity).

1987a   *The Theory of Communicative Action*. II. *The Critique of Functionalist Reason* (trans. T. McCarthy; London: Polity).

1987b   'Theodor W. Adorno a) Ein philosophierende Intellektueller b) Ur-geschichte der Subjektivität und verwilderte Selbstbehauptung', in *Philosophisch-politische Profile* (Frankfurt am Main: Suhrkamp): 160-79.

Hager, F., and H. Pfütze

1990   *Das unerhört Moderne: Berliner Adorno-Tagung* (Lüneburg: Dietrich zu Klampen Verlag).

Hahn, H.F.

1966   *The Old Testament in Modern Research* (Philadelphia: Fortress Press).

Halliday, M.A.K.

1973a   'The Functional Basis of Language', in Bernstein (ed.) 1973: 343-66.

1973b   *Explorations in the Functions of Language* (London: Edward Arnold).

1975   *Learning How to Mean: Explorations in the Development of Language* (London: Edward Arnold).

1978   *Language as Social Semiotic: The Social Interpretation of Language and Meaning* (London: Edward Arnold).

1985   *An Introduction to Functional Grammar* (London: Edward Arnold).

Halliday, M.A.K., and R.P. Fawcett (eds.)

1987   *New Developments in Systemic Linguistics*. I. *Theory and Description* (London: Pinter).

Halliday, M.A.K., and R. Hasan

1976   *Cohesion in English* (London: Longmans).

1985   *Language, Context, and Text: Aspects of Language in a Social-Semiotic Perspective* (Geelong, Victoria, Australia: Deakin University Press).

Halliday, M.A.K., A. McIntosh and P. Strevens

1964   *The Linguistic Sciences and Language Teaching* (London: Longmans).

Hallo, W.

1977   'New Moons and Sabbaths: A Case-study in the Contrastive Approach', *HUCA* 48: 1-18.

Hammershaimb, E.

1970   *The Book of Amos: A Commentary* (trans. J. Sturdy; Oxford: Basil Blackwell).

Handel, W.H.

1993   *Contemporary Sociological Theory* (Englewood Cliffs, NJ: Prentice–Hall).

Handler, R.

1983   'An Interview with Clifford Geertz', *CurrAnth* 32.5: 603-13.

Harris, M.

1979   *Cultural Materialism: The Struggle for a Science of Culture* (New York: Vintage Books).

Hasan, R.

1973   'Code, Register and Social Dialect', in Bernstein (ed.) 1973: 253-92.

1987   'The Grammarian's Dream: Lexis as Most Delicate Grammar', in Halliday and Fawcett (eds.) 1987: 184-211.

Hasel, G.F.

1991   *Understanding the Book of Amos: Basic Issues in Current Interpretations* (Grand Rapids: Baker Book House).

Haugen, E.
1950   'Problems of Bilingualism', *Lingua* 2: 271-90.
1972   'Dialect, Language, Nation', in J.B. Pride and J. Holmes (eds.), *Sociolinguistics: Selected Readings* (Harmondsworth: Penguin Books): 97-111.

Hayes, J.H.
1988   *Amos the Eighth-Century Prophet: His Times and his Preaching* (Nashville: Abingdon Press).

Headland, T.N., K.L. Pike, and M. Harris
1990   *Emics and Etics: The Insider/Outsider Debate* (Frontiers of Anthropology, 7; Newbury Park: Sage).

Heider, G.C.
1985   *The Cult of Molek: A Reassessment* (JSOTSup, 43; Sheffield: Sheffield Academic Press).

Hemer, C.J.
1987   'Reflections on the Nature of New Testament Greek Vocabulary', *TynBul* 38: 65-92.

Hengel, M.
1985   *Studies in the Gospel of Mark* (trans. J. Bowden; Philadelphia: Fortress Press).

Herion, G.A.
1986   'The Impact of Modern and Social Scientific Assumptions on the Reconstruction of Israelite History', *JSOT* 34: 3-33.

Hess, R.S.
1992   'Yahweh and his Asherah? Religious Pluralism in the Old Testament World', in A.D. Clarke and B.W. Winter (eds.), *One God, One Lord: Christianity in a World of Religious Pluralism* (Carlisle: Paternoster Press; Grand Rapids: Eerdmans, 2nd edn): 13-42.

Hill, C.
1988   *A Turbulent, Seditious, and Factious People: John Bunyan and his Church* (Oxford: Oxford University Press).

Hirsch, E.D.
1967   *Validity in Interpretation* (New Haven, CT: Yale University Press).
1976   *Aims of Interpretation* (Chicago: University of Chicago Press).

Hoelscher, G.
1923   *Ezra–Nehemiah* (HSAT; Tübingen: J.C.B. Mohr).

Hoffmeier, J.K.
1998   'Once Again the "Plumb Line" of Amos 7.7-9: An Interpretive Clue from Egypt?', in M. Lubetski, C. Gottlieb and S. Keller (eds.), *Boundaries of the Ancient World: A Tribute to Cyrus H. Gordon* (JSOTSup, 273; Sheffield: Sheffield Academic Press): 304-19.

Hoglund, K.
1992   *Achaemenid Imperial Administration in Syria-Palestine and the Missions of Ezra and Nehemiah* (SBLDS, 125; Atlanta, CA: Scholars Press).

Hohendahl, P.U.
1995   *Prismatic Thought: Theodor W. Adorno* (Lincoln: University of Nebraska Press).

Holladay, J.S., Jr
    1987   'Religion in Israel and Judah under the Monarchy: An Explicitly Archae-
            ological Approach', in Miller *et al.* (eds.) 1987: 249-99.
Holm, J.
    1988   *Pidgins and Creoles*. I. *Theory and Structure* (Cambridge Language Sur-
            veys; Cambridge: Cambridge University Press).
Holmberg, B.
    1990   *Sociology and the New Testament: An Appraisal* (Minneapolis: Fortress
            Press).
Horkheimer, M.
    1987   *Gesammelte Schriften*, V (Frankfurt am Main: S. Fischer Verlag).
Horrell, D.G.
    1999   *Social-Scientific Approaches to Biblical Interpretation* (Edinburgh: T. &
            T. Clark).
Horrocks, G.
    1997   *Greek: A History of the Language and its Speakers* (Longman Linguistics
            Library; London: Longmans).
Horsely, R.A.
    1989   *Sociology and the Jesus Movement* (New York: Crossroad).
    1995   *Galilee: History, Politics and People* (Valley Forge, PA: Trinity Press
            International).
    1996   *Archaeology, History and Society in Galilee: The Social Context of Jesus
            and the Rabbis* (Valley Forge, PA: Trinity Press International).
Horsely, R.A., and N.A. Silberman
    1997   *The Message and the Kingdom: How Jesus and Paul Ignited a Revolution
            and Transformed the Ancient World* (New York: Penguin Putnam).
Hudson, R.A.
    1980   *Sociolinguistics* (CTL; Cambridge: Cambridge University Press).
Hurst, L.D.
    1986   'The Neglected Role of Semantics in the Search for the Aramaic Words
            of Jesus', *JSNT* 28: 63-80.
Hurtado, L.W.
    1989   *Mark* (New International Biblical Commentary; Peabody, MA: Hendrick-
            son).
Irarrázaval, D.
    1991   'Religión popular', in I. Ellacuría and J. Sobrino (eds.), *Mysterium Lib-
            erationis: Conceptos fundamentales de la teología de la liberación*
            (2 vols.; Colección Teología Latinoamericana, 16; San Salvador, El
            Salvador: UCA, 1993), II: 345-75.
Jacobs, P.F.
    1985   'A Note on the Interpretation of Amos 4:1', *JBL* 104.1: 109-10.
Jameson, F.
    1981   *The Political Unconscious: Narrative as a Socially Symbolic Act* (Ithaca,
            NY: Cornell University Press).
Japhet, S.
    1981   'People and Land in the Restoration Period', in G. Strecker (ed.), *Das
            Land Israel in biblischer Zeit* (Göttingen: Vandenhoeck & Ruprecht):
            103-25.

Jarvis, S.
    1998   *Adorno: A Critical Introduction* (Cambridge: Polity Press).
Jay, M.
    1973   *The Dialectical Imagination: A History of the Frankfurt School and the Institute of Social Research, 1923–1950* (Berkeley: University of California Press).
Jeremias, J.
    1998   *The Book of Amos* (trans. D.W. Stott; OTL; Louisville, KY: Westminster/ John Knox Press).
Jobling, D.
    1990   'Writing the Wrongs of the World: The Deconstruction of the Biblical Text in the Context of Liberation Theologies', *Semeia* 51: 81-118.
    1992   'Deconstruction and the Political Analysis of Texts: A Jamesonian Reading of Psalm 72', in Jobling and Pippin (eds.) 1992: 95-127.
Jobling, D., and T. Pippin (eds.)
    1992   *Ideological Criticism of Biblical Texts* (Semeia, 59: Atlanta, GA: Scholars Press).
Joosten, J.
    1997   *People and Land in the Holiness Code* (Leiden: E.J. Brill).
Joseph, J.E.
    1987   *Eloquence and Power: The Rise of Language Standards and Standard Languages* (London: Pinter).
Kee, A.
    1990   *Marx and the Failure of Liberation Theology* (London: SCM Press; Philadelphia: Trinity Press International).
Kee, H.C.
    1977   *Community of the New Age: Studies in Mark's Gospel* (London: SCM Press).
Keel, O.
    1998   *Goddesses and Trees, New Moon and Yahweh: Ancient Near Eastern Art and the Hebrew Bible* (JSOTSup, 261; Sheffield: Sheffield Academic Press).
Keel, O., and C. Uehlinger
    1998   *Gods, Goddesses, and Images of God in Ancient Israel* (trans. T.H. Trapp; Minneapolis: Fortress Press).
Keesing, R.M.
    1974   'Theories of Culture', *AnnRevAnth* 3: 73-97.
    1987   'Anthropology as Interpretive Quest', *CurrAnth* 28.2: 161-76.
King, P.J.
    1988   *Amos, Hosea, Micah: An Archaeological Commentary* (Philadelphia: Westminster Press).
Kippenberg, H.
    1982   *Religion und Klassenbildung im antiken Judäa: Eine religionssoziologische Studie zum Verhältnis von Tradition und gesellschaftlichen Entwicklung* (SUNT, 14; Göttingen: Vandenhoeck & Ruprecht, 2nd edn).
Kitzberger, I.R.
    1998   *The Personal Voice in Biblical Studies* (London: Routledge).

Klein, W.
  1986   *Second Language Acquisition* (CTL; Cambridge: Cambridge University
             Press).
Knohl, I.
  1995   *The Sanctuary of Silence: The Priestly Torah and the Holiness School*
             (Minneapolis: Fortress Press).
Kohlmann, U.
  1997   *Dialektik der Moral: Untersuchungen zur Moralphilosophie Adornos*
             (Lüneburg: Dietrich zu Klampen).
Kracauer, S.
  1980   *Neue Deutscher Biographie*, 12 (Berlin: Duncker & Humbolt).
Kselman, T.A.
  1986   'Ambivalence and Assumption in the Concept of Popular Religion', in
             Levine (ed.) 1986: 24-41.
Laato, A.
  1996   *History and Ideology in the Old Testament Prophetic Literature: A
             Semiotic Approach to the Reconstruction of the Proclamation of the His-
             torical Prophets* (ConBOT, 41; Stockholm: Almqvist & Wiksell).
Labov, W.
  1972   *Sociolinguistic Patterns* (Oxford: Basil Blackwell).
Labuschagne, C.J.
  1966   'Amos' Conception of God and the Popular Theology of his Time',
             OTWSA 7–8: 122-33.
Lane Fox, R.
  1973   *Alexander the Great* (London: Dial Press).
Lane, W.L.
  1974   *The Gospel According to Mark* (NICNT; Grand Rapids: Eerdmans).
Lang, B.
  1984   'Max Weber und Israels Propheten: Eine kritische Stellungnahme',
             ZRGG 36.2: 156-65.
Lang, B. (ed.)
  1985   *Anthropological Approaches to the Old Testament* (Issues in Religion and
             Theology, 8; Philadelphia: Fortress Press; London: SPCK).
Lanternari, V.
  1982   'La religion populaire: Prospective historique et anthropologique', *ASSR*
             53.1: 121-43.
Leech, G.N.
  1983   *Principles of Pragmatics* (London: Longmans).
Lemche, N.P.
  1985   *Early Israel: Anthroplogical and Historical Studies on the Israelite Soci-
             ety before the Monarchy* (VTSup, 37; Leiden: E.J. Brill).
  1990   'On the Use of "System Theory", "Macro-Theories", and "Evolutionistic
             Thinking" in Modern Old Testament Research and Biblical Arch-
             aeology', *SJOT* 2: 73-88.
Levenson, J.D.
  1993   *The Hebrew Bible, the Old Testament, and Historical Criticism: Jews
             and Christians in Biblical Studies* (Louisville, KY: Westminster/John
             Knox Press).

Levine, D.H.
  1986   *Religion and Political Conflict in Latin America* (Chapel Hill: University
            of North Carolina Press).
  1993   'Popular Groups, Popular Culture, and Popular Religion', in D.H. Levine
            (ed.), *Constructing Culture and Power in Latin America* (Comparative
            Studies in Society and History: Ann Arbor: University of Michigan
            Press): 171-225.
Levinson, S.C.
  1983   *Pragmatics* (CTL; Cambridge: Cambridge University Press).
Lévi-Strauss, C.
  1963   *Structural Anthropology* (London: Basic Books).
  1964   *Mythologiques*. I. *Le cruxe et le cuit* (Paris: Plon).
Lewis, T.J.
  1989   *Cults of the Dead in Ancient Israel and Ugarit* (HSM, 39; Atlanta, GA:
            Scholars Press).
Löbig, M., and G. Schweppenhäuser (eds.)
  1984   *Hamburger Adorno-Symposium* (Lüneburg: Dietrich zu Klampen Ver-
            lag).
Long, B.O.
  1996   'W.F. Albright as Prophet-Reformer: A Theological Paradigm Inscribed
            in Scholarly Practice', in Reid (ed.) 1996: 152-72.
Loretz, O.
  1989   'Die babylonischen Gottesnamen Sukkut und Kajjamanu in Amos 5,26:
            Ein Beitrag zur jüdischen Astrologie', *ZAW* 101.2: 286-89.
Löwy, M.
  1996   *The War of Gods: Religion and Politics in Latin America* (London:
            Verso).
Maduro, O.
  1982   *Religion and Social Conflict* (trans. R.R. Barr; Maryknoll, NY: Orbis
            Books).
Mahan, B., and L.D. Richesin (eds.)
  1981   *The Challenge of Liberation Theology: A First World Response*
            (Maryknoll, NY: Orbis Books).
Maldonado, L.
  1985   *Introducción a la religiosidad popular* (Presencia Teológica, 21; San-
            tander, Spain: Sal Terrae).
Malina, B.J.
  1986   *Christian Origins and Cultural Anthropology: Practical Models for Bib-
            lical Interpretation* (Atlanta, GA: John Knox Press).
  1991   'Reading Theory Perspective: Reading Luke–Acts', in J.H. Neyrey (ed.),
            The Social World of Luke–Acts: Models for Interpretation (Peabody,
            MA: Hendrickson): 3-23.
  1993   *The New Testament World: Insights from Cultural Anthropology* (Louis-
            ville, KY: Westminster/John Knox Press, rev. edn).
  1996   'Rhetorical Criticism and Social-Scientific Criticism: Why Won't
            Romanticism Leave Us Alone?', in S.E. Porter and T.H. Olbricht (eds.),
            *Rhetoric, Scripture and Theology: Essays from the 1994 Pretoria Con-
            ference* (JSNTSup, 131; Sheffield: Sheffield Academic Press): 72-101.

Malinowski, B.
    1923   'The Problem of Meaning in Primitive Languages', in C.K. Ogden and
                I.A. Richards (eds.), *The Meaning of Meaning* (New York: Harcourt,
                Brace): 296-336.
Maloney, E.C.
    1980   *Semitic Interference in Marcan Syntax* (SBLDS, 51; Chico, CA: Scholars
                Press).
Mann, C.S.
    1986   *Mark* (AB, 27; New York: Doubleday).
Mannheim, K.
    1936   *Ideology and Utopia: An Introduction to the Sociology of Knowledge*
                (trans. L. Wirth and E. Shils; New York: Harcourt Brace Jovanovich).
Marcus, G.E., and M.M.J. Fischer
    1986   *Anthropology as Cultural Critique: An Experimental Moment in the
                Social Sciences* (Chicago: University of Chicago Press).
Martin, W.
    1986   *Recent Theories of Narrative* (Ithaca, NY: Cornell University Press).
Martin-Achard, R.
    1984   *Amos: L'homme, le message, l'influence* (Geneva: Labor et Fides).
Marx, K.
    1970   'A Contribution to the Critique of Hegel's "Philosophy of Right" ', in
                J. O'Malley (ed.), *Critique of Hegel's 'Philosophy of Right'* (trans. A.
                Jolin and J. O'Malley; Cambridge: Cambridge University Press).
Marx, K., and F. Engels
    1959   *Basic Writings on Politics and Philosophy* (ed. L.S. Feuer; Garden City,
                NY: Anchor Books).
Matthews, V.H., and D.J. Benjamin
    1993   *Social World of Ancient Israel 1250–587 BCE* (Peabody, MA: Hendrick-
                son).
Matthiessen, M.
    1992   'Interpreting the Textual Metafunction', in Davies and Ravelli (eds.)
                1992: 37-81.
    1993   'Register in the Round: Diversity in a Unified Theory of Register Analy-
                sis', in Ghadessy (ed.) 1993: 221-92.
Mayes, A.D.H.
    1989   *The Old Testament in Sociological Perspective* (London: Marshall
                Pickering).
McKay, J.W.
    1973   *Religion in Judah under Assyrians 722–609 BC* (SBT, 26; Naperville, IL:
                Allenson).
Melrose, R.
    1988   'Systemic Linguistics and the Communicative Language Syllabus', in
                Fawcett and Young (eds.) 1988: 78-93.
Mendenhall, G.
    1974   'The Shady Side of Wisdom: The Date and Purpose of Genesis 3', in H.
                Bream, R.D. Heim, and C.A. Moore (eds.), *A Light unto my Path*
                (Philadelphia: Temple University Press): 319-34.

Meyer, E.
    1896   *Die Entstehung des Judentums: Eine Historische Untersuchung* (Halle:
                Niemeyer).
Meyers, C.
    1988   *Discovering Eve: Ancient Israelite Women in Context* (Oxford: Oxford
                University Press).
Miller, J.H.
    1987   'Presidential Address 1986: The Triumph of Theory, the Resistance to
                Reading, and the Question of Material Base', *PMLA* 102: 281-91.
Miller, P.D., Jr, P.D. Hanson and S.D. McBride (eds.)
    1987   *Ancient Israelite Religion* (Festchrift F.M. Cross; Philadelphia: Fortress
                Press).
Miranda, J.P.
    1974   *Marx and the Bible: A Critique of the Philosophy of Oppression* (trans. J.
                Eagleson; Maryknoll, NY: Orbis Books).
Mires, F.
    1986   *En nombre de la cruz: Discusiones teológicas y políticas frente al holo-
                causto de los indios (período de conquista)* (San José, Costa Rica: DEI).
    1987   *La colonización de las almas: Misión y conquista en Hispanoamérica*
                (San José, Costa Rica: DEI).
Moberly, R.W.L.
    1992   *The Old Testament of the Old Testament: Patriarchal Narratives and
                Mosaic Yahwism* (Minneapolis: Fortress Press).
Moor, J.C. de
    1997   *The Rise of Yahwism: The Roots of Israelite Monotheism* (rev. edn;
                BETL, 91; Leuven: Leuven University Press).
Moritz, P.
    1992   *Kritik des Paradigmenwechsels: Mit Horkheimer gegen Habermas*
                (Lüneburg: Dietrich zu Klampen Verlag).
Mosala, I.J.
    1989a   *Biblical Hermeneutics and Black Theology in South Africa* (Grand
                Rapids: Eerdmans).
    1989b   'Black Theology', unpublished paper.
    1993   'A Materialist Reading of Micah', in Gottwald and Horsley (eds.) 1993:
                264-95.
Mowinckel, S.
    1964   *Studien zu dem Buche Ezra-Nehemiah* (Oslo: Universitetsforlaget).
Mullen, E.T.
    1987   *Ethnic Myths and Pentateuchal Foundations* (Atlanta, GA: Scholars
                Press).
Munson, H., Jr
    1986   'Geertz on Religion: The Theory and the Practice', *Religion* 16.1: 19-32.
Murphy, R.E.
    1990   *The Song of Songs: A Commentary on the Book of Canticles or the Song
                of Songs* (Hermeneia; Minneapolis: Fortress Press).
Neher, A.
    1981   *Amos: Contribution à l'étude du prophétisme* (Bibliothèque d'Histoire de
                la Philosophie; Paris: Libraire Philosophique J. Vrin, 2nd rev. edn).

Newmeyer, F.J. (ed.)
    1988   *Linguistics: The Cambridge Survey.* IV. *Language: The Socio-Cultural Context* (Cambridge: Cambridge University Press).
Newsom, C.A., and S.H. Ringe (eds.)
    1992   *The Women's Bible Commentary* (London: SPCK; Louisville, KY: Westminster/John Knox Press).
Niditch, S.
    1987   *Underdogs and Tricksters: A Prelude to Biblical Folklore* (San Francisco: Harper & Row).
    1996   *Oral World and Written Word: Ancient Israelite Literature* (Louisville, KY: Westminster/John Knox Press).
Niehoff-Panagiotidis, J.
    1994   *Koine und Diglossie* (Wiesbaden: Otto Harrassowitz).
Noble, P.R.
    1995   'The Literary Structure of Amos: A Thematic Analysis', *JBL* 114.2: 209-26.
    1998   'Amos and Amaziah in Context: Synchronic and Diachronic Approaches in Amos 7–8', *CBQ* 60.3: 423-39.
Norris, C.
    1990   *What's Wrong with Postmodernism: Critical Theory and the Ends of Postmodernism* (New York: Harvester Wheatsheaf).
Núñez, E.A., and W.D. Taylor
    1996   *Crisis and Hope in Latin America: An Evangelical Perspective* (Pasadena: Wm Carey Library, rev. edn).
Oden, R.A.
    1987   *The Bible without Theology* (San Francisco: Harper & Row).
Olyan, S.M.
    1988   *Asherah and the Cult of Yahweh in Israel* (SBLMS, 34; Atlanta, GA: Scholars Press).
    1991   'The Oaths of Amos 8.14', in G.A. Anderson and S.M. Olyan (eds.), *Priesthood and Cult in Ancient Israel* (JSOTSup, 125; Sheffield: Sheffield Academic Press): 121-49.
Ong, W.
    1987   'The Pyschodynamics of Oral Memory and Narrative: Some Implications for Biblical Studies', in R. Masson (ed.), *The Pedagogy of God's Image: Essays on Symbol and the Religious Imagination* (Chico, CA: Scholars Press): 55-73.
Overholt, T.W.
    1990   'Prophecy in History: The Social Reality of Intermediation', *JSOT* 48: 3-29.
    1996a   *Cultural Anthropology and the Old Testament* (Guides to Biblical Scholarship; Minneapolis: Fortress Press).
    1996b   'Elijah and Elisha in the Context of Israelite Religion', in Reid (ed.) 1996: 94-111.
Pablo II, Juan [John Paul II]
    1983   *Viaje apostólico a Centroamérica, 2–9 de marzo de 1983* (Madrid: BAC).

Palmer, F.R.
  1994   *Grammatical Roles and Relations* (CTL; Cambridge: Cambridge University Press).
Palmer, L.R.
  1980   *The Greek Language* (London: Faber & Faber).
Palmer, M.W.
  1995   *Levels of Constituent Structure in New Testament Greek* (SBG, 4; New York: Peter Lang).
Parker, C.
  1996   *Popular Religion and Modernization in Latin America: A Different Logic* (trans. R.R. Barr; Maryknoll, NY: Orbis Books).
Pasto, J.
  1998   'When the End Is the Beginning? or When the Biblical Past Is the Political Present: Some Thoughts on Ancient Israel, "Post-Exilic Judaism", and the Politics of Biblical Scholarship', *SJOT* 12.2: 157-202.
Patterson, A.
  1990   'Intention', in F. Lentricchia and F. McLaughlin (eds.), *Critical Terms for Literary Study* (Chicago: Univerity of Chicago Press): 135-46.
Paul, S.M.
  1990   *Amos* (Hermeneia; Minneapolis: Fortress Press).
Pearson, B.W.R., and S.E. Porter
  1997   'The Genres of the New Testament', in Porter (ed.) 1997: 131-65.
Peterson, A.
  1998   'Varieties of Popular Catholicism: A Parish Study', *SocComp* 45.3: 399-45.
Petersen, D.L.
  1979   'Max Weber and Sociological Study of Ancient Israel', in H. Johnson (ed.), *Religious Change and Continuity* (San Francisco: Jossey–Bass): 117-49.
Petersen, N.R.
  1980   'When is the End Not the End? Literary Reflections on the Ending of Mark's Narrative', *Int* 34.2: 151-66.
Petersen, R.M.
  1995   'Time, Resistance, and Reconstruction: Rethinking Kairos Theology' (unpublished PhD, University of Chicago, Chicago).
Pike, K.
  1964   'Towards a Theory of the Structure of Human Behaviour', in D. Hymes (ed.), *Language in Culture and Society* (New York: Harper & Row): 154-61.
Pippin, T.
  1996   'Ideology, Ideological Criticism, and the Bible', *CR:BS* 4: 51-78.
Pixley, J.
  1987   *On Exodus: A Liberation Perspective* (Maryknoll, NY: Orbis Books).
  1988   '¿Exige el dios verdadero sacrificios cruentos?', *RIBLA* 2: 109-31.
  1992   *Biblical History: A People's History* (Minneapolis: Fortress Press).
Polley, M.E.
  1989   *Amos and the Davidic Empire: A Socio-Historical Approach* (New York: Oxford University Press).

Poole, S.
  1995   *Our Lady of Guadelupe: The Origins and Sources of a Mexican National Symbol, 1531–1797* (Tucson: University of Arizona Press).

Pope, M.H.
  1972   'A Divine Banquet at Ugarit', in J. Efird (ed.), *The Use of the Old Testament in the New and Other Essays* (Festschrift W.F. Stinespring; Durham: University of North Carolina Press): 153-80.
  1981   'The Cult of the Dead at Ugarit', in G.D. Young (ed.), *Ugarit in Retrospect* (Winona Lake, IN: Eisenbrauns): 159-79.

Porter, S.E.
  1989   *Verbal Aspect in the Greek of the New Testament, with Reference to Tense and Mood* (SBG, 1; New York: Peter Lang).
  1993   'Word Order and Clause Structure in New Testament Greek: An Unexplored Area of Greek Linguistics Using Philippians as a Test Case', *FN* 6: 177-206.
  1994   'Jesus and the Use of Greek in Galilee', in B. Chilton and C.A. Evans (eds.), *Studying the Historical Jesus: Evaluations of the State of Current Research* (NTTS, 19; Leiden: E.J. Brill): 129-47.
  1996   'The Case for Case Revisited', *Jian Dao* 6: 13-28.
  1997a   'The Greek Papyri of the Judaean Desert and the World of the Roman East', in S.E. Porter and C.A. Evans (eds.), *The Scrolls and the Scriptures: Qumran Fifty Years After* (RILP, 3; JSPSup, 26; Sheffield: Sheffield Academic Press): 293-311.
  1997b   'The Greek Language of the New Testament', in Porter (ed.) 1997: 99-130.
  1999   'Resurrection, the Greeks, and the New Testament', in S.E. Porter, M.A. Hayes and D. Tombs, *Resurrection* (RILP, 5; JSNTSup, 186; Sheffield: Sheffield Academic Press): 52-87.
  forthcoming 'Jesus in the Light of Other Scriptural Traditions', *Theology Wales*.

Porter, S.E. (ed.)
  1997   *Handbook to Exegesis of the New Testament* (NTTS, 25; Leiden: E.J. Brill).

Prewitt, T.J.
  1990   *The Elusive Covenant: A Structural-Semiotic Reading of Genesis* (Advances in Semiotics; Bloomington, IN: Indiana University Press).

Prior, M.
  1997   *The Bible and Colonialism: A Moral Critique* (The Biblical Seminar, 48; Sheffield; Sheffield Academic Press).

Pritchard, J.B. (ed.)
  1969   *Ancient Near Eastern Texts Relating to the Old Testament* (Princeton, NJ: Princeton University Press, 3rd edn).

Provan, I.W.
  1995   'Ideologies, Literary and Critical: Reflections on Recent Writing on the History of Israel', *JBL* 114.2: 585-606.

Puech, E.
  1977   'Milkom, le dieu Ammonite, en Amos I 15', *VT* 27.2: 117-25.

Rademacher, C.

1993   *Versöhnung oder Verständigung? Kritik der Habermasschen Adorno-Revision* (Lüneburg: Dietrich zu Klampen Verlag).

Ramsay, W.M.

1915   *The Bearing of Recent Discovery on the Trustworthiness of the New Testament* (London: Hodder & Stoughton).

Reed, J.T.

1995   'Modern Linguistics and the New Testament: A Basic Guide to Theory, Terminology, and Literature', in S.E. Porter and D. Tombs (eds.), *Approaches to New Testament Study* (JSNTSup, 120; Sheffield: Sheffield Academic Press): 222-65.

1997a   *A Discourse Analysis of Philippians: Method and Rhetoric in the Debate over Literary Integrity* (JSNTSup, 136; Sheffield: Sheffield Academic Press).

1997b   'Discourse Analysis', in Porter (ed.) 1997: 189-217.

Reid, S.B. (ed.)

1996   *Prophets and Paradigms: Essays in Honor of Gene Tucker* (JSOTSup, 229; Sheffield: Sheffield Academic Press).

Reiser, M.

1984   *Syntax und Stil des Markusevangeliums im Licht der hellenistischen Volksliteratur* (WUNT, 2.11; Tübingen: J.C.B. Mohr [Paul Siebeck]).

Rendtorff, R.

1996   'The Ger in the Priestly Laws of the Pentateuch', in Brett (ed.) 1996: 77-87.

Ribeiro de Oliveira, P. de A.

1994   'The Political Ambivalence of Popular Religion', *SocComp* 41.4: 513-23.

Rice, K.A.

1980   *Geertz and Culture* (Studies in Cultural Analysis; Ann Arbor: University of Michigan Press).

Richard, P.

1996   'Biblical Interpretation from the Perspective of Indigenous Cultures of Latin America (Mayas, Kunas, and Quechuas)', in Brett (ed.) 1996: 297-314.

Richard, P. *et al.*

1980   *La lucha de los dioses: Los ídolos de la opresión y la búsqueda del Dios Liberador* (San José, C.R.: DEI; Managua, Nicaragua: Centro Antonio Valdivieso).

Ricoeur, P.

1986   *Lectures on Ideology and Utopia* (ed. G.H. Taylor; New York: Columbia University Press).

Ringe, S.H.

1992   'When Women Interpret the Bible', in Newsom and Ringe (eds.) 1992: 1-9.

1995   'The New Testament and the Ethics of Compromise: *Compromiso* with the God of Life or Compromise with the Ideology of Power?', in Rogerson, Davies, and Carroll R. (eds.) 1995: 232-47.

Ritsert, J.

1997   *Kleines Lehrbuch der Dialektik* (Darmstadt: Wissenschaftliche Buchgesellschaft).

Rivera, L.N.
    1992   *A Violent Evangelism: The Political and Religious Conquest of the Americas* (Louisville, KY: Westminster/John Knox Press).

Rodd, C.S.
    1979   'Max Weber and Ancient Judaism', *SJT* 32: 457-69.
    1981   'On Applying a Sociological Theory to Biblical Studies', *JSOT* 19: 95-106.

Rogerson, J.W.
    1970a   'The Hebrew Conception of "Corporate Personality": A Reexamination', *JTS* 21: 1-16.
    1970b   'Structural Anthropology and the Old Testament', *BSO(A)S* 33: 490-500.
    1974   *Myth in Old Testament Interpretation* (BZAW, 143; Berlin: W. de Gruyter).
    1978   *Anthropology and the Old Testament* (Oxford: Basil Blackwell).
    1985   'The Use of Sociology in Old Testament Studies', in J.A. Emerton (ed.), *Congress Volume, Salamanca 1983* (VTSup, 36; Leiden: E.J. Brill, 1985): 245-56.
    1986   'Was Early Israel a Segmentary Society?', *JSOT* 36: 17-26.
    1987   *Anthropology and the Old Testament* (Growing Points in Theology; Oxford: Basil Blackwell).
    1989   'Anthropology and the Old Testament', in Clements (ed.) 1989: 17-37.
    1990   'What Does It Mean to Be Human? The Central Question of Old Testament Theology', in Clines, Fowl and Porter (eds.) 1990: 285-98.
    1995a   *The Bible and Criticism in Victorian England: Profiles of F.D. Maurice and William Robertson Smith* (JSOTSup, 201; Sheffield: Sheffield Academic Press).
    1995b   'Discourse Ethics and Biblical Ethics', in Rogerson, Davies and Carroll R. (eds.) 1995: 17-26.
    1995c   'The Old Testament and Christian Morality', *HeyJ* 36.4: 422-30.

Rogerson, J., M. Davies and M.D. Carroll R. (eds.)
    1995   *The Bible and Ethics: The Second Sheffield Colloquium* (JSOTSup, 207; Sheffield: Sheffield Academic Press).

Rogerson, J.W., and P.R. Davies
    1989   *The Old Testament World* (Cambridge: Cambridge University Press).

Rohrbaugh, R. (ed.)
    1996   *The Social Science and New Testament Interpretation* (Peabody, MA: Hendrickson).

Rorty, R.
    1992   'The Pragmatist's Progress', in U. Eco *et al.* (eds.), *Interpretation and Overinterpretation* (Cambridge: Cambridge University Press): 89-108.

Rosenbaum, S.N.
    1990   *Amos of Israel: A New Interpretation* (Macon, GA: Mercer University Press).

Rowland, C., and M. Corner
    1990   *Liberating Exegesis: The Challenge of Liberation Theology to Biblical Studies* (Biblical Foundations in Theology; London: SPCK).

Rudolph, W.
    1947   *Ezra und Nehemia* (HAT; Tübingen: J.C.B. Mohr).

Ruether, R.R.
    1983   *Sexism and God-Talk: Towards a Feminist Theology* (London: SCM
                Press).
Runciman, W.G.
    1983   *A Treatise on Social Theory*. I. *The Methodology of Social Theory* (Cam-
                bridge: Cambridge University Press).
Russell, L.M. (ed.)
    1985   *Feminist Interpretation of the Bible* (Philadelphia: Westminster Press).
Said, E.W.
    1983   *The World, the Text, and the Critic* (Cambridge, MA: Harvard University
                Press).
    1985   *Orientalism* (Harmondsworth: Penguin Books).
Sampson, G.
    1980   *Schools of Linguistics* (Stanford: Stanford University Press).
Sarna, N.
    1966   *Understanding Genesis* (Heritage of Biblical Israel, 1; New York:
                Schocken Books, 1966).
Sasson, J.M.
    1981   'On Choosing Models for Recreating Israelite Pre-Monarchic History',
                JSOT 21: 3-24.
Saussure, F. de
    1916   *Cours de linguistique générale* (Paris: Payot).
Scheer, B.
    1997   *Einführung in die philosophische Ästhetik* (Darmstadt: Wissenschaftliche
                Buchgesellschaft).
Schiffrin, D.
    1987   *Discourse Markers* (Cambridge: Cambridge University Press).
Schmidt, B.
    1996   *Israel's Beneficent Dead: Ancestor Cult and Necromancy in Ancient
                Israelite Religion and Tradition* (Winona Lake, IN: Eisenbrauns; reprint
                of Tübingen: J.C.B. Mohr, 1994).
Scholes, R.
    1985   *Protocols of Reading* (New Haven, CT: Yale University Press).
Schreiter, R.J.
    1985   *Constructing Local Theologies* (Maryknoll, NY: Orbis Books).
Schultz, C.
    1980   'The Political Tensions Reflected in Ezra–Nehemiah', in C.D. Evans *et
                al.* (eds.), *Scripture in Context: Essays on the Comparative Method*
                (Pittsburgh: Pickwick Press): 221-44.
Schüssler Fiorenza, E.
    1981   'Towards a Feminist Biblical Hermeneutics: Biblical Interpretation and
                Liberation Theology', in Mahan and Richesin 1981: 91-112.
    1983   *In Memory of Her: A Feminist Theological Reconstruction of Christian
                Origins* (London: SCM Press).
    1984   *Bread Not Stone: The Challenge of Feminist Biblical Interpretation*
                (Boston: Beacon Press).
Schweppenhäuser, G.
    1996   *Theodor W. Adorno zur Einführung* (Hamburg: Junius Verlag).

Scott, J.C.
    1990   *Domination and the Arts of Resistance: Hidden Transcripts* (New Haven, CT: Yale University Press).

Segal, J.B.
    1976   'Popular Religion in Ancient Israel', *JJS* 27.1: 1-22.

Segovia, F., and M. Tolbert (eds.)
    1995a   *Reading from this Place: Social Location and Biblical Interpretation in Global Perspective*, I (Minneapolis: Fortress Press).
    1995b   *Reading from this Place: Social Location and Biblical Interpretation in Global Perspective*, II (Minneapolis: Fortress Press).
    1998   *Teaching the Bible: The Discourses and Politics of Biblical Pedagogy* (Maryknoll, NY: Orbis Books).

Segundo, J.L.
    1976   *The Liberation of Theology* (trans. J. Drury; Maryknoll, NY: Orbis Books).
    1984   *Faith and Ideologies. I. Jesus of Nazareth Yesterday and Today* (Maryknoll, NY: Orbis Books).
    1985   'The Shift within Latin American Theology', *JTSA* 52.1: 17-29.

Shanks, H., and J. Meinhardt (eds.)
    1997   *Aspects of Monotheism: How God Is One* (Washington, DC: Biblical Archaeology Society).

Sicre, J.L.
    1979   *Los dioses olvidados: Poder y riqueza en los profetas preexílicos* (Estudios de Antiguo Testamento, 1; Madrid: Cristiandad).
    1984   *'Con los pobres de la tierra': La justicia social en los profetas de Israel* (Madrid: Cristiandad, 1984).

Skinner, J.
    1930   *Prophecy and Religion: Studies in the Life of Jeremiah* (Cambridge: Cambridge University Press).

Smith, D.L.
    1989   *The Religion of the Landless: The Social Context of the Babylonian Exile* (Bloomington, IN: Meyer Stone).

Smith, M.S.
    1990   *The Early History of God: Yahweh and the Other Deities in Ancient Israel* (London: Harper & Row).

Smith, W.R.
    1927   *Lectures on the Religion of the Semites: The Fundamental Institutions* (Edinburgh: A. & C. Black, 3rd edn).

Smith-Christopher, D. (ed.)
    1995   *Text and Experience: Towards a Cultural Exegesis of the Bible* (The Biblical Seminar, 35; Sheffield: Sheffield Academic Press).

Sperber, D., and D. Wilson
    1986   *Relevance* (Oxford: Basil Blackwell).

Steinberg, N.
    1993   *Kinship and Marriage in Genesis: A Household Economics Perspective* (Minneapolis: Fortress Press).

Sternberg, M.
    1985   *The Poetics of Biblical Narrative* (Bloomington, IN: Indiana University Press).
    1992   'Biblical Poetics and Sexual Politics', *JBL* 111.3: 463-88.
Sugirtharajah, R.S. (ed.)
    1991   *Voices from the Margin: Interpreting the Bible in the Third World* (Mary-knoll, NY: Orbis Books).
Swete, H.B.
    1909   *The Gospel According to St Mark* (London: Macmillan, 3rd edn).
Taylor, C.
    1985   'Understanding and Ethnocentrism', in *idem, Philosophy and the Human Sciences* (Cambridge: Cambridge University Press): 116-33.
Taylor, D.B.
    1992   *Mark's Gospel as Literature and History* (London: SCM Press).
Taylor, G.H.
    1986   'Editor's Introduction', in Ricoeur (ed.) 1986: ix-xxxvi.
Taylor, V.
    1952   *The Gospel According to St Mark* (London: Macmillan).
Teodorsson, S.-T.
    1977   *The Phonology of Ptolemaic Koine* (Studia Graeca et Latina Gothoburg-ensia, 36; Gothenburg: Acta Universitatis Gothoburgensis).
    1979   'Phonological Variation in Classical Attic and the Development of Koine', *Glotta* 57: 61-75.
Thistelton, A.C.
    1992   *New Horizons in Biblical Hermeneutics: The Theory and Practice of Transforming Biblical Reading* (Grand Rapids: Zondervan).
Thompson, J.B.
    1981   *Critical Hermeneutics: A Study in the Thought of Jürgen Habermas and Paul Ricoeur* (Cambridge: Cambridge University Press).
    1984   *Studies in the Theory of Ideology* (Berkeley: University of California Press).
    1990   *Ideology and Modern Culture: Critical Social Theory in the Era of Mass Communication* (Stanford: Stanford University Press).
Thumb, A.
    1901   *Die griechische Sprache im Zeitalter des Hellenismus: Beiträge zur Geschichte und Beurteilung der KOINH* (Strassburg: Trübner).
    1909   *Handbuch der griechischen Dialekte* (Indogermanische Bibliothek, 1.8; Heidelberg: Carl Winter).
Tiedemann, R. (ed.)
    1989   *Frankfurter Adorno Blätter* V (Munich: edition text + kritik).
Tiedemann, R.
    1989   ' "Gegen-wärtige Vorwelt": Zu Adornos Begriff des Mythischen (I)', in Tiedemann (ed.) 1998: 9-36.
Tigay, J.H.
    1986   *You Shall Have No Other Gods: Israelite Religion in the Light of Hebrew Inscriptions* (HSS, 31; Atlanta, GA: Scholars Press).

Tonkin, E.
  1992   *Narrating our Past: The Social Construction of Oral History* (Cambridge:
             Cambridge University Press).

Toorn, K. van der
  1992   'Anat-Yahu, Some Other Deities and the Jews of Elephantine', *Numen*
             39.1: 80-101.
  1996   *Family Religion in Babylonia, Syria, and Israel* (Leiden: E.J. Brill).
  1997   'Worshipping Stones: On the Deification of Cult Symbols', *JNSL* 23.1: 1-
             14.
  1998   'Currents in the Study of Israelite Religion', *CR:BS* 6: 9-30.

Towler, R.
  1974   *Homo Religiosus: Sociological Problems in the Study of Religion*
             (Sociology and Social Welfare Series; London: Constable).

Tracy, D.
  1981   'Introduction', in Mahan and Richesin (eds.) 1981: 1-3.
  1987   *Plurality and Ambiguity: Hermeneutics, Religion, Hope* (San Francisco:
             Harper & Row).

Trible, P.
  1978   'Love's Lyrics Redeemed', in *idem*, *God and the Rhetoric of Sexuality*
             (OBT; Philadelphia: Fortress Press).

Turner, B.S.
  1994   *Orientalism, Postmodernism and Globalism* (London: Routledge).

Turner, M.
  1995   'Modern Linguistics and the New Testament', in J.B. Green (ed.), *Hear-
             ing the New Testament: Strategies for Interpretation* (Grand Rapids:
             Eerdmans): 146-74.

Ure, J., and J. Ellis
  1977   'Register in Descriptive Linguistics and Linguistic Sociology', in
             O. Uribe-Villegas (ed.), *Issues in Sociolinguistics* (The Hague: Mouton):
             197-243.

Veeser, H.A. (ed.)
  1996   *Confessions of the Critics* (London: Routledge).

Ventola, E.
  1988   'Text Analysis in Operation: A Multilevel Approach', in Fawcett and
             Young (eds.) 1988: 52-77.

Vorländer, H.
  1986   'Aspects of Popular Religion in the Old Testament', in N. Greinochen
             and N. Mette (eds.), *Concilium: Popular Religion* (Edinburgh: T. & T.
             Clark): 63-70.

Vrijhof, P.H., and J. Waardenburg (eds.)
  1979   *Official and Popular Religion: Analysis of a Theme for Religious Studies*
             (Religion and Society, 19; The Hague: Mouton).

Wardaugh, R.
  1992   *An Introduction to Sociolinguistics* (Oxford: Basil Blackwell, 2nd edn).

Watt, J.W.
  1997   *Code-Switching in Luke and Acts* (Berkeley Insights in Linguistics and
             Semiotics, 31; New York: Peter Lang).

Watts, J.D.W.
> 1972 'A Critical Analysis of Amos 4:1ff.', *Society of Biblical Literature Annual Meeting Proceedings*, II (Missoula, MT: Scholars Press): 489-500.
> 1997 *Vision and Prophecy in Amos* (Macon, GA: Mercer University Press, rev. edn).

Weber, M.
> 1952 *Ancient Judaism* (ed. and trans. H.H. Gerth and D. Martindale; Glencoe, IL: Free Press).
> 1993 *The Sociology of Religion* (Boston: Beacon Press).

Weigl, M.
> 1995 'Eine "unendliche Geschichte": אף (Am 7,7-8)', *Bib* 76.3: 343-87.

Weinberg, J.
> 1992 *Citizen-Temple Community* (trans. D.L. Smith; JSOTSup, 151; Sheffield: Sheffield Academic Press).

Weinfeld, M.
> 1972 'The Worship of Molech and of the Queen of Heaven and its Background', *UF* 4: 133-54.

Weinreich, U.
> 1953 *Languages in Contact: Findings and Problems* (New York: Linguistic Circle of New York).

Wellhausen, J.
> 1957 *Prolegomena to the History of Ancient Israel* (Cleveland: Meridian).

Werbner, P., and T. Modood (eds.)
> 1997 *Debating Cultural Hybridity* (London: Zed Books).

Werman, C.
> 1997 'Jubilees 30: Building a Paradigm for the Ban on Intermarriage', *HTR* 90.1: 1-22.

West, C.
> 1985 'Afterword: The Politics of American Neo-pragmatism', in J. Rajchman and C. West (eds.), *Post-Analytic Philosophy* (New York: Columbia University Press): 259-95.

West, G.O.
> 1992 'Some Parameters of the Hermeneutic Debate in the South African Context', *JTSA* 80.1: 3-13.
> 1993 'The Interface between Trained Readers and Ordinary Readers in Liberation Hermeneutics—A Case Study: Mark 10:17-22', *Neot* 27.1: 165-80.
> 1995a *Biblical Hermeneutics of Liberation: Modes of Reading the Bible in the South African Context* (Maryknoll, NY: Orbis Books; Pietermaritzburg: Cluster Publications, 2nd edn).
> 1995b 'And the Dumb Do Speak: Articulating Incipient Readings of the Bible in Marginalized Communities', in Rogerson, Davies and Carroll R. (eds.) 1995: 174-92.
> 1996 'Reading the Bible Differently: Giving Shape to the Discourses of the Dominated', *Semeia* 73: 21-41.
> 1999 *The Academy of the Poor: Towards a Dialogical Reading of the Bible* (Sheffield: Sheffield Academic Press).

Whitelam, K.W.
    1989   'Israelite Kinship: The Royal Ideology and Its Opponents', in Clements (ed.) 1989: 119-39.

    1996   *The Invention of Ancient Israel: The Silencing of Palestinian History* (London: Routledge).

Whybray, N.
    1987   *The Making of the Pentateuch* (JSOTSup, 53; Sheffield: Sheffield Academic Press).

Wifstrand, A.
    1947   'Stylistic Problems in the Epistles of James and Peter', *ST* 1: 170-82.

Wilcken, U.
    1967   *Alexander the Great* (trans. G.C. Richards: New York: W.W. Norton [1931]).

Williams, A.J.
    1979   'A Further Suggestion about Amos IV 1-3', *VT* 29.2: 206-11.

Williams, G.
    1992   *Sociolinguistics: A Sociological Critique* (London: Routledge).

Williams, P.W.
    1980   *Popular Religion in America: Symbolic Change and the Modernization Process in Historical Perspective* (Prentice–Hall Studies in Religion; Englewood Cliffs, NJ: Prentice–Hall).

Williamson, H.G.M.
    1985   *Ezra, Nehemiah* (WBC, 16; Waco, TX: Word Books).

    1990   'The Prophet and the Plumb-Line: A Redaction-Critical Study of Amos vii', in A.S. van der Woude (ed.), *In Quest of the Past: Studies on Israelite Religion, Literature, and Prophetism* (OTS, 26; Leiden: E.J. Brill): 101-22.

Wilson, R.R.
    1984   *Sociological Approaches to the Old Testament* (Guides to Biblical Research; Philadelphia: Fortress Press).

Wimsatt, W.K., and M. Beardsley
    1972 [1946]   'The Intentional Fallacy', in D. Lodge (ed.), *20th Century Literary Criticism* (London: Longman): 334-45.

Wolf, E.R.
    1999   *Envisioning Power: Ideologies of Dominance and Crisis* (Berkeley: University of California Press).

Wolff, H.W.
    1977   *Joel and Amos* (trans. W. Lanzen, S.D. McBride, Jr and C.A. Muenchlow; Hermeneia; Philadelphia: Fortress Press).

Wong, S.S.M.
    1994   'What Case is This Case? An Application of Semantic Case in Biblical Exegesis', *Jian Dao* 1: 49-73.

    1997   *A Classification of Semantic Case-Relations in the Pauline Epistles* (SBG, 9; New York: Peter Lang).

Yee, G. (ed.)
    1995   'Ideological Criticism: Judges 17–21 and the Dismembered Body', in G. Yee (ed.), *Judges and Method: New Approaches in Biblical Studies* (Minneapolis: Fortress Press): 147-67.

Young, R.
    1995   *Colonial Desire: Hybridity in Theory, Culture and Race* (London: Routledge).

Zenger, E. *et al.*
    1995   *Einleitung in das Alte Testament* (Stuttgart: W. Kohlhammer).

Zizek, S.
    1994   'The Spectre of Ideology', in S. Zizek (ed.), *Mapping Ideology* (London: Verso): 1-33.

INDEXES

INDEX OF REFERENCES

OLD TESTAMENT

NEW TESTAMENT

INDEX OF AUTHORS

Levinson, S.C. 223
Lewis, T.J. 175
Löbig, M. 25
Long, B.O. 148
Loretz, O. 179
Luckman, T. 115
Lukács, G. 26

Maduro, O. 160
Maldonado, L. 159
Malina, B.J. 13, 14, 197
Malinowski, B. 199
Maloney, E.C. 216
Mann, C.S. 212
Marcus, G.E. 154
Martin-Achard, R. 172
Marx, K. 112, 113, 120, 121
Matthews, V.H. 14
Matthiessen, M. 200, 203
Mayes, A.D.H. 13, 14, 64
McIntosh, A. 197
McKay, J.W. 179
Meyer, E. 136, 144
Meyers, C.L. 14, 16, 82-84, 88, 98, 104
Michaelis, J.G. 13
Miller, J.H. 50
Miranda, J.P. 169
Mires, F. 158
Moor, J.C. de 150, 179
Moore, S.D. 212
Moritz, P. 26
Mosala, I.J. 19, 75-81, 88-90, 98, 99, 104, 105
Mowinckel, S. 134
Müler-Doohm, S. 26
Mullen, E.T. 65
Müller-Lauter, W. 46
Munson, H. Jr 156
Murphy, R.E. 36
Murray, G. 29

Neher, A. 173
Newmeyer, F.J. 190
Newsome, C.A. 18

Niditch, S. 104, 163
Niehoff-Panagiotidis, J. 191
Nietzsche, F. 29
Noble, P.R. 176, 177
Norris, C. 70
Noth, M. 105

Oden, R.A. 63
Olyan, S.M. 180, 188
Ong, W. 104
Overholt, T.W. 14, 157, 158, 173

Palmer, F.R. 215
Palmer, M.W. 193, 213
Parker, C. 160, 162
Pasto, J. 15
Patterson, A. 60
Paul, S.M. 171, 179, 180
Pearson, B.W.R. 202
Petersen, D.L. 16
Petersen, N.R. 222
Petersen, R.M. 94
Peterson, A. 160
Pfütze, H. 25
Pike, K. 66
Pike, K.L. 166
Pixley, J.V. 17, 19
Polley, M.E. 170, 184
Poole, S. 162
Pope, M.H. 175
Popper, K. 49
Porter, S.E. 192, 193, 202, 210, 214, 217, 218, 224, 225, 227
Prewitt, T.J. 63
Prior, M. 18
Pritchard, J.B. 29
Provan, I.W. 15
Puech, E. 173

Rademacher, C. 26
Ramsay, W.M. 195
Reed, J.T. 197, 198, 200, 202, 210, 211
Reiser, M. 220
Rendtorff, R. 53

JOURNAL FOR THE STUDY OF THE OLD TESTAMENT
SUPPLEMENT SERIES